Better Homes and Gardens

Our Best Recipes

Meredith Consumer Marketing
Des Moines, Iowa

Better Homes and Gardens.

Our Best Recipes

MEREDITH CONSUMER MARKETING
Vice President, Consumer Marketing: Janet Donnelly
Consumer Marketing Product Director: Heather Sorensen
Consumer Marketing Product Manager: Wendy Merical
Business Director: Ron Clingman
Senior Production Manager: Al Rodruck

WATERBURY PUBLICATIONS, INC.
Editorial Director: Lisa Kingsley
Associate Editor: Tricia Bergman
Creative Director: Ken Carlson
Associate Design Director: Doug Samuelson
Graphic Designer: Mindy Samuelson
Contributing Copy Editors: Gretchen Kauffman, Peg Smith
Contributing Indexer: Elizabeth T. Parson

BETTER HOMES AND GARDENS® MAGAZINE
Editor in Chief: Gayle Goodson Butler
Creative Director: Michael D. Belknap
Senior Deputy Editor: Nancy Wall Hopkins
Editorial Assistant: Renee Irey

MEREDITH NATIONAL MEDIA GROUP
President: Tom Harty

MEREDITH CORPORATION
Chairman and Chief Executive Officer: Stephen M. Lacy

In Memoriam: E.T. Meredith III (1933–2003)

Our seal assures you that every recipe in *Better Homes and Gardens*® *Our Best Recipes* has been tested in the Better Homes and Gardens® Test Kitchen. This means that each recipe is practical and reliable, and meets our high standards of taste appeal. We guarantee your satisfaction with this book for as long as you own it.

All of us at Meredith Consumer Marketing are dedicated to providing you with information and ideas to enhance your home. We welcome your comments and suggestions. Write to us at: Meredith Consumer Marketing, 1716 Locust St., Des Moines, IA 50309-3023.

Pictured on front cover:
Blueberry Ice Cream Pie, page 290

contents

48

248

268

our treasured heritage

FOR GENERATIONS, *Better Homes and Gardens*® has been a part of the fabric of food and family for our readers. Since 1922—when the magazine made its debut—we have made it our mission to make the lives of American families easier, more comfortable, and enriched by time spent in the kitchen and around the table with the people they love most. We have responded enthusiastically to new technology (the invention of the refrigerator in the 1930s) and with care to social trends and new realities (the influx of women into the workplace in the 1970s). We'll even take a little credit for popularizing one of the country's most beloved food-centric activities—backyard grilling and barbecuing—in the 1950s. We look forward to inspiring and supporting cooks and the families they love for decades to come.

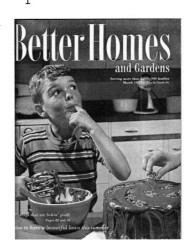

Past, Present, Future:

Our Best Recipes **celebrates** the very best of our *Better Homes and Gardens*® heritage. The editors spent months combing through our collections to assemble the cream of the crop. The result: more than 350 of the best recipes we've ever published, all in one volume. The recipes in this book offer a mix of beloved classics and new favorites—as well as quick and simple fare for every day and splurges for company and special occasions.

Every recipe in this book is tested and approved by the *Better Homes and Gardens*® Test Kitchen, so you know it tastes great and works every time. When the Test Kitchen opened in 1928, we pioneered a recipe style that offered precise ingredient amounts and thoroughly descriptive methods. Cooks came to *Better Homes and Gardens*® for recipes they could count on. They still do.

We know you're interested in feeding your family as healthfully and with as much speed and efficiency as possible—most days, anyway. (There is always that luxurious Sunday afternoon spent cooking or the indulgent dessert for a special occasion.) That's why every recipe in this book includes timings for preparation of ingredients and cooking times, as well as full nutritional profiles, so you can plan your days accordingly. We also know life is all about balance.

There is something for everyone and every occasion in this book. With chapters that cover Appetizers to Desserts—and everything in between—you will always find just what you're looking for on these pages. Serve up cocktails and Strawberry-Goat Cheese Bruschetta (page 26) or Bacon-and-Cheese-Stuffed Mushrooms (page 13) to friends or stir up a big pot of All-American Cheeseburger Soup, complete with pickles and toasted buns on the side (page 121)—for your family. Indulge in Honey-Glazed Buttermilk Oatmeal Coffee Cake (page 264) or S'mores Bread Pudding (page 279).

Our Best Recipes **gives you** one more reason to trust *Better Homes and Gardens*®. It is a reflection of where we have been and a glimpse of where we are going. It is a look, in fact, at where we will always go—straight to the hearts of our readers and their families through the most sincere and direct route we know of: their stomachs. We hope these recipes will help you fondly remember favorite meals and times spent with friends and family—and help you make new memories too.

CHÈVRE-FIG SPREAD,
RECIPE PAGE 31

appetizers & snacks

ENTERTAINING IS EASY with this collection of crowd-pleasing , party-friendly nibbles. Not planning a party? Once you check out these delicious bites, you might just change your mind!

BLUE CHEESE AND BACON MINI CORN DOGS

Blue Cheese and Bacon Mini Corn Dogs

PREP 30 minutes
COOK 2 minutes per batch

- 1   cup all-purpose flour
- ⅔   cup yellow cornmeal
- 2   tablespoons sugar
- 1½ teaspoons baking powder
- ½   teaspoon dry mustard
- ¼   teaspoon salt
- 1   tablespoon shortening
- ¾   cup milk
- ¼   cup blue cheese
- 1   egg
- 3   slices bacon, crisp-cooked and finely crumbled or chopped
      Oil for deep-frying
- 6   jumbo beef hot dogs, cut in half crosswise
- 12 6-inch wooden skewers
      Honey mustard or mustard
- 1   recipe Blue Cheese Dip (optional)
      Fresh snipped parsley (optional)

1. In large bowl combine flour, cornmeal, sugar, baking powder, dry mustard, and salt. Cut in the shortening until mixture resembles fine crumbs. In a blender combine milk, blue cheese, and egg; cover and blend until almost smooth. Add egg mixture to flour mixture along with bacon; mix well. (Batter will be thick.)
2. Meanwhile, heat 1 inch of oil in a heavy large skillet over medium heat to 365°F (should take about 15 minutes).
3. Insert skewers into ends of hot dogs. Hold skewered hot dogs over bowl of cornmeal mixture. Spoon cornmeal mixture on hot dogs, then slightly spread to completely cover.

Place coated hot dogs, 3 or 4 at a time, lengthwise in hot oil. Turn hot dogs with tongs after about 10 seconds of cooking to prevent batter from sliding off. Cook for 2 minutes more or until golden brown, turning to brown evenly. Remove and drain on a baking sheet lined with paper towels. Keep warm in a 200°F oven while frying remaining hot dogs. Serve warm with honey mustard and/or, if desired, Blue Cheese Dip. If desired, sprinkle with parsley. Makes 12 servings.

Blue Cheese Dip In a medium bowl combine ⅔ cup mayonnaise, ¼ cup sour cream, 2 ounces crumbled blue cheese, 1 teaspoon Worcestershire sauce, and ⅛ teaspoon black pepper. Cover and chill until ready to serve.

EACH SERVING *259 cal, 15 g fat, 49 mg chol, 564 mg sodium, 23 g carb, 1 g fiber, 9 g pro.*

GARDEN SLIDERS

Garden Sliders

START TO FINISH 30 minutes

- 1 15- to 16-ounce can Great Northern or cannellini beans, rinsed and drained
- 2 tablespoons olive oil
- 2 cloves garlic, minced (1 teaspoon)
- ½ teaspoon Italian seasoning, crushed
- 1 medium yellow summer squash, cut into ¼-inch slices
- 24 ¼-inch slices baguette
- 2 medium plum tomatoes, cut into ¼-inch slices
- 1 small cucumber, cut into ¼-inch slices
  Small celery top sprigs, small tomato wedges, and/or pickle slices (optional)

1. For bean spread, in a blender or food processor combine beans, 1 tablespoon of the oil, garlic, and seasoning. Cover; blend or process until smooth. Season with *salt* and *black pepper*.
2. Toss squash slices with remaining 1 tablespoon olive oil. Grill squash in grill basket directly over medium coals for about 5 minutes or just until squash is tender, turning once.
3. Spread one side of each bread slice with bean spread. Top half the bread with tomato, squash, and cucumber slices. Top with remaining bread slices, spread sides down. If desired, secure sandwiches, topped with celery sprigs, tomato wedges, and/or pickle slices, with wooden picks. Makes 12 servings.
EACH SERVING *120 cal, 2 g fat, 0 mg chol, 289 mg sodium, 23 g carb, 3 g fiber, 6 g pro.*

Fontina-Stuffed Meatball Kabobs

PREP 30 minutes   GRILL 10 minutes

- 1 egg, lightly beaten
- ⅓ cup grated Parmesan cheese
- 2 cloves garlic, minced
- 1 teaspoon dried Italian seasoning
- 1½ pounds lean ground beef
- 2 ounces thinly sliced prosciutto, chopped
- 16 ½-inch fontina cheese cubes (1½ ounces)
- 8 canned artichoke hearts, drained and halved
- 1 6- to 8-ounce package fresh cremini mushrooms
- 1 pint grape tomatoes
- 1 recipe Balsamic Glaze
  Fresh basil (optional)

1. Combine egg, Parmesan, garlic, seasoning, ½ teaspoon *salt*, and ⅛ teaspoon *black pepper*. Add beef and prosciutto; mix well. Divide into 16 portions; shape around cheese cubes. On sixteen 8- to 10-inch skewers thread meatballs, artichokes, mushrooms, and tomatoes, leaving ¼ inch between. Prepare Balsamic Glaze; set aside.
2. On a charcoal grill place kabobs on greased rack of grill directly over medium coals. Grill 10 minutes or until meat is no longer pink (160°F), turning and brushing with half the glaze halfway through. To serve, drizzle with remaining glaze and, if desired, sprinkle with fresh basil. Makes 16 servings.
Balsamic Glaze In a small saucepan combine ⅓ cup balsamic vinegar; 2 teaspoons olive oil; 1 clove garlic, minced; ¼ teaspoon salt; ¼ teaspoon dried Italian seasoning; and ⅛ teaspoon black pepper. Bring to boiling; reduce heat. Simmer, uncovered, 4 minutes or until reduced to about ¼ cup.
EACH SERVING *269 cal, 15 g fat, 91 mg chol, 673 mg sodium, 8 g carb, 2 g fiber, 24 g pro.*

ITALIAN MEATBALLS

Italian Meatballs

PREP 35 minutes
BAKE 22 minutes at 400°F

Nonstick cooking spray
2 eggs, lightly beaten
½ cup Italian-style dry bread crumbs
⅓ cup grated Parmesan cheese
4 cloves garlic, minced
½ teaspoon salt
½ teaspoon black pepper
2 pounds lean ground turkey
8 ounces sweet Italian turkey sausage, casings removed
2 tablespoons olive oil
1 teaspoon smoked paprika or paprika
1 cup Smoky Tomato Sauce Small fresh basil leaves (optional)

1. Preheat oven to 400°F. Lightly coat a 15×10×1-inch baking pan with cooking spray.

2. In an extra-large bowl mix eggs, bread crumbs, cheese, garlic, salt, and pepper. Add turkey and sausage; mix well. With damp hands or an ice cream scoop, form twenty-four to thirty 1¾- to 2-inch meatballs (about 3 tablespoons each). Transfer to prepared baking sheet.

3. Combine oil and paprika; brush on meatballs. Bake meatballs 22 minutes or until cooked through (165°F). With a slotted spoon, transfer meatballs to a large serving bowl; toss with Smoky Tomato Sauce. If desired, top with basil. Makes 12 to 15 servings.

Smoky Tomato Sauce In a Dutch oven heat 2 tablespoons olive oil over medium-high heat. Add 1 large onion, finely chopped; 8 cloves garlic, minced; 2 teaspoons dried or 2 tablespoons chopped fresh basil; 2 teaspoons dried or 2 tablespoons chopped fresh oregano. Cook, stirring occasionally, until onion is tender, about 4 minutes. Add two 28-ounce cans crushed tomatoes, ⅓ cup tomato paste, 1½ teaspoons smoked paprika or paprika, ½ teaspoon

salt, and ½ teaspoon black pepper. Bring to a boiling; reduce heat to medium-low. Simmer, covered, stirring occasionally, for 20 minutes. Makes 7 cups.

EACH SERVING *180 cal, 7 g fat, 89 mg chol, 416 mg sodium, 6 g carb, 1 g fiber, 24 g pro.*

Apricot-Glazed Ham Balls

PREP 20 minutes
BAKE 20 minutes at 350°F
COOK 4 hours (low) or 1½ hours (high)

1 egg, beaten
½ cup graham cracker crumbs
2 tablespoons unsweetened pineapple juice
1 teaspoons dry mustard
¼ teaspoon salt
8 ounces ground cooked ham
8 ounces ground pork
½ cup snipped dried apricots
1 18-ounce jar apricot preserves
⅓ cup unsweetened pineapple juice
1 tablespoon cider vinegar
½ teaspoon ground ginger

1. Preheat oven to 350°F. For meatballs, in a large bowl combine egg, cracker crumbs, the 2 tablespoons pineapple juice, dry mustard, and salt. Add ham, pork, and snipped apricots; mix well. Shape mixture into 30 meatballs.

2. Arrange meatballs in a 15×10×1-inch baking pan. Bake, uncovered, about 20 minutes or until cooked through (160°F). Drain off fat.

3. Place cooked meatballs in 3½- or 4-quart slow cooker. In a small bowl combine apricot preserves, the ⅓ cup pineapple juice, vinegar, and ginger. Pour over meatballs in cooker.

4. Cover and cook on low-heat setting for 4 to 5 hours or on high-heat setting for 1½ to 2 hours. Gently stir just before serving. Serve with short skewers or toothpicks. If desired, keep warm on warm or low-heat setting up to 2 hours. Makes 30 servings.

EACH SERVING *97 cal, 3 g fat, 17 mg chol, 151 mg sodium, 15 g carb, 0 g fiber, 3 g pro.*

APRICOT-GLAZED
HAM BALLS

BACON-AND-CHEESE-STUFFED MUSHROOMS

TURKEY MEATBALLS IN PEACH SAUCE

Bacon-and-Cheese-Stuffed Mushrooms

PREP 30 minutes
BAKE 12 minutes at 400°F

    3   cups soft bread crumbs
    2   tablespoons olive oil
   12   3- to 4-inch-diameter fresh
        portobello mushrooms
    2   cups finely shredded Colby and
        Monterey Jack cheese
    8   slices bacon, crisp-cooked,
        drained, and crumbled
   ½   cup bottled creamy Italian salad
        dressing
    4   green onions, sliced
    2   cloves garlic, minced
   12   cherry tomatoes, thinly sliced

1. Preheat oven to 400°F. Place bread
crumbs in a 3-quart baking pan; toss
with oil. Bake, uncovered, for 5 minutes
or until lightly toasted, stirring once.
Cool on a wire rack.
2. Meanwhile, clean mushrooms; remove
and discard stems and gills. Pat dry with
paper towels. Place mushrooms, rounded
sides down, on two baking sheets.
3. In a bowl combine 1 cup of the
toasted bread crumbs, cheese, bacon,
salad dressing, green onions, and garlic.
Spoon filling into mushroom caps.
Top with tomato slices. Sprinkle with
remaining crumbs. Bake for 12 minutes
or until mushrooms are tender. Cut in
half to serve. Makes 24 servings.
EACH SERVING *109 cal, 8 g fat, 11 mg chol,
253 mg sodium, 6 g carb, 1 g fiber, 5 g pro.*

Creole Turkey Meatballs

PREP 25 minutes
BAKE 25 minutes at 375°F

    1   egg, lightly beaten
   ½   cup finely chopped sweet green
        pepper
   ½   cup quick-cooking rolled oats
   ½   cup chopped onion
    2   tablespoons milk
    1   teaspoon dried Italian
        seasoning, crushed
    1   teaspoon salt-free garlic and
        herb seasoning blend
    1   teaspoon Creole seasoning
    2   cloves garlic, minced
    1   pound ground raw turkey or
        chicken

1. Preheat oven to 375°F. Lightly grease
a 15×10×1-inch pan; set aside. In a large
bowl combine egg, sweet pepper, oats,
onion, milk, Italian seasoning, salt-free
seasoning, Creole seasoning, and garlic.
Add turkey; mix well.
2. Shape mixture into 30 meatballs.
Place meatballs in a single layer in the
prepared baking pan.
3. Bake, uncovered, about 25 minutes
or until cooked through (165°F).
4. Serve meatballs with short skewers or
toothpicks. Makes 30 servings.
EACH SERVING *33 cal, 2 g fat, 19 mg chol,
37 mg sodium, 2 g carb, 0 g fiber, 3 g pro.*

Turkey Meatballs in Peach Sauce

PREP 35 minutes   COOK 22 minutes

    1   egg, beaten
   ¼   cup fine dry bread crumbs
   ¼   cup finely chopped shallot
    1   teaspoon grated fresh ginger
   ⅛   teaspoon salt
    1   pound ground raw turkey
    1   tablespoon cooking oil
    1   15- to 16-ounce can peach slices
        (juice pack)
   ¼   cup ketchup
    2   tablespoon soy sauce
    2   tablespoon butter, melted
   ¼   cup dried tart cherries

1. In a large mixing bowl combine egg,
bread crumbs, shallot, ½ teaspoon of
the ginger, and the salt; add turkey and
mix well. Shape into 24 meatballs.
2. In an extra-large skillet cook
meatballs in hot oil over medium heat
for 18 to 20 minutes or until browned
and no longer pink (165°F), turning
occasionally to brown evenly. Drain fat.
3. Meanwhile, drain peaches, reserving
¼ cup juice. In a blender or food
processor combine drained peaches,
reserved juice, ketchup, soy sauce,
melted butter, and remaining ginger.
Cover and blend or process until
smooth. Add peach sauce and cherries
to skillet. Bring to boiling. Reduce heat
and simmer, uncovered, for 1 minute
or until heated through, stirring gently
to coat meatballs. Serve warm. Makes
6 servings.
EACH SERVING *264 cal, 14 g fat, 105 mg chol,
632 mg sodium, 20 g carb, 1 g fiber, 16 g pro.*

HOT AND SASSY
CHICKEN WINGS

SAUCY APRICOT 'N' SPICED MEATBALLS

CRANBERRY-SAUCED SAUSAGES

Hot and Sassy Chicken Wings

PREP 25 minutes MARINATE 2 hours
BAKE 40 minutes at 375°F

- 20 chicken wings
- 2 cups white wine vinegar
- ½ cup packed brown sugar
- ½ cup honey
- 4 teaspoons garlic powder
- 4 teaspoons bottled hot pepper sauce
- 2 teaspoons salt
- 2 teaspoons dried thyme, crushed
- 1 teaspoon cayenne pepper
  Nonstick cooking spray

1. Cut off and discard wing tips. Cut each wing at the joint to make 2 pieces. Place wing pieces in a large resealable plastic bag; set aside.
2. For marinade, in a medium bowl stir together vinegar, brown sugar, honey, garlic powder, hot pepper sauce, salt, thyme, and cayenne pepper. Pour over wings in bag; seal bag. Marinate in the refrigerator for 2 to 4 hours, turning bag occasionally.
3. Preheat oven to 375°F. Line a 15×10×1-inch baking pan with foil. Lightly coat a large roasting rack with cooking spray; set rack in prepared pan. Drain chicken wings, reserving marinade. Place wings on roasting rack; set aside.
4. Transfer marinade to a medium saucepan. Bring to boiling over medium-high heat. Boil gently, uncovered, about 10 minutes or until marinade is reduced to about ½ cup and is thick and slightly syrupy, stirring occasionally.

5. Brush wings on both sides with some of the reduced marinade. Bake for 30 minutes. Turn wings over; brush with remaining marinade. Bake about 10 minutes or until chicken is no longer pink. Makes 16 servings.
EACH SERVING *205 cal, 10 g fat, 47 mg chol, 339 mg sodium, 16 g carb, 0 g fiber, 11 g pro.*

Saucy Apricot 'n' Spiced Meatballs

PREP 25 minutes
BAKE 15 minutes at 350°F

- ½ cup soft bread crumbs
- 2 tablespoons fat-free milk
- 1 egg white
- ¼ cup finely chopped onion
- ¼ cup finely snipped dried apricots
- ½ teaspoon salt
- 1 clove garlic, minced
- ¼ teaspoon ancho chili powder or chili powder
- 6 ounces lean ground pork
- 6 ounces ground raw turkey breast
- ½ cup apricot nectar
- 1 teaspoon cornstarch
- ¼ teaspoon chili powder
- ⅛ teaspoon salt
- ⅛ teaspoon ground nutmeg

1. Preheat oven to 350°F. Line a 15×10×1-inch baking pan with foil; lightly grease foil. In a bowl combine bread crumbs and milk. Let stand 5 minutes. Stir in egg white, onion, dried apricots, salt, garlic, and chili powder. Add ground pork and turkey; mix well.
2. Shape mixture into 24 meatballs. Place meatballs in the baking pan. Bake, uncovered, for 15 minutes or until meatballs are cooked through (160°F).

3. For the spiced apricot sauce, in a small saucepan combine apricot nectar, cornstarch, chili powder, salt, and nutmeg. Cook and stir over medium heat until thickened and bubbly. Cook and stir 1 minute more.
4. Place meatballs in a 1½-quart slow cooker. Add spiced apricot sauce; stir gently to coat. Keep warm in slow cooker on warm or low-heat setting up to 2 hours. Serve meatballs with short skewers or toothpicks. Makes 24 servings.
EACH SERVING *38 cal, 2 g fat, 8 mg chol, 78 mg sodium, 3 g carb, 0 g fiber, 3 g pro.*

Cranberry-Sauced Sausages

START TO FINISH 20 minutes

- 1 16-ounce can jellied cranberry sauce
- ⅔ cup ketchup
- 2 tablespoons lemon juice
- 1 teaspoon dry mustard
- ¼ teaspoon ground allspice
- 1 16-ounce package small cooked smoked sausage links

1. In a saucepan combine cranberry sauce, ketchup, lemon juice, dry mustard, and allspice. Stir in sausage links. Cook over medium-high heat about 10 minutes or until heated through, stirring occasionally.
2. Serve immediately or keep warm, covered, in a 1½- or 2-quart slow cooker on low-heat setting up to 2 hours. Makes 16 servings.
EACH SERVING *134 cal, 7 g fat, 20 mg chol, 393 mg sodium, 13 g carb, 0 g fiber, 11 g pro.*

FLAMIN' CAJUN RIBLETS

Flamin' Cajun Riblets

PREP 20 minutes COOK 5 hours
(low) or 2½ hours (high)

- 3 pounds pork loin back ribs
- 1 tablespoon Cajun seasoning
- 1 cup bottled chili sauce
- ½ cup finely chopped onion
- 1 serrano pepper, seeded and finely chopped (see tip, page 35)
- 2 tablespoons quick-cooking tapioca, crushed
- 1 teaspoon finely shredded lemon peel
- 1 tablespoon lemon juice
- 1 teaspoon bottled hot pepper sauce

1. Sprinkle ribs with Cajun seasoning; rub in with your fingers. Cut ribs into single rib portions. Place ribs in a 3½- or 4-quart slow cooker.
2. In a medium bowl combine chili sauce, onion, serrano pepper, tapioca, lemon peel, lemon juice, and hot pepper sauce. Pour sauce over ribs.
3. Cover and cook on low-heat setting for 5 to 6 hours or on high-heat setting for 2½ to 3 hours. Serve immediately or keep covered on warm or low-heat setting up to 2 hours. Makes 12 servings.
EACH SERVING *231 cal, 17 g fat, 57 mg chol, 369 mg sodium, 7 g carb, 1 g fiber, 12 g pro.*

Mediterranean Chicken Pinwheels

PREP 45 minutes
BAKE 25 minutes at 400°F
COOL 15 minutes

- 4 skinless, boneless chicken breast halves (about 1½ pounds)
  Black pepper
- 4 ounces sliced prosciutto
- 3 ounces goat cheese (chèvre), crumbled
- ¼ cup snipped fresh basil
- ¼ cup oil-packed dried tomatoes, drained and chopped
- 2 tablespoons pine nuts, toasted and chopped (see tip, page 31)
- 1 tablespoon olive oil
- ⅔ cup Italian panko (Japanese-style bread crumbs)
  Pitted olives, drained marinated artichoke hearts, and/or crackers
- 1 recipe Seasoned Mayonnaise

TURKEY KIELBASA BITES

1. Preheat oven to 400°F. Place chicken breast halves between plastic wrap. Pound with the flat side of a meat mallet to about ¼-inch thickness. Remove top sheet of plastic wrap. Lightly sprinkle chicken with *pepper*. Place chicken narrow side toward you. Divide prosciutto among breast halves to within ½ inch of edges. Sprinkle with goat cheese, basil, tomatoes, and pine nuts. Roll up from narrow side; secure with wooden toothpicks.
2. Brush chicken rolls with oil. Place bread crumbs in a shallow dish. Coat chicken rolls with bread crumbs; place in a 9×2-inch square pan. Bake, uncovered, 25 minutes or until cooked through (170° F). Cool 15 minutes. Cut into ½-inch-slices.
3. Serve pinwheels with olives, artichoke hearts, and/or crackers and Seasoned Mayonnaise. Makes 20 servings.
Seasoned Mayonnaise In a medium bowl stir together ½ cup mayonnaise, 1 teaspoon lemon or lime juice, and 2 cloves garlic, minced. Cover and chill.
EACH SERVING *137 cal, 8 g fat, 29 mg chol, 392 mg sodium, 4 g carb, 1 g fiber, 12 g pro.*

Turkey Kielbasa Bites

PREP 10 minutes
COOK 2½ hours(low)

- 1 orange
- 1 16-ounce package cooked turkey kielbasa, cut in 1-inch pieces
- 1 12-ounce carton cranberry-orange or cranberry-raspberry crushed fruit
- 1 tablespoon Dijon mustard
- ¼ teaspoon crushed red pepper

1. Using the fine grate on a shredder, remove the zest from the orange. Section and chop the orange.
2. In a 1½-quart slow cooker combine kielbasa, cranberry-orange crushed fruit, Dijon mustard, and crushed red pepper.
3. Cover and cook on low-heat setting for 2½ to 3 hours. Serve immediately or keep warm up to 1 hour. Serve kielbasa with wooden toothpicks. Makes 10 servings.
EACH SERVING *126 cal, 4 g fat, 28 mg chol, 441 mg sodium, 15 g carb, 0 g fiber, 7 g pro.*

MANDARIN APRICOT CHICKEN WINGS

chicken pieces with bacon. Thread each skewer with a bacon-wrapped chicken piece, a green onion piece, and a sweet pepper strip. Place in a 15×10×1-inch baking pan.

3. Bake for 8 minutes. Brush with teriyaki glaze. Bake about 16 minutes or until bacon is cooked through. Makes 24 servings.

EACH SERVING *114 cal, 9 g fat, 24 mg chol, 325 mg sodium, 1 g carb, 0 g fiber, 7 g pro.*

Fajita-Style Quesadillas

START TO FINISH **30 minutes**

- ½ medium red or green sweet pepper, seeded and cut into bite-size strips
- ½ medium onion, halved and thinly sliced
- 1 fresh serrano pepper, halved, seeded, and cut into thin strips (see tip, page 35)
- 2 teaspoons vegetable oil
- 4 6-inch white corn tortillas Nonstick cooking spray
- ½ cup shredded Monterey Jack cheese (2 ounces)
- 2 thin slices tomato, halved crosswise
- 1 tablespoon snipped fresh cilantro Light sour cream (optional) Cilantro and lime wedges (optional)

1. In an extra-large skillet cook sweet pepper, onion, and serrano pepper in hot oil over medium-high heat for 3 minutes or just until vegetables are tender. Remove from heat.
2. Lightly coat one side of each tortilla with cooking spray. On uncoated side of 2 tortillas divide half the cheese. Top each with half the sweet pepper mixture, tomato slices, cilantro, remaining cheese, then remaining tortillas, coated sides up.
3. In the same skillet cook quesadillas over medium heat for 4 minutes per side or until cheese is melted and tortillas are lightly browned. Cut each quesadilla into 4 wedges. Serve warm and, if desired, with sour cream, additional cilantro, and lime wedges. Makes 8 servings.

EACH SERVING *61 cal, 4 g fat, 6 mg chol, 41 mg sodium, 5 g carb, 1 g fiber, 2 g pro.*

Mandarin Apricot Chicken Wings

PREP **15 minutes**
BAKE **25 minutes at 400°F**

- 16 chicken wing drummettes
- ⅔ cup bottled sweet-and-sour sauce
- ½ cup snipped dried apricots
- ⅓ cup bottled hoisin sauce
- ¼ cup soy sauce
- 2 tablespoons honey
- 2 cloves garlic, minced
- ¼ teaspoon ground ginger
- ¼ teaspoon five-spice powder
- 1 tablespoon sesame seeds, toasted (see tip, page 31) Green onion (optional) Dried apricot halves (optional)

1. Preheat oven to 400°F. Arrange drummettes in a single layer in a baking pan or roasting pan lined with foil. Bake drummettes for 20 minutes.
2. Meanwhile, in a small saucepan stir together sweet-and-sour sauce, snipped apricots, hoisin sauce, soy sauce, honey, garlic, ginger, and five-spice powder. Bring to boiling; reduce heat. Simmer, uncovered, for 5 minutes. Remove from heat.

3. Brush about ¼ cup of the sauce mixture over drummettes. Sprinkle with sesame seeds. Bake about 5 minutes more or until drummettes are no longer pink in the center. Serve with remaining sauce. If desired, garnish with green onion and serve with dried apricot halves. Makes 8 servings.

EACH SERVING *129 cal, 8 g fat, 44 mg chol, 411 mg sodium, 11 g carb, 0 g fiber, 8 g pro.*

Teriyaki Chicken Rumaki

PREP **25 minutes**
STAND **30 minutes**
BAKE **24 minutes at 375°F**

- 1 pound skinless, boneless chicken breast halves
- 12 slices bacon, halved crosswise
- 6 green onions, trimmed and each cut into 4 pieces
- 1 cup thin red sweet pepper strips
- ⅓ cup teriyaki glaze

1. Soak twenty-four 4- to 6-inch wooden skewers in water for at least 30 minutes. Drain before using.
2. Preheat oven to 375°F. Cut chicken into twenty-four 1½-inch pieces. Wrap

FAJITA-STYLE QUESADILLAS

CRAB-TOPPED SHRIMP

smooth. Beat in mayonnaise, mustard, and salt. Stir in crabmeat, green onion, and roasted red pepper until combined.

3. Butterfly shrimp by cutting through the rounded side almost to opposite side. Open shrimp and place, cut side down, in prepared baking pan. Divide crab mixture among shrimp, shaping the mixture into a mound. Bring shrimp tails up and over the crab mixture.

4. Bake about 10 minutes or until shrimp are opaque. Serve warm. Makes 16 servings.

EACH SERVING *38 cal, 2 g fat, 23 mg chol, 90 mg sodium, 0 g carb, 0 g fiber, 4 g pro.*

Marinated Shrimp Scampi

PREP **35 minutes**

MARINATE **1 hour** BROIL **4 minutes**

2 pounds extra-jumbo fresh or frozen shrimp in shells
¼ cup olive oil
¼ cup dry white wine
6 cloves garlic, minced
2 teaspoons finely shredded lemon peel
½ teaspoon crushed red pepper
½ teaspoon salt
2 tablespoons snipped fresh parsley
Lemon wedges

1. Thaw shrimp, if frozen. Peel and devein shrimp, leaving tails intact. Rinse shrimp and pat dry with paper towels. Place shrimp in a large resealable plastic bag in a shallow bowl.

2. In a small bowl combine olive oil, wine, garlic, lemon peel, crushed red pepper, and salt. Pour over shrimp. Seal bag and toss gently to coat. Marinate in the refrigerator for 1 hour.

3. Remove shrimp from marinade, reserving marinade. Arrange shrimp on unheated broiler pan. Broil 4 to 5 inches from heat for 2 minutes. Turn shrimp over and brush with reserved marinade; broil 2 minutes more or until shrimp turn opaque.

4. To serve, mound shrimp on a platter; sprinkle with parsley and squeeze lemon wedges over shrimp. Makes 10 servings.

EACH SERVING *126 cal, 4 g fat, 138 mg chol, 193 mg sodium, 2 g carb, 1 g fiber, 19 g pro.*

Shrimp Brochette with Chipotle-Lime Cream

START TO FINISH **45 minutes**

1 8-ounce package cream cheese, softened
1 avocado, halved, seeded, peeled, and cut up
1 small jalapeño, seeded and finely chopped (see tip, page 35)
1 tablespoon snipped fresh cilantro
1 tablespoon lime juice
¼ teaspoon ground chipotle chile pepper
40 toasted baguette slices
1 7-ounce package frozen peeled, cooked salad shrimp, thawed and well drained
2 green onions, very finely chopped
1 tablespoon cilantro, very finely chopped

1. In a large mixing bowl beat cream cheese with an electric mixer on medium until smooth. Add avocado, jalapeño, 1 tablespoon snipped cilantro, lime juice, and the chipotle chile pepper. Beat until smooth and fluffy. Place in a large resealable plastic bag. Snip off one corner of the bag.

2. Pipe chipotle-lime cream on baguette slices. Top with shrimp. Combine green onions and chopped cilantro; sprinkle over chipotle-lime cream. Makes 40 servings.

EACH SERVING *67 cal, 3 g fat, 16 mg chol, 115 mg sodium, 8 g carb, 1 g fiber, 3 g pro.*

Crab-Topped Shrimp

PREP **35 minutes**

BAKE **10 minutes at 425°F**

16 large fresh or frozen shrimp in shells
2 tablespoons cream cheese, softened
2 tablespoons mayonnaise
1 teaspoon Dijon mustard
⅛ teaspoon salt
1 6.5-ounce can lump crabmeat, drained and flaked
2 tablespoons finely chopped green onion
2 tablespoons finely chopped roasted red sweet pepper

1. Thaw shrimp, if frozen. Peel and devein shrimp, leaving tails intact. Rinse shrimp; pat dry with paper towels. Preheat oven to 425°F. Line a 15×10×1-inch baking pan with foil.

2. In a medium bowl beat cream cheese with an electric mixer on medium until

MARINATED SHRIMP
SCAMPI

BACON-PEACH PINWHEELS

Bacon-Peach Pinwheels

PREP 30 minutes
BAKE 15 minutes at 375°F

4	ounces blue cheese, crumbled
1	3-ounce package cream cheese, softened
4	slices bacon
⅓	cup finely chopped onion
⅓	cup peach preserves
1	tablespoon balsamic vinegar
1	8-ounce package refrigerated crescent dough for recipes
⅓	cup pecans, toasted and finely chopped (see tip, page 31)
½	teaspoon dried basil
	Crumbled blue cheese (optional)
	Thinly sliced green onions (optional)

1. Preheat oven to 375°F. In a small mixing bowl beat cheeses on medium to high until fluffy. In a large skillet cook bacon until crisp; drain and crumble. Reserve 1 tablespoon drippings in skillet; cook and stir onion in drippings over medium heat until tender. Remove from heat; stir in preserves and vinegar. **2.** Unroll dough. Cut into two 3×10-inch rectangles. On each rectangle spread half the cheese mixture to within ¼ inch of one long edge. Top cheese with bacon, pecans, and basil. Beginning at a long edge, roll up each rectangle. Press seams to seal. Cut each roll into 10 slices. Place, cut sides down, on ungreased baking sheet. Bake 15 minutes or until golden brown. Spoon onion mixture on rolls. Remove from baking sheet. Serve warm. Sprinkle additional cheese and top with green onions. Makes 20 servings.
EACH SERVING *124 cal, 8 g fat, 11 mg chol, 221 mg sodium, 9 g carb, 0 g fiber, 3 g pro.*

Antipasto Pinwheels

STAND 30 minutes   PREP 15 minutes
CHILL 30 minutes

12	thin slices provolone cheese (6 to 7 ounces)
½	cup Gorgonzola cheese, softened (2 ounces)
1	tablespoon milk
12	thin slices sopressata or premium Genoa salami (4 ounces)
12	large fresh basil leaves
	Assorted crackers or flatbread (optional)

1. Let provolone cheese stand at room temperature for 30 minutes. In a small bowl combine Gorgonzola and milk. **2.** To make each roll, on waxed paper slightly overlap 6 slices of provolone to form a rectangle. Top with 6 slices of salami and 6 basil leaves. Spoon half the Gorgonzola mixture on the basil leaves. Roll, beginning from the narrow side of the rectangle, using waxed paper to lift and roll. Wrap roll in waxed paper or plastic wrap and place, seam side down, on a platter. Repeat to make second roll. Refrigerate wrapped rolls at least 30 minutes and up to overnight. Cut rolls into ½-inch slices. Serve with crackers or flatbread. Makes 10 servings.
EACH SERVING *122 cal, 10 g fat, 28 mg chol, 426 mg sodium, 1 g carb, 0 g fiber, 8 g pro.*

Bacon-Cheddar Cheese Balls

PREP 40 minutes   STAND 45 minutes
CHILL 2 hours

1	pound extra-sharp cheddar cheese, finely shredded
2	8-ounce packages reduced-fat cream cheese (Neufchâtel)
1	2-ounce jar sliced pimientos, rinsed, drained, patted dry, and chopped
¼	cup apricot preserves
2	tablespoons milk
1	teaspoon Worcestershire sauce
¼	teaspoon bottled hot pepper sauce
8	to 10 slices bacon, crisp-cooked and crumbled
⅓	cup pistachio nuts, chopped
	Celery stalks, cucumber slices, apricot halves, and/or toasted baguette slices

1. In an extra-large mixing bowl combine cheddar and cream cheeses; let stand to come to room temperature. Add pimientos, apricot preserves, milk, Worcestershire, hot pepper sauce, and about half the cooked bacon. Beat with an electric mixer on medium until almost smooth. **2.** Cover and refrigerate cheese mixture 2 hours or up to overnight. Divide into two portions. On waxed paper shape portions into balls. Up to 4 hours before serving, roll one cheese ball in bacon pieces and one in pistachio nuts. **3.** Serve with celery, cucumber, apricot, and/or toasted bread slices. Makes 18 servings.
EACH SERVING *218 cal, 17 g fat, 49 mg chol, 361 mg sodium, 6 g carb, 1 g fiber, 11 g pro.*

**BACON-CHEDDAR
CHEESE BALLS**

BACON-AVOCADO
DEVILED EGGS

Bacon-Avocado Deviled Eggs

PREP 45 minutes CHILL 4 hours

AVOCADO PESTO-STUFFED TOMATOES

- 12 eggs
- 5 slices thick-sliced bacon, chopped
- ½ cup mayonnaise
- 1 tablespoon country Dijon mustard
- 2 teaspoons caper juice or sweet or dill pickle juice
  Few dashes bottled hot pepper sauce
- ¼ teaspoon freshly ground black pepper
- 1 ripe firm avocado, halved, seeded, and peeled
- 1 teaspoon lemon juice
  Snipped fresh chives (optional)

1. Place eggs in a single layer in a 1½-quart saucepan or Dutch oven. Add enough cold water to cover the eggs by at least 1 inch. Bring to a rapid boil over high heat (water will have large rapidly breaking bubbles). Remove from heat, cover, and let stand for 15 minutes; drain. Run cold water over the eggs or place them in ice water until cool enough to handle; drain. Peel eggs and slice in half lengthwise. Remove yolks and place in a large bowl. Set whites aside.
2. Meanwhile, fry the bacon in a medium skillet over medium heat until crisp. Drain on paper towels, crumble, and set aside. Mash egg yolks with a fork. Mix in the mayonnaise, mustard, caper juice, hot pepper sauce, and pepper.
3. Chop the avocado into ½-inch pieces; toss with lemon juice. Place pieces of avocado in the hollow of each egg white. Spoon or pipe egg yolk mixture into egg white halves. Sprinkle with bacon pieces, any remaining avocado pieces, and, if desired, snipped chives. Cover and chill up to 4 hours. Makes 30 servings.
EACH SERVING *95 cal, 8 g fat, 109 mg chol, 147 mg sodium, 1 g carb, 0 g fiber, 4 g pro.*

Avocado Pesto-Stuffed Tomatoes

START TO FINISH 45 minutes

- 30 cherry tomatoes (about 1¼ pints)
- ½ medium avocado, seeded, peeled, and cut up
- 2 ounces cream cheese, softened
- 2 tablespoons homemade or purchased basil pesto
- 1 teaspoon lemon juice
  Snipped fresh basil (optional)

1. Cut a thin slice from the top of each tomato. (If desired, cut a thin slice from bottoms of tomatoes so they stand upright.) With a small spoon or small melon baller, carefully hollow out the tomatoes. Line a baking sheet with paper towels. Invert tomatoes on the towels. Let stand about 30 minutes to drain.
2. Meanwhile, for filling, in a food processor bowl combine avocado, cream cheese, pesto, and lemon juice. Cover; process until smooth. Spoon filling into a pastry bag fitted with a large plain round or open star tip.
3. Place tomatoes, open sides up, on a serving platter. Pipe filling into the tomato cups. Serve immediately or cover loosely and refrigerate up to 4 hours. If desired, sprinkle with snipped basil before serving. Makes 30 servings.
EACH SERVING *18 cal, 1 g fat, 2 mg chol, 16 mg sodium, 1 g carb, 0 g fiber, 0 g pro.*

ITALIAN PEPPERONI-
CHEESE PUFFS

1 tablespoon butter, melted
½ cup coarsely chopped pecans
2 slices bacon, crisp-cooked,
    drained, and crumbled
    Snipped fresh chives (optional)

1. Preheat oven to 325°F. In a medium
mixing bowl combine ½ cup butter and
cream cheese. Beat with an electric
mixer on medium until smooth. Stir in
flour. Divide dough into 24 pieces; shape
into balls. Press balls onto the bottoms
and up the sides of 24 ungreased
1¾-inch muffin cups. Set aside.
2. For filling, in a medium bowl beat
egg, brown sugar, and melted butter
until combined. Stir in pecans and
bacon. Spoon about 1 heaping teaspoon
of the filling into each pastry-lined
muffin cup.
3. Bake for 25 minutes or until pastry
is golden brown and filling is puffed.
Cool slightly in pan. Carefully transfer
tassies to a wire rack; cool. If desired,
sprinkle with chives. Makes 24 servings.
EACH SERVING *118 cal, 8 g fat, 25 mg chol,
62 mg sodium, 11 g carb, 0 g fiber, 2 g pro.*

Strawberry-Goat
Cheese Bruschetta

PREP 15 minutes   BROIL 4 minutes

2 8-ounce baguettes
2 tablespoons olive oil
2 4-ounce logs goat cheese
    (chèvre)
3 cups sliced strawberries
1 cup arugula
    Olive oil
    Sea salt or coarse salt
    Freshly ground black pepper
    Snipped fresh herbs

1. Preheat broiler. Halve baguettes
crosswise, then lengthwise. Place,
cut sides up, on a large baking sheet.
Brush with the 2 tablespoons oil.
Broil 3 to 4 inches from heat for 1½ to
2 minutes or until lightly toasted.
2. Slice and divide cheese among toasts.
Top with sliced berries. Broil 2 minutes
or until cheese and berries soften.
Remove from broiler; top with arugula.
Drizzle with additional oil. Sprinkle
with salt, pepper, and herbs. Makes
8 servings.
EACH SERVING *346 cal, 16 g fat, 22 mg chol,
616 mg sodium, 37 g carb, 2 g fiber, 13 g pro.*

Italian Pepperoni-
Cheese Puffs

PREP 30 minutes
BAKE 15 minutes per batch at 450°F

⅔ cup water
2 tablespoons shortening
¾ cup all-purpose flour
2 eggs
⅓ cup finely chopped pepperoni
⅓ cup finely shredded Romano
    cheese
1 tablespoons snipped fresh
    parsley
    Dash garlic powder
    Dash black pepper
    Purchased pizza sauce, warmed
    (optional)

1. Preheat oven to 450°F. Lightly grease
a large baking sheet; set aside. In a
medium saucepan combine the water
and shortening. Bring to boiling. Add
flour all at once, stirring vigorously.
Cook and stir until mixture forms
a ball. Remove from heat. Cool for
10 minutes. Add eggs, one at a time,
beating well with a wooden spoon after
each addition. Stir in pepperoni, cheese,
parsley, garlic powder, and pepper.
2. Using half the dough, drop dough by
rounded teaspoons into small mounds
2 inches apart on the prepared baking
sheet. Bake for 15 minutes or until firm
and golden brown, rotating pan halfway
through baking. Transfer to a wire
rack. Repeat with remaining dough.
Serve warm. If desired, serve with pizza
sauce. Makes 20 servings.
EACH SERVINGS *57 cal, 4 g fat, 25 mg chol,
81 mg sodium, 4 g carb, 0 g fiber, 2 g pro.*

Bacon-Pecan Tassies

PREP 30 minutes
BAKE 25 minutes at 325°F

½ cup butter, softened
1 3-ounce package cream cheese,
    softened
1 cup all-purpose flour
1 egg
¾ cup packed brown sugar

STRAWBERRY-GOAT CHEESE BRUSCHETTA

CARAWAY
VEGGIES

Smoked Salmon Toasts

PREP 20 minutes
BAKE 14 minutes at 325°F

- 8 slices pumpernickel bread
- 2 tablespoons butter, melted
- 1 8-ounce package cream cheese, softened
- 1 tablespoon lemon juice
- 1 4-ounce piece smoked salmon, flaked, with skin and bones removed
- 1 3.5-ounce jar capers, drained
- 1 hard-cooked egg, chopped
- ¼ cup finely chopped red onion

1. Preheat oven to 325°F. Remove crusts from bread slices. Flatten bread slices with a rolling pin. Cut each slice into four pieces. Brush both sides of each bread piece with melted butter. Press each bread piece into a 1¾-inch muffin cup. Bake for 14 minutes. Remove toast cups immediately from muffin cups and place on a wire rack to cool.
2. In a medium mixing bowl stir together cream cheese and lemon juice. Fold in salmon, capers, egg, and onion until combined. Spoon heaping tablespoons of the filling into toast cups. Serve at once or chill for 1 to 2 hours. Makes 32 servings.

EACH SERVING 59 cal, 4 g fat, 17 mg chol, 201 mg sodium, 4 g carb, 1 g fiber, 2 g pro.

Marinated Feta and Olives

PREP 30 minutes MARINATE 4 hours

- 1 pound feta cheese, cut into ½-inch cubes
- 1 cup pitted Kalamata olives
- 1 cup pitted green olives
- ½ cup bottled roasted red sweet peppers, cut into strips
- 1 red onion, cut into thin wedges
- ½ cup olive oil
- ½ cup balsamic vinegar
- 4 cloves garlic, minced
- 1 tablespoon snipped fresh thyme leaves
- 2 teaspoons snipped fresh oregano
- ½ teaspoon cracked black pepper

1. In a large glass bowl combine cheese cubes, the olives, sweet peppers, and onion wedges.

MARINATED FETA AND OLIVES

2. In a screw-top jar combine olive oil, vinegar, garlic, thyme, oregano, and pepper. Cover and shake well. Pour over mixture in bowl; toss gently to coat.
3. Cover and marinate in the refrigerator for 4 to 6 hours before serving. Serve with picks. Makes 20 servings.

EACH SERVING 138 cal, 12 g fat, 20 mg chol, 444 mg sodium, 4 g carb, 1 g fiber, 3 g pro.

Caraway Veggies

PREP 45 minutes CHILL 2 hours

- 1½ pounds baby-cut carrots
- 6 cups cauliflower florets
- 2 medium red and/or green sweet peppers, cut into strips
- ¾ cup salad oil
- 1 tablespoon caraway seeds, crushed
- 1 cup white wine vinegar
- ½ teaspoon salt
- ½ teaspoon crushed red pepper

1. In a medium saucepan cook carrots, covered, in a small amount of boiling water about 3 minutes or until crisp-tender. Drain; rinse with cold water.

Drain well. In a large saucepan cook cauliflower, covered, in a small amount of boiling water about 3 minutes or until crisp-tender. Drain; rinse with cold water. Drain well. Place carrots, cauliflower, and sweet pepper in separate resealable plastic bags.
2. For marinade, in a medium saucepan combine oil and caraway seeds. Cook and stir over low heat for 4 minutes or until oil is warm and slightly fragrant; cool slightly. In a large glass measure whisk together the oil mixture, vinegar, salt, and crushed red pepper.
3. Pour about ½ cup of the marinade over the carrots, about 1 cup of the marinade over the cauliflower, and the remaining marinade over the sweet pepper. Seal bags; turn to coat. Chill for 2 to 6 hours, turning bags often.
4. To serve, drain vegetables, discarding marinade. Arrange vegetables on a serving platter. Makes 12 servings.

EACH SERVING 85 cal, 5 g fat, 0 mg chol, 85 mg sodium, 9 g carb, 3 g fiber, 2 g pro.

REUBEN SPREAD

**RIPE OLIVE
CHEESE BALLS**

Chèvre-Fig Spread

START TO FINISH 25 minutes
CHILL up to 24 hours

¾ cup snipped dried figs
¾ cup crumbled goat cheese
  (chèvre) (3 ounces)
½ cup light sour cream
3 tablespoons snipped fresh basil
2 tablespoons milk
1 tablespoon snipped fresh thyme
  Salt and black pepper
½ cup chopped walnuts, toasted*
  Fresh thyme sprigs (optional)
  Toasted baguette slices or
  crackers

1. In a heatproof bowl pour boiling
water over figs to cover; let stand
15 minutes. Drain.
2. In a medium bowl stir together
cheese, sour cream, basil, milk, and
thyme. Season to taste with salt and
pepper. Stir in drained figs and half the
walnuts. Cover and refrigerate up to
24 hours.
3. To serve, transfer spread to serving
bowl. Sprinkle with remaining walnuts
and, if desired, fresh thyme sprigs.
Serve with baguette slices or crackers.
Makes 12 servings.
EACH SERVING *100 cal, 7 g fat, 10 mg chol,
45 mg sodium, 8 g carb, 1 g fiber, 4 g pro.*

Reuben Spread

PREP 15 minutes
COOK 2½ hours (low)

16 ounces cooked corned beef,
  finely chopped
1 16-ounce jar sauerkraut, rinsed,
  drained, and snipped
1½ cups shredded Swiss cheese

1 cup bottled Thousand Island
  salad dressing
1 3-ounce package cream cheese,
  cut up
1 tablespoon prepared horseradish
1 teaspoon caraway seeds
  Rye crisp bread or rye crackers
  Pickle slices (optional)

1. In a 3½- or 4-quart slow cooker
combine corned beef, sauerkraut, Swiss
cheese, salad dressing, cream cheese,
horseradish, and caraway seeds. Cover
and cook on low-heat setting for 2½ to
3 hours. Stir before serving.
2. Serve immediately or keep warm,
covered, on low-heat setting up to
2 hours. Serve with rye crisp bread and, if
desired, pickles. Makes 20 servings.
***Tip** To toast whole nuts or large pieces,
spread them in a shallow pan. Bake them
in a 350°F oven for 5 to 10 minutes,
shaking the pan once or twice. Toast
coconut in the same way, but watch it
closely to prevent burning. Toast finely
chopped or ground nuts or sesame seeds
in a dry skillet over medium heat. Stir
often to prevent burning.
EACH SERVING *157 cal, 13 g fat, 38 mg
chol, 531 mg sodium, 3 g carb, 1 g fiber, 7 g pro.*

Ripe Olive
Cheese Balls

PREP 15 minutes STAND 30 minutes
CHILL 4 hours

2 8-ounce packages cream cheese
½ cup butter
½ cup crumbled blue cheese
1 4.5-ounce can sliced pitted ripe
  olives, drained
2 tablespoons chopped green
  onion or snipped fresh chives
  Assorted crackers, flatbread,
  dried dates and/or dried
  apricots, and walnut halves

1. Place cream cheese, butter, and
blue cheese in a large mixing bowl; let
stand for 30 minutes to reach room
temperature. Beat with an electric
mixer on low until smooth. Stir in
olives and green onion. Cover and chill
for at least 4 hours or up to 24 hours.
2. Loosely shape mixture into 2 balls;
cover and chill until serving time. Serve
cheese balls with assorted crackers
and/or dried fruits. Makes 46 servings.
EACH SERVING *55 cal, 6 g fat, 14 mg chol,
69 mg sodium, 1 g carb, 0 g fiber, 1 g pro.*

RICOTTA, GORGONZOLA, AND HONEY SPREAD

1 4-ounce or two 2-ounce jars diced pimientos, drained
½ cup finely chopped green sweet pepper
⅓ cup finely chopped onion
1 small fresh jalapeño, stemmed, seeded, and minced (see tip, page 35)
1 tablespoon Worcestershire sauce
¼ teaspoon cayenne pepper
   Optional stir-ins: crumbled crisp-cooked bacon, toasted pecans, chopped green onions, and/or diced tomatoes
   Dippers: celery sticks, carrot sticks, pita chips, and/or crackers

1. In an extra-large mixing bowl beat cream cheese for 30 seconds. Gradually beat in remaining cheeses. Beat in mayonnaise. Stir in pimientos, sweet pepper, onion, jalapeño, Worcestershire, and cayenne.
2. Add stir-ins or divide the pimiento cheese into portions and add a different stir-in to each. Serve with dippers. Makes 20 servings.

EACH SERVING *220 cal, 20 g fat, 39 mg chol, 275 mg sodium, 3 g carb, 1 g fiber, 8 g pro.*

Cranberry Spread

PREP 10 minutes STAND 1 hour

2 tablespoons orange juice
2 tablespoons amaretto or orange juice
½ cup dried cranberries
1 8-ounce package cream cheese, softened
3 tablespoons butter, softened
1 teaspoon finely shredded orange peel
   Gingersnaps and/or crackers

1. In a small bowl combine orange juice and amaretto. Stir in dried cranberries. Cover and let stand for 1 hour. Drain and reserve liquid.
2. In a medium bowl beat together cream cheese and butter until fluffy. Stir in cranberries, orange peel, and enough of the reserved liquid for spreading consistency. Serve with gingersnaps and/or crackers. Makes 12 servings.

EACH SERVING *114 cal, 10 g fat, 28 mg chol, 77 mg sodium, 5 g carb, 0 g fiber, 1 g pro.*

Ricotta, Gorgonzola, and Honey Spread

PREP 25 minutes CHILL 1 hour

1 15-ounce carton whole-milk ricotta cheese
6 ounces Gorgonzola cheese, crumbled
½ teaspoon snipped fresh thyme or ¼ teaspoon dried thyme, crushed
¼ teaspoon snipped fresh rosemary or ⅛ teaspoon dried rosemary, crushed
1 tablespoon honey
36 toasted baguette slices
   Sliced apples, fresh thyme, and/or toasted chopped walnuts (see tip, page 31)
   Honey

1. Place ricotta in a large mixing bowl. Beat with an electric mixer on medium for 2 minutes. Stir in Gorgonzola, thyme, and rosemary until combined. Fold in 1 tablespoon honey just until combined. Spoon cheese mixture into a serving bowl. Cover and chill 1 to 24 hours.
2. To serve, spread on baguette slices and top with apple slices, additional thyme, and/or walnuts. Drizzle with honey. Makes 36 servings.

EACH SERVING *91 cal, 3 g fat, 10 mg chol, 182 mg sodium, 12 g carb, 1 g fiber, 4 g pro.*

Four-Cheese Pimiento Dip

START TO FINISH 35 minutes

1 3-ounce package cream cheese, softened
2 cups extra-sharp cheddar cheese, shredded (8 ounces)
2 cups shredded extra-sharp white cheddar cheese (8 ounces)
1 cup Gruyère cheese, shredded (4 ounces)
1 cup mayonnaise

**FOUR-CHEESE
PIMIENTO DIP**

**HOT ARTICHOKE
AND BANANA
PEPPER DIP**

Onion-Horseradish Dip

START TO FINISH 20 minutes

- 1 8-ounce wedge blue cheese
- 1 8-ounce carton sour cream
- ½ cup whipping cream
- ½ medium red onion
- 2 cloves garlic, minced
- 1 to 2 teaspoons prepared horseradish
  Additional chopped red onion
  Cut-up vegetables

1. In a large bowl crumble about three-fourths of the blue cheese. Add sour cream, whipping cream, red onion, garlic, and horseradish. Use an immersion blender to blend cheese mixture until almost smooth. (Or place ingredients in a blender or food processor and blend or process until almost smooth.) Spoon into a serving bowl. Top with remaining blue cheese and red onion. Serve with vegetables. Makes 20 servings.

EACH SERVING *85 cal, 8 g fat, 23 mg chol, 170 mg sodium, 1 g carb, 0 g fiber, 3 g pro.*

Hot Artichoke and Banana Pepper Dip

PREP 25 minutes

BAKE 25 minutes at 400°F

- 3 9-ounce packages frozen artichoke hearts, cooked, drained, and coarsely chopped
- 1 cup finely chopped yellow, red, or green sweet pepper
- 8 ounces Parmigiano-Reggiano or Parmesan cheese, finely shredded
- 1½ cups light mayonnaise dressing
- 1 medium banana pepper, seeded and cut into rings
- 1 tablespoon chopped fresh garlic
- 2 teaspoons ground cumin
  Assorted crackers

1. Preheat oven to 400° F. In a bowl mix together artichoke hearts, sweet pepper, cheese, mayonnaise, banana pepper, garlic, and cumin. Transfer dip to a 1½-quart baking dish.
2. Bake, uncovered, for 25 minutes or until top is lightly browned and dip is hot throughout. Makes 16 servings.

EACH SERVING *101 cal, 8 g fat, 11 mg chol, 251 mg sodium, 5 g carb, 2 g fiber, 4 g pro.*

Triple-Smoked Salmon-Pepper Spread

PREP 55 minutes

BAKE 25 minutes at 350°F

- 1 large green sweet pepper
- 1 8-ounce package reduced-fat cream cheese (Neufchâtel), softened
- ¼ cup light sour cream
- 2 tablespoons fat-free milk
- ½ cup thinly sliced green onions
- 2 cloves garlic, minced
- ½ teaspoon smoked paprika or paprika
- ½ teaspoon finely chopped chipotle pepper in adobo sauce*
- 4 ounces hot-style smoked salmon, flaked, with skin and bones removed
  Toasted whole grain crackers

1. Line a baking sheet with foil. Cut green peppers into quarters, removing stems, seeds, and membranes. Place pepper quarters, skin sides up, on prepared baking sheet. Broil 4 to 5 inches from the heat for 10 minutes or until pepper skins are charred. Wrap pepper quarters in the foil; let stand 15 minutes or until cool enough to handle. Peel off and discard skin. Chop pepper.
2. Preheat oven to 350°F. In a large mixing bowl beat cream cheese with an electric mixer on medium until smooth. Beat in sour cream and milk until smooth. Reserve ¼ cup of the green onions; stir in remaining green onions, garlic, paprika, and chipotle pepper. Gently fold in salmon and chopped green pepper. Spread in a 1-quart gratin dish.
3. Bake for 25 minutes or until heated through, stirring once halfway through baking. Sprinkle with reserved green onions. Serve warm with toasted whole grain crackers. Makes 12 servings.
***Tip** Because chile peppers contain oils that can burn skin and eyes, avoid direct contact with them as much as possible. When working with chile peppers, wear rubber or plastic gloves. If your bare hands touch the peppers, wash your hands and nails well with soap and warm water.

EACH SERVING *81 cal, 6 g fat, 24 mg chol, 192 mg sodium, 3 g carb, 0 g fiber, 4 g pro.*

CARAMELIZED ONION-BLUE CHEESE DIP

ASIAGO DIP

MEXICAN SEVEN-LAYER DIP

Caramelized Onion-Blue Cheese Dip

START TO FINISH 35 minutes

- 2 tablespoons olive oil
- 2 large sweet onions, halved and cut into slivers
- 16 ounces cremini mushrooms, chopped
- 1 8-ounce package reduced-fat cream cheese (Neufchâtel), softened
- ⅔ cup crumbled blue cheese
- ½ cup fat-free milk
- 2 teaspoons snipped fresh thyme
- ¼ teaspoon salt
- ¼ teaspoon black pepper
  Pear slices, melba toast, and/or whole grain crackers

1. In a large nonstick skillet heat olive oil over medium heat. Add onion. Cover and cook for 10 minutes, stirring occasionally. Uncover and add mushrooms. Cook, uncovered, for 8 minutes or until mushrooms are tender and onion is golden brown, stirring occasionally.
2. Add cream cheese, blue cheese, milk, thyme, salt, and pepper to onion mixture. Cook and stir over low heat until mixture is melted. Serve warm with pear slices, melba toast, and/or whole grain crackers. Makes 16 servings.
EACH SERVING *99 cal, 7 g fat, 15 mg chol, 172 mg sodium, 6 g carb, 1 g fiber, 4 g pro.*

Asiago Dip

PREP 25 minutes COOK 3 hours (low) or 1½ hours (high)

- ½ cup chicken broth or water
- 2 ounces dried tomatoes (not oil-packed)
- 1 16-ounce carton sour cream
- ¾ cup finely shredded Asiago cheese
- ⅔ cup mayonnaise
- 2 ounces cream cheese, cut up
- ½ cup sliced fresh mushrooms
- ½ cup thinly sliced green onions
  Thinly sliced green onions
  Baguette-style French bread slices, topped with finely shredded Asiago cheese and toasted

1. In a small saucepan bring broth to boiling. Remove from heat. Add dried tomatoes; cover and let stand for 5 minutes. Drain, discarding liquid. Chop tomatoes.
2. Meanwhile, in a 1½- or 2-quart slow cooker combine sour cream, ¾ cup Asiago cheese, mayonnaise, cream cheese, mushrooms, and ½ cup green onions. Stir in chopped tomatoes.
3. Cover and cook on low-heat setting for 3 to 4 hours or on high-heat setting for 1½ to 2 hours. Stir well before serving. If desired, keep warm in slow cooker on low-heat setting up to 2 hours. Sprinkle dip with additional green onions and serve with toasted cheese-topped baguette slices. Makes 14 servings.
EACH SERVING *196 cal, 19 g fat, 29 mg chol, 269 mg sodium, 4 g carb, 1 g fiber, 4 g pro.*

Mexican Seven-Layer Dip

PREP 20 minutes CHILL 4 hours

- 1 16-ounce can refried beans
- ½ cup bottled salsa
- ½ 14-ounce package refrigerated guacamole
- 1 8-ounce carton sour cream
- 1 cup shredded cheddar or taco cheese
- ¼ cup sliced green onions
- ¼ cup sliced pitted ripe olives
- 1 cup chopped, seeded tomato
- 8 cups tortilla chips or crackers

1. In a medium bowl combine refried beans and salsa; spread onto a 12-inch platter or 2-quart baking dish. Carefully layer guacamole and sour cream over bean mixture. Top with cheese, green onions, and olives. Cover and chill for 4 to 24 hours.
2. Before serving, sprinkle with chopped tomato. Serve with tortilla chips. Makes 16 servings.
EACH SERVING *179 cal, 11 g fat, 15 mg chol, 340 mg sodium, 16 g carb, 3 g fiber, 5 g pro.*

CHEESY SHRIMP DIP

1. In a 3½- or 4-quart slow cooker stir together cream cheese, fontina cheese, and Parmesan cheese. Stir in half-and-half, green onions, wine, mustard, and cayenne pepper.

2. Cover and cook on low-heat setting for 3 hours or on high-heat setting for 1½ hours.

3. Thaw shrimp, if frozen. Chop shrimp; stir shrimp and lemon peel into cheese mixture.

4. Serve immediately or keep warm, covered, on warm or low-heat setting up to 2 hours. Serve with vegetables. Makes 15 servings.

EACH SERVING *283 cal, 20 g fat, 124 mg chol, 625 mg sodium, 3 g carb, 0 g fiber, 18 g pro.*

Club Sandwich Dip
PREP 20 minutes COOK 1 hour (high)

- 1 pound smoked turkey, chopped
- 8 ounces cooked ham, chopped
- 8 ounces process Swiss or American cheese, torn
- 1 8-ounce package cream cheese, cut up
- 1 cup light mayonnaise
- 2 teaspoons Dijon mustard
- 6 slices bacon, crisp-cooked, drained, and crumbled
- ½ cup cherry or grape tomatoes, coarsely chopped
  Whole wheat toast points and/or assorted cut-up vegetables

1. In a 3½- or 4-quart slow cooker combine turkey, ham, process cheese, cream cheese, mayonnaise, and mustard.

2. Cover and cook on high-heat setting for 1 to 2 hours or until cheeses are melted, stirring after 1 hour.

3. Serve immediately or keep warm, covered, on warm or low-heat setting up to 2 hours, stirring occasionally. Before serving, stir in half the bacon. Top with the remaining bacon and tomatoes. Serve with toast points. Makes 20 servings.

EACH SERVING *177 cal, 13 g fat, 46 mg chol, 578 mg sodium, 3 g carb, 0 g fiber, 11 g pro.*

Very Veggie Dip
START TO FINISH 20 minutes

- 1 8-ounce carton light sour cream
- ½ 8-ounce package reduced-fat cream cheese (Neufchâtel)
- 1 tablespoon fat-free milk
- ¼ cup finely chopped red or yellow sweet pepper
- ¼ cup finely chopped zucchini
- 2 tablespoons shredded carrot
- 1 tablespoon snipped fresh chives
- ¼ teaspoon salt
- ¼ teaspoon black pepper
  Fresh cut-up vegetables, whole grain crackers, and/or multigrain tortilla chips

1. In a medium mixing bowl beat sour cream, cream cheese, and milk with an electric mixer on low to medium until smooth. Stir in sweet pepper, zucchini, carrot, and chives. Stir in salt and pepper.

2. Serve with vegetables, crackers, and/or tortilla chips. Makes 16 servings.

EACH SERVING *39 cal, 3 g fat, 10 mg chol, 76 mg sodium, 2 g carb, 0 g fiber, 1 g pro.*

Cheesy Shrimp Dip
PREP 20 minutes
COOK 3 hours (low) or 1½ hours (high)

- 2 8-ounce packages cream cheese, cubed
- 2 cups shredded fontina cheese
- ½ cup finely shredded Parmesan cheese
- 1 cup half-and-half or light cream
- ½ cup sliced green onions
- 2 tablespoons dry white wine
- 2 tablespoons Dijon mustard
- ¼ teaspoon cayenne pepper
- 1 pound fresh or frozen peeled and deveined cooked shrimp
- 2 teaspoons finely shredded lemon peel
  Assorted cut-up vegetables

CLUB SANDWICH DIP

SPINACH AND ROASTED RED PEPPER DIP

CHILE CON QUESO

Spinach and Roasted Red Pepper Dip

PREP 20 minutes
BAKE 15 minutes at 350°F

½ cup shredded part-skim mozzarella cheese
½ cup plain low-fat yogurt
½ cup mayonnaise
¼ cup grated Parmesan cheese
1 tablespoon all-purpose flour
1 teaspoon Dijon mustard
¼ cup thinly sliced green onions
¾ cup bottled roasted red sweet peppers, drained and chopped
1 cup loosely packed fresh spinach leaves, coarsely chopped
3 red and/or yellow sweet peppers, seeded and cut into strips
Assorted crackers or flatbread

1. Preheat oven to 350°F. In a large bowl stir together mozzarella cheese, yogurt, mayonnaise, 2 tablespoons of the Parmesan cheese, flour, and mustard. Stir in 2 tablespoons of the green onions, the roasted red peppers, and spinach. Spread dip evenly into a 1-quart ungreased ovenproof shallow dish. Sprinkle with the remaining 2 tablespoons Parmesan cheese.
2. Bake, uncovered, for 15 minutes or until edges are bubbly and dip is heated through. Sprinkle with the remaining 2 tablespoons green onions. Serve with sweet pepper strips, crackers, and/or flatbread. Makes 36 servings.
EACH SERVING *21 cal, 2 g fat, 3 mg chol, 47 mg sodium, 1 g carb, 0 g fiber, 1 g pro.*

Chili con Queso

START TO FINISH 25 minutes

1 cup finely chopped onion
2 tablespoons butter
2⅔ cups chopped, seeded tomatoes
2 4-ounce cans diced green chile peppers
1 teaspoon ground cumin
1 cup Monterey Jack cheese with jalapeño peppers, shredded
2 teaspoons cornstarch
2 8-ounce packages cream cheese, cubed
Tortilla chips

1. In a large saucepan cook onion in butter until tender. Stir in tomatoes, undrained chile peppers, and cumin. Heat to boiling; reduce heat. Simmer, uncovered, for 10 minutes, stirring occasionally.
2. Toss shredded Monterey Jack cheese with cornstarch. Gradually add cheese mixture to saucepan, stirring until cheese is melted. Gradually add cream cheese, stirring until cheese is melted and smooth. Serve with chips. Makes 20 servings.
EACH SERVING *58 cal, 5 g fat, 16 mg chol, 79 mg sodium, 5 g carb, 0 g fiber, 2 g pro.*

Italian Grinder Dip

PREP 25 minutes
COOK 4 hours (low) or 2 hours (high)

1 pound ground beef
1 pound bulk Italian sausage
1 cup chopped onion
3 cloves garlic, minced
¾ cup chopped green sweet pepper
1 4-ounce can sliced mushrooms, drained
1 teaspoon fennel seeds, crushed
1 teaspoon dried oregano, crushed
1 teaspoon dried basil, crushed
½ teaspoon crushed red pepper
1 15-ounce can pizza sauce
Sliced garlic bread and/or ciabatta bread, toasted
Shredded mozzarella cheese

1. In a large skillet cook ground beef, sausage, onion, and garlic over medium-high heat until meat is browned, using a wooden spoon to break up meat as it cooks. Drain off fat.
2. In a 3½- or 4-quart slow cooker combine meat mixture, sweet pepper, mushrooms, fennel seeds, oregano, basil, and crushed red pepper. Stir in pizza sauce.
3. Cover and cook on low-heat setting for 4 to 5 hours or on high-heat setting for 2 to 2½ hours. Serve on toasted bread and sprinkle with cheese. Makes 22 servings.
EACH SERVING *148 cal, 12 g fat, 32 mg chol, 217 mg sodium, 3 g carb, 1 g fiber, 7 g pro.*

ITALIAN GRINDER DIP

RICOTTA DIP FOR FRUIT

1 tablespoon extra virgin olive oil
1 clove garlic, minced
½ teaspoon salt
¼ teaspoon freshly ground black pepper
    Corn chips or tortilla chips

1. In a medium bowl stir together the tomatillos, tomatoes, oranges, avocado, cilantro, lime juice, jalapeño, oil, garlic, salt, and black pepper. Cover and chill for 1 to 4 hours. Stir before serving. Serve with corn chips or tortilla chips. Makes 16 servings.

EACH SERVING *193 cal, 11 g fat, 0 mg chol, 274 mg sodium, 23 g carb, 0 g fiber, 2 g pro.*

S'mores Fondue
START TO FINISH **20 minutes**

⅓ cup unsweetened cocoa powder
¼ cup sugar
2 tablespoons cornstarch
¼ teaspoon ground cinnamon
2½ cups low-fat milk
⅔ cup marshmallow creme
    Low-fat milk
    Graham cracker sticks and/or assorted fruit dippers (strawberries, banana chunks, and/or apple wedges)

1. In a medium saucepan combine cocoa powder, sugar, cornstarch, and cinnamon. Gradually whisk in the 2½ cups milk. Stir on medium heat until thickened and bubbly; reduce heat. Stir for 2 minutes more. Remove from heat. Stir in marshmallow creme until well combined.
2. Transfer chocolate mixture to a 1- or 1½-quart slow cooker or a fondue pot. Keep warm up to 2 hours on low heat. Stir occasionally and add additional milk to thin as needed. Serve warm with graham cracker sticks and/or fruit dippers. Makes 14 servings.

EACH SERVING *54 cal, 1 g fat, 2 mg chol, 23 mg sodium, 11 g carb, 1 g fiber, 2 g pro.*

Ricotta Dip for Fruit
PREP **15 minutes** CHILL **24 hours**

½ cup low-fat ricotta cheese
4 ounces cream cheese, softened
3 tablespoons orange juice
2 tablespoons powdered sugar
1 6-ounce container vanilla low-fat yogurt
6 cups cubed cantaloupe, cubed honeydew melon, pineapple chunks, and/or strawberries

1. For dip, in a blender or food processor combine ricotta cheese, cream cheese, orange juice, and powdered sugar. Cover and blend or process until smooth. In a medium bowl stir together cheese mixture and yogurt. If desired, cover and chill dip up to 24 hours.

2. Serve with assorted fresh fruit. Makes 12 servings.

EACH SERVING *94 cal, 4 g fat, 14 mg chol, 72 mg sodium, 12 g carb, 1 g fiber, 3 g pro.*

Tomatillo Salsa
PREP **25 minutes** CHILL **1 hour**

3 medium tomatillos, peeled and chopped
2 plum tomatoes, seeded, and chopped
2 medium oranges, peeled, seeded, and chopped
1 avocado, halved, seeded, peeled, and chopped
2 tablespoons chopped fresh cilantro
2 tablespoons lime juice
1 small fresh jalapeño, halved, seeded, and finely chopped (see tip, page 35)

S'MORES FONDUE

SWEET-HOT
PEANUTS

WHITE CHOCOLATE SNACK MIX

STRAWBERRIES WITH CITRUS DIP

Sweet-Hot Peanuts

PREP 10 minutes
BAKE 30 minutes at 250°F

    2 tablespoons sugar
    2 tablespoons olive oil
    1 to 2 teaspoons ground chipotle
       chile pepper
 1½   teaspoons chili powder
    1 teaspoon five-spice powder
    3 cups dry-roasted peanuts

1. Preheat oven to 250°F. Line
a 15×10×1-inch baking pan with
parchment paper or foil; set aside.
2. In a large bowl combine sugar, oil,
chipotle chile pepper, chili powder, and
five-spice powder. Add peanuts; toss
gently to coat.
3. Spread peanuts in an even layer in
the prepared pan. Bake for 30 minutes,
stirring twice. Cool in pan on a wire
rack. Makes 12 servings.
EACH SERVING *244 cal, 20 g fat, 0 mg chol,
302 mg sodium, 10 g carb, 0 g fiber, 9 g pro.*

White Chocolate Snack Mix

START TO FINISH 45 minutes

    1 cup bite-size wheat or rice
       shredded square biscuits cereal
    1 cup broken graham crackers,
       graham crackers with cinnamon-
       sugar topping, or chocolate-
       covered graham crackers
    1 cup pretzel sticks
    1 cup broken rice cakes
  ½ cup tiny marshmallows
  ½ cup raisins or mixed dried fruit
       bits
  ½ cup whole or slivered almonds or
       cashews
    8 ounces white baking chocolate,
       chopped
    3 tablespoons whipping cream
    2 teaspoons light-color corn syrup
  ¼ teaspoon almond extract

1. Line a large baking sheet with waxed
paper or parchment paper; set aside.
In a large bowl gently combine cereal,
graham crackers, pretzels, rice cakes,
marshmallows, raisins, and nuts.
2. In a medium saucepan combine
white chocolate, cream, and corn
syrup. Cook and stir over low heat until
nearly melted; remove from heat and
stir gently until smooth. Stir in almond
extract.

3. Pour warm chocolate mixture over
cereal mixture; toss gently to coat.
Immediately spread snack mix onto
the prepared baking sheet. Cool until
chocolate is set (up to 12 hours). Break
into pieces. Makes 28 servings.
EACH SERVING *105 cal, 5 g fat, 4 mg chol,
75 mg sodium, 14 g carb, 1 g fiber, 2 g pro.*

Strawberries with Citrus Dip

START TO FINISH 15 minutes

    1 6-ounce carton plain low-fat
       yogurt
  ⅓ cup light whipped dessert
       topping, thawed
    2 tablespoons powdered sugar
    2 teaspoons finely shredded
       orange, lemon, and/or lime peel
    1 tablespoon orange juice
    3 cups small strawberries

1. For dip, in a medium bowl stir
together yogurt, dessert topping,
powdered sugar, orange peel, and
orange juice.
2. Wash strawberries but do not remove
stems. Drain on several layers of paper
towels. Serve berries with dip. Makes
8 servings.
EACH SERVING *56 cal, 1 g fat, 1 mg chol,
15 mg sodium, 9 g carb, 1 g fiber, 1 g pro.*

**CURRIED CHICKEN
STEW, RECIPE PAGE 84**

poultry

THE BEST OF THE BIRD Whether you like it fried, stuffed, or roasted, poultry is a perennial favorite. It's versatile, mild-flavored, and always a smart choice for supper.

Cheddar-Stuffed Turkey Burgers with Peach Ketchup

PREP 30 minutes COOK 20 minutes

- 4 medium peaches, peeled, pitted, and cut up
- ¼ cup sugar
- 2 tablespoons cider vinegar
- 1 teaspoon chili powder
- ⅛ teaspoon cinnamon
  Dash cayenne pepper
- 2 pounds ground turkey or ground beef
- ½ teaspoon salt
- ¼ teaspoon black pepper
- 2 to 3 ounces white cheddar or Havarti cheese, shredded (½ to ¾ cup)
- 1 tablespoon canola oil
- 8 hamburger buns, split and toasted
  Leaf lettuce (optional)
  Additional peach slices (optional)

1. For peach ketchup, in a blender or food processor combine cut-up peaches, sugar, cider vinegar, chili powder, cinnamon, and cayenne pepper. Cover and blend or process until smooth.
2. In a large bowl lightly mix turkey with half the peach ketchup, salt, and black pepper. Divide into 8 balls. Make an indentation in center of each ball and fill with some cheese. Shape meat around cheese. Flatten into patties.
3. In a very large skillet heat oil over medium heat. Cook half the patties about 5 minutes or until well browned. Turn and cook 5 minutes more or until no pink remains (165°F). Cook remaining patties.
4. If desired, serve patties on lettuce-lined buns with additional peach slices and remaining peach ketchup. Makes 8 servings.
EACH SERVING *388 cal, 16 g fat, 97 mg chol, 505 mg sodium, 35 g carb, 2 g fiber, 26 g pro.*

Turkey Steaks with Spinach, Pears, and Blue Cheese

START TO FINISH 20 minutes

- 2 turkey breast tenderloins (1 to 1¼ pounds)
- 1 teaspoon dried sage, crushed
  Salt and freshly ground black pepper
- 2 tablespoons butter
- 1 6-ounce package fresh baby spinach
- 1 large pear, cored and thinly sliced
- ¼ cup crumbled blue cheese

1. Horizontally split tenderloins to make four ½-inch-thick steaks. Rub turkey with sage; sprinkle with salt and pepper. In an extra-large skillet cook steaks in 1 tablespoon of the butter over medium-high heat for 14 minutes or until no longer pink (170°F), turning once. (Reduce heat to medium if turkey browns too quickly.) Remove from skillet. Add spinach to skillet. Cook and stir just until wilted.
2. Meanwhile, in small skillet cook pear slices in remaining 1 tablespoon butter over medium to medium-high heat for 5 minutes or until tender and lightly browned, stirring occasionally.
3. Serve steaks with spinach and pears. Top with blue cheese. Makes 4 servings.
EACH SERVING *240 cal, 9 g fat, 92 mg chol, 380 mg sodium, 8 g carb, 2 g fiber, 31 g pro.*

CHEDDAR-STUFFED TURKEY BURGERS WITH PEACH KETCHUP

TURKEY MANICOTTI

Turkey Manicotti

PREP 30 minutes   COOK 30 minutes
BAKE 25 minutes at 350°F
STAND 10 minutes

12 dried manicotti tubes
½ cup chopped onion
4 cloves garlic, minced
2 tablespoons olive oil
2 14.5-ounce cans fire-roasted diced tomatoes, undrained
⅓ cup dry red wine
2 tablespoons tomato paste
2 cups chopped cooked turkey
1 cup shredded mozzarella cheese
½ 15-ounce carton ricotta cheese
½ 8-ounce tub cream cheese spread with chives and onion
¼ cup grated Parmesan cheese
1 teaspoon dried basil, crushed
½ teaspoon dried oregano, crushed
¼ teaspoon salt
¼ teaspoon black pepper

1. Cook manicotti according to package directions; drain. Rinse with cold water; drain again and set aside. Meanwhile, for sauce, in a large saucepan cook onion and garlic in hot oil over medium-high heat until onion is tender. Stir in undrained tomatoes, wine, and tomato paste. Bring to boiling; reduce heat. Cover and simmer for 30 minutes.
2. Preheat oven to 350°F. For filling, in a large bowl combine turkey, ½ cup of the mozzarella cheese, the ricotta, cream cheese spread, Parmesan, basil, oregano, salt, and pepper. Using a small spoon, carefully fill each manicotti tube with about ¼ cup filling. Arrange filled shells in one 3-quart baking pan. Pour sauce over shells; sprinkle with remaining ½ cup mozzarella cheese. Cover pan with foil.
3. Bake for 30 minutes or until heated through. Let stand, covered, for 10 minutes before serving. Makes 6 servings.

EACH SERVING 503 cal, 22 g fat, 83 mg chol, 777 mg sodium, 42 g carb, 2 g fiber, 30 g pro.

CRAN-TURKEY ENCHILADAS

Cran-Turkey Enchiladas

PREP 30 minutes
BAKE 50 minutes at 350°F

Nonstick cooking spray
2 cups shredded cooked turkey
1 16-ounce can whole cranberry sauce
1 15-ounce can black beans, rinsed and drained
1½ cups bottled salsa
1 cup shredded Colby and Monterey Jack cheese
½ cup sour cream
3 green onions, sliced
¼ cup snipped fresh cilantro
1 teaspoon ground cumin
½ teaspoon salt
½ teaspoon black pepper
8 7- to 8-inch whole wheat or regular flour tortillas
1 teaspoon bottled hot pepper sauce

1. Preheat oven to 350°F. Lightly coat a 3-quart rectangular baking dish with cooking spray; set aside. For filling, in a large bowl stir together turkey, half the cranberry sauce, beans, ½ cup of the salsa, ¾ cup of the cheese, sour cream, green onions, cilantro, cumin, salt, and pepper. Spoon about ⅔ cup filling on each tortilla. Roll up tortillas around filling. Place, seam sides down, in prepared dish; set aside.
2. For sauce, in a bowl stir together remaining cranberry sauce, remaining salsa, and hot pepper sauce. Spoon over filled tortillas. Cover with foil. Bake for 45 minutes. Uncover; top with remaining cheese. Bake 5 minutes more or until heated through and cheese is melted. Makes 8 servings.

EACH SERVING 406 cal, 12 g fat, 45 mg chol, 963 mg sodium, 57 g carb, 6 g fiber, 22 g pro.

TURKEY
SALTIMBOCCA

Turkey Saltimbocca

START TO FINISH **30 minutes**

¼ cup all-purpose flour
½ teaspoon salt
½ teaspoon dried sage, crushed
¼ teaspoon black pepper
4 turkey cutlets
2 tablespoons vegetable oil
4 slices cooked ham
4 slices fontina or Swiss cheese
¼ cup dry white wine
¼ cup reduced-sodium chicken broth

1. In a shallow dish combine flour, salt, sage, and pepper. Set aside.
2. Place each turkey cutlet between two pieces of plastic wrap. Using the flat side of a meat mallet, lightly pound turkey, working from center to edges, to about ¼-inch thickness. Remove plastic wrap. Dip cutlets into flour, turning to coat both sides; shake off excess.
3. In an extra-large nonstick skillet heat oil over medium-high heat. Add cutlets; cook about 2 minutes or until browned on bottom. Turn cutlets over; top each with 1 slice of the ham and 1 slice of the cheese. Add wine and broth; cook about 2 minutes more or until cheese is melted and sauce is thickened.
4. Transfer cutlets to a serving platter. Spoon pan drippings over cutlets. Makes 4 servings.

EACH SERVING *282 cal, 14 g fat, 66 mg chol, 774 mg sodium, 7 g carb, 1 g fiber, 28 g pro.*

Herb-Roasted Turkey

PREP **30 minutes**   CHILL **overnight**
ROAST **3 hours at 350°F**
STAND **1 hour 30 minutes**

1 15- to 17-pound whole fresh free-range turkey
4 tablespoons unsalted butter
15 fresh sage leaves
Sea salt and freshly ground black pepper
4 sprigs fresh rosemary
2 onions, quartered
1 apple, quartered
2 cups dry white wine
2 cups unfiltered apple juice

1. Rinse turkey inside and out; remove giblets and neck from the cavities.
2. Loosen skin of turkey breast. Place 2 tablespoons butter and 4 sage leaves under skin of each breast. Season turkey cavity and skin with salt and pepper. Place 2 rosemary sprigs, 1 onion, half the apple, and 4 sage leaves in large cavity. Pour the wine and apple juice in roasting pan; add remaining onion, apple, sage, and rosemary. Place turkey breast, side down, in pan. Cover; refrigerate overnight.

3. Remove turkey from refrigerator; let stand 1 hour at room temperature. Preheat oven to 350°F. Skewer neck skin to back. Tie drumsticks to tail using kitchen string.
4. Roast turkey, breast side down, for 1½ hours, spooning pan drippings over the turkey every 30 to 45 minutes. Turn turkey breast side up.* Cut string between drumsticks. Roast 1½ to 2 hours longer, spooning over pan drippings every 30 to 45 minutes or until turkey juices run clear when a small knife is inserted in thickest part of thigh (180°F in thigh and 165°F in breast). Lightly tent turkey with foil if it becomes brown too quickly.
5. Remove turkey from oven; spoon pan drippings over it. Move turkey to a cutting board (reserve pan drippings for Herb Gravy). Let stand 30 to 45 minutes. Makes 8 servings, plus leftovers.
*To turn the turkey, insert large tongs into the center cavity and wear rubber gloves or use a piece of foil to hold it as you rotate it.

EACH SERVING *331 cal, 10 g fat, 177 mg chol, 162 mg sodium, 5 g carb, 0 g fiber, 48 g pro.*

Herb Gravy

START TO FINISH **20 minutes**

4 tablespoons unsalted butter
4 tablespoons all-purpose flour
2 teaspoons fresh thyme
1 teaspoon chopped fresh sage
1 cup reserved pan juices from cooked turkey
2 cups reduced-sodium chicken broth
Sea salt and freshly ground pepper

1. Melt butter in a skillet over medium-high heat until sizzling hot. Slowly stir in flour, reduce heat to medium, then cook, stirring constantly until flour is light brown, about 2 minutes. Stir in thyme and sage. Slowly whisk in pan liquids from the turkey and the chicken broth; season with salt and pepper to taste. Cook and stir for 2 minutes or until gravy comes to boiling and begins to thicken. Makes 12 (¼-cup) servings.
EACH SERVING *54 cal, 4 g fat, 11 mg chol, 154 mg sodium, 3 g carb, 0 g fiber, 1 g pro.*

HERB-ROASTED
TURKEY WITH
HERB GRAVY

TURKEY REUBEN LOAF

WHITE BEAN AND SAUSAGE PASTA

Turkey and Sweet Potato Shepherd's Pies

PREP 40 minutes
BAKE 20 minutes at 375°F

1½ pounds sweet potatoes, peeled and cut into 2-inch pieces
2   cloves garlic, halved
¼   cup fat-free milk
½   teaspoon salt
12 ounces uncooked ground turkey breast
½   cup chopped onion
1¼ cups coarsely chopped zucchini
1   cup chopped carrots
½   cup frozen whole kernel corn
¼   cup water
1   8-ounce can tomato sauce
2   tablespoons Worcestershire sauce
2   teaspoons snipped fresh sage
⅛   teaspoon black pepper

1. Preheat oven to 375°F. In a medium saucepan cook sweet potatoes and garlic, covered, in enough lightly salted boiling water to cover for 15 minutes or until tender; drain. Mash with a potato masher or beat with an electric mixer on low. Gradually add milk and salt, mashing or beating to make potato mixture light and fluffy. Cover and keep warm.
2. Meanwhile, in a large skillet cook turkey and onion over medium heat until meat is browned, stirring with a wooden spoon to break up turkey as it cooks. Drain if needed. Stir in zucchini, carrots, corn, and the water. Bring to boiling; reduce heat. Simmer, covered,

for 5 minutes or until vegetables are tender.
3. Add tomato sauce, Worcestershire sauce, snipped sage, and pepper to turkey mixture; heat through. Divide turkey mixture among four ungreased 10-ounce ramekins, spreading evenly. Spoon mashed sweet potato mixture in mounds onto turkey mixture.
4. Bake, uncovered, for 20 minutes or until heated through. Makes 4 servings.
EACH SERVING 268 cal, 1 g fat, 42 mg chol, 824 mg sodium, 41 g carb, 7 g fiber, 24 g pro.

Turkey Reuben Loaf

PREP 15 minutes
BAKE 12 minutes at 400°F

1   cup mayonnaise
½   cup pickle relish
2   tablespoons ketchup
4   cups shredded cabbage
4   teaspoons vinegar
2   teaspoons caraway seeds
1   unsliced oblong loaf of bread
12 ounces Havarti cheese, sliced
1   pound cooked turkey, sliced or chopped

1. Preheat oven to 400°F. For sauce, in a bowl combine mayonnaise, pickle relish, and ketchup. In another bowl combine cabbage, vinegar, and caraway seeds.
2. Slice bread lengthwise. Hollow out some of the bread. Spread some of the sauce on cut sides of bread; reserve remaining for serving. Arrange half the cheese slices on bottom half of bread. Top with cabbage mixture, turkey, and remaining cheese. Top with top half of bread. Wrap tightly in foil and place on baking sheet. Bake for 10 minutes.

Carefully unwrap and bake 2 minutes more, until bread is crisp and cheese is melted.
3. To serve, cut loaf in slices with a sharp serrated knife. Pass remaining sauce. Makes 8 servings.
EACH SERVING 640 cal, 40 g fat, 85 mg chol, 931 mg sodium, 37 g carb, 5 g fiber, 31 g pro.

White Bean and Sausage Pasta

START TO FINISH 20 minutes

2   cups dried rigatoni
1   15-ounce can white kidney (cannellini), Great Northern, or navy beans, rinsed and drained
1   14.5-ounce can Italian-style stewed tomatoes, undrained
4   ounces cooked smoked turkey sausage, halved lengthwise and cut into ½-inch slices
⅓   cup snipped fresh basil
¼   cup shredded Asiago or Parmesan cheese

1. Cook pasta according to package directions. Drain; return pasta to saucepan.
2. Meanwhile, in a large saucepan combine beans, undrained tomatoes, and sausage. Cook and stir until heated through. Add bean mixture and fresh basil to pasta; stir gently to combine. To serve, sprinkle each serving with cheese. Makes 4 servings.
EACH SERVING 432 cal, 10 g fat, 46 mg chol, 961 mg sodium, 65 g carb, 7 g fiber, 25 g pro.

BALSAMIC-GLAZED CHICKEN TENDERS

HERBED CHICKEN, ORZO, AND ZUCCHINI

Herbed Chicken, Orzo, and Zucchini

START TO FINISH 20 minutes

- 1 cup dried orzo
- 4 small skinless, boneless chicken breast halves (1 to 1¼ pounds)
- 1 teaspoon dried basil
- 3 tablespoons olive oil
- 2 medium zucchini, sliced
- 2 tablespoons red wine vinegar
- 1 tablespoon snipped fresh dill
  Lemon wedges (optional)
  Snipped fresh dill (optional)

1. Prepare orzo according to package directions; drain. Cover and keep warm.
2. Meanwhile, sprinkle chicken with the basil; season with *salt* and *black pepper.* In large skillet heat 1 tablespoon of the olive oil. Add chicken and cook 12 minutes or until no longer pink (170°F), turning once. Remove from skillet. Add zucchini to skillet; cook for 3 minutes or until crisp-tender.
3. In a bowl whisk together vinegar, remaining olive oil, and the 1 tablespoon fresh dill. Add orzo; toss. Season with *salt* and *pepper.* Serve chicken with orzo, zucchini, and, if desired, lemon wedges. If desired, sprinkle with dill. Makes 4 servings.
EACH SERVING *390 cal, 12 g fat, 66 mg chol, 233 mg sodium, 35 g carb, 3 g fiber, 33 g pro.*

Balsamic-Glazed Chicken Tenders

START TO FINISH 25 minutes

- 1 small orange
- ⅔ cup cinnamon applesauce
- ¼ cup balsamic vinegar
- ½ teaspoon ground cardamom or ¼ teaspoon ground nutmeg
- ½ teaspoon salt
- ½ teaspoon black pepper
- 1 pound chicken tenders
- 2 teaspoons vegetable oil
  Fresh thyme sprigs (optional)

1. Finely shred peel from orange; set aside. Juice orange. In a saucepan combine applesauce, vinegar, cardamom, juice from the orange, salt, and pepper. Bring to boiling over high heat. Reduce heat to low. Cook, uncovered, 10 minutes, stirring occasionally. Remove from heat; cover to keep warm.
2. Lightly season chicken with salt and pepper. Heat oil in an extra-large nonstick skillet over medium-high heat. Add chicken; cook until golden brown on bottom, about 4 minutes. Turn chicken and add ½ cup of the applesauce mixture to skillet. Cook 2 minutes more or until chicken is cooked through.
3. To serve, spoon some of the applesauce mixture on each plate; top

with chicken, orange peel, and fresh thyme. Pass remaining sauce. Makes 4 servings.
EACH SERVING *208 cal, 4 g fat, 66 mg chol, 207 mg sodium, 15 g carb, 1 g fiber, 27 g pro.*

Smoky Chicken Pizzas

PREP 20 minutes
BAKE 10 minutes at 425°F

- 1 large red onion, thinly sliced
- ¼ cup olive oil
- ½ teaspoon crushed red pepper
- 4 individual-size packaged baked pizza crusts or flatbreads
- 12 ounces fully cooked chicken, shredded
- 4 ounces smoked mozzarella, shredded
- 1 cup arugula
  Crushed red pepper

1. Preheat oven to 425°F. In a large skillet cook onion in 1 tablespoon hot oil over medium heat for 10 minutes, stirring occasionally. Set aside.
2. Combine remaining oil and crushed red pepper; drizzle some on pizza crusts. Place on very large baking sheet(s). Top crusts with chicken, onions, and cheese. Bake for 10 minutes or until cheese is melted and pizzas are heated through. Top with greens; drizzle any remaining oil and sprinkle additional crushed red pepper. Makes 4 servings.
EACH SERVING *783 cal, 36 g fat, 98 mg chol, 1,074 mg sodium, 69 g carb, 3 g fiber, 46 g pro.*

COQ AU VIN

Coq au Vin

PREP 20 minutes
BAKE 45 minutes at 350°F
COOK 20 minutes

2½ pounds chicken drumsticks and/or thighs, skin removed
2 tablespoons vegetable oil
Salt
Black pepper
2 tablespoons butter or margarine
3 tablespoons all-purpose flour
1¼ cups Pinot Noir or Burgundy wine
¼ cup chicken broth or water
1 cup whole fresh mushrooms
1 cup very thinly sliced carrots
18 frozen small whole onions, thawed
1½ teaspoons snipped fresh marjoram
1½ teaspoons snipped fresh thyme
2 cloves garlic, minced
2 slices bacon, crisp-cooked, drained, and crumbled
Snipped fresh parsley (optional)
Hot cooked noodles (optional)

1. Preheat oven to 350°F. In an extra-large skillet cook chicken, half at a time, in hot oil over medium heat for 10 to 15 minutes or until browned, turning occasionally. Transfer chicken to a 3-quart baking dish. Sprinkle chicken with salt and pepper. Set aside.
2. In the same skillet melt butter over medium heat. Stir in flour until smooth. Gradually stir in wine and broth. Cook and stir until boiling. Halve any large mushrooms. Stir mushrooms, carrots, onions, marjoram, thyme, and garlic into wine mixture. Return just to boiling. Pour vegetable mixture over chicken.
3. Cover with foil. Bake about 45 minutes or until chicken is no longer pink (180°F). Transfer Coq au Vin to a serving platter. Sprinkle with bacon. If desired, sprinkle with parsley and serve with hot cooked noodles. Makes 6 servings.

EACH SERVING 286 cal, 13 g fat, 95 mg chol, 321 mg sodium, 8 g carb, 1 g fiber, 24 g pro.

OVEN-FRIED BUTTERMILK CHICKEN

Oven-Fried Buttermilk Chicken

PREP 25 minutes   MARINATE 4 hours
BAKE 45 minutes at 400°F

2½ pounds meaty chicken pieces (breast halves,* thighs, and/or drumsticks)
1 cup buttermilk
¾ teaspoon salt
½ 8-ounce package crisp rye crackers
1 tablespoon Greek seasoning
¼ cup butter or margarine, melted
2 eggs, beaten
1 tablespoon water

1. If desired, skin chicken. Place chicken in a resealable plastic bag set in a bowl. For marinade, in a small bowl stir together buttermilk and salt. Pour over chicken. Seal bag; turn to coat chicken. Marinate in the refrigerator for at least 4 hours or up to 24 hours, turning bag occasionally.

2. Drain chicken, discarding marinade. In a blender or food processor combine crackers and Greek seasoning. Blend or process until crackers are crushed; transfer to a shallow dish.
3. Preheat oven to 400°F. Lightly grease a 3-quart rectangular baking pan; set aside. Add melted butter to crushed crackers; toss together. In another shallow dish combine eggs and the water. Dip chicken pieces, one at a time, in egg mixture, then roll in cracker mixture to coat. Arrange chicken in prepared baking pan, making sure pieces do not touch.
4. Bake, uncovered, for 45 minutes or until chicken pieces are tender and no longer pink (170°F for breasts; 180°F for thighs and drumsticks). Makes 6 servings.
*If breast halves are large, cut them in half before marinating.

EACH SERVING 388 cal, 20 g fat, 162 mg chol, 476 mg sodium, 18 g carb, 5 g fiber, 33 g pro.

LEMON CHICKEN
WITH OLIVES
AND RICOTTA

4. Spoon ricotta mixture into bowls. Top with noodles, chicken, olive mixture, remaining lemon peel, and fresh rosemary. Pass lemon wedges. Makes 4 servings.

EACH SERVING *443 cal, 19 g fat, 130 mg chol, 1,053 mg sodium, 30 g carb, 4 g fiber, 39 g pro.*

Pan-Seared Chicken with Cherry-Tarragon Sauce

START TO FINISH 30 minutes

- ¼ cup all-purpose flour
- 2 teaspoons smoked paprika
- 1 teaspoon dry mustard
- ¼ teaspoon salt
- ¼ teaspoon black pepper
- 8 skinless, boneless chicken thighs
- 2 tablespoons olive oil
- 2 cups fresh or frozen pitted dark sweet cherries, thawed if frozen
- 2 tablespoons snipped fresh tarragon
- 3 cloves garlic, minced
- 1 cup dry red wine or cherry juice
- ½ cup chicken broth
- 2 tablespoons butter
- 2 cups hot cooked couscous, rice, or pasta

1. In a shallow dish combine flour, paprika, mustard, salt, and pepper. Coat chicken with flour mixture.
2. In a very large skillet cook chicken in hot oil over medium to medium-high heat for 8 to 10 minutes or until chicken is no longer pink, turning once. Remove from pan. Cover; keep warm.
3. Add cherries, tarragon, and garlic to skillet. Cook and stir over medium heat for 1 minute. Stir in wine and broth. Simmer, uncovered, 3 to 5 minutes or until sauce is reduced to about 2 cups. Stir in butter until melted. Season to taste with salt and pepper.
4. To serve, spoon sauce over chicken and serve with couscous. If desired, sprinkle with additional fresh tarragon. Makes 4 servings.

EACH SERVING *573 cal, 21 g fat, 180 mg chol, 631 mg sodium, 40 g carb, 3 g fiber, 44 g pro.*

Lemon Chicken with Olives and Ricotta

START TO FINISH 27 minutes

- 8 no-boil (oven-ready) lasagna noodles
- 1 teaspoon + 1 tablespoon olive oil
- 1 Meyer lemon or regular lemon
- 4 small skinless, boneless chicken breast halves, halved crosswise
- 1 cup garlic-stuffed or pitted green olives
- 1 cup ricotta cheese
- ½ teaspoon salt
- ½ teaspoon black pepper
  Fresh rosemary (optional)

1. In a Dutch oven bring 3 inches water to boiling. Add noodles and 1 teaspoon olive oil; cover. Cook for 6 minutes or until tender; drain. Lay noodles in single layer on waxed paper. Cover and set aside.
2. Meanwhile, shred lemon peel; halve lemon. Juice 1 half; cut remaining in wedges. Season chicken with salt, pepper, and half of the lemon peel. In very large skillet heat 1 tablespoon oil over medium-high heat. Add chicken; cook 10 minutes or until no pink remains, turning once. Add olives; heat through. Remove from heat.
3. In microwave-safe bowl combine ricotta, the lemon juice, salt, and pepper. Heat on high 30 seconds, stirring once.

PAN-SEARED CHICKEN WITH CHERRY-TARRAGON SAUCE

SAUCY BBQ CHICKEN

Saucy BBQ Chicken

PREP 10 minutes BROIL 27 minutes

- 8 small chicken drumsticks
- 1 large onion, cut into 6 slices
- 1 cup ketchup
- ¼ cup molasses
- 3 to 4 tablespoons cider vinegar
- 2 tablespoons packed brown sugar
- 1 teaspoon smoked paprika
  Several dashes bottled hot pepper sauce
  Fresh parsley

1. Preheat broiler. Broil chicken on unheated rack of broiler pan 4 to 5 inches from heat for 10 minutes.
2. Lightly brush onion slices with olive oil. Remove pan from oven. Turn and move chicken to one end of pan. Place onion slices, in single layer, on opposite end of pan. Broil 15 minutes or until chicken is no longer pink and juices run clear (180°F).
3. Meanwhile, in a small saucepan combine ketchup, molasses, vinegar, brown sugar, paprika, and pepper sauce. Bring to boiling over medium heat. Remove from heat; keep warm. Remove onions. Broil chicken 2 minutes more; brush with sauce during last minute.
4. Chop 2 of the onion slices; stir into sauce. Serve chicken with onion slices and parsley. Makes 4 servings.

EACH SERVING 426 cal, 16 g fat, 118 mg chol, 801 mg sodium, 40 g carb, 1 g fiber, 30 g pro.

Chicken and Pasta with Gorgonzola Sauce

START TO FINISH 30 minutes

- 1½ pounds skinless, boneless chicken breast halves, cut crosswise into ½-inch slices
- ½ teaspoon salt
- ½ teaspoon black pepper
- 3 tablespoons olive oil
- 8 ounces stemmed fresh cremini, shiitake, and/or button mushrooms, sliced
- 2 cups whipping cream
- 1 cup crumbled Gorgonzola cheese
- ⅔ cup grated Parmesan cheese
- ¼ cup snipped fresh parsley
- 12 to 16 ounces dried pasta, cooked and drained

CHICKEN AND PASTA WITH GORGONZOLA SAUCE

1. Sprinkle chicken with ¼ teaspoon of the salt and ¼ teaspoon of the pepper.
2. In a large nonstick skillet heat 2 tablespoons of the oil over medium-high heat. Add chicken; cook and stir until brown. Remove from skillet. Add the remaining 1 tablespoon oil and mushrooms. Cook for 5 minutes or until mushrooms are softened and liquid is evaporated, stirring occasionally.
3. Return chicken to skillet; stir in cream. Bring to boiling; reduce heat. Boil gently, uncovered, for 3 minutes. Stir in ½ cup of the Gorgonzola cheese, the Parmesan cheese, the remaining ¼ teaspoon salt, and the remaining ¼ teaspoon pepper. Cook and stir about 1 minute or until cheeses are melted.
4. Add chicken mixture, the remaining ½ cup Gorgonzola cheese, and parsley to hot cooked pasta; toss gently to combine. Makes 6 servings.

EACH SERVING *800 cal, 48 g fat, 200 mg chol, 753 mg sodium, 47 g carb, 2 g fiber, 45 g pro.*

Chicken Pasta Casserole

PREP 30 minutes
BAKE 35 minutes at 350°F

8 ounces dried bow tie pasta
2 tablespoons olive oil
6 cloves garlic, minced
1 pound skinless, boneless chicken breast halves, cut into 1-inch pieces
1 teaspoon dried basil, crushed
½ teaspoon salt
¼ teaspoon black pepper

CHICKEN PASTA CASSEROLE

1 medium onion, chopped
½ cup chopped red sweet pepper
1 cup frozen cut asparagus
1 8-ounce container cream cheese spread with chive and onion
¾ cup half-and-half or light cream
½ cup panko (Japanese-style bread crumbs)
¼ cup sliced almonds
1 tablespoon butter, melted

1. Preheat oven to 350°F. Cook pasta according to package directions; drain. Return pasta to pan.
2. Meanwhile, in a large skillet heat oil; add garlic and cook for 30 seconds. Season chicken with basil, salt, and pepper. Add chicken to the skillet; cook 3 minutes or until no pink remains. Remove from skillet. Add onion and sweet pepper to skillet; cook until tender. Stir in asparagus and cooked chicken. Remove from heat and set aside.
3. Stir cheese into pasta until melted. Stir in chicken mixture and half-and-half. Transfer to a 2-quart rectangular baking dish. In a small bowl combine bread crumbs, almonds, and butter; sprinkle over casserole.
4. Bake, uncovered, for 35 minutes or until heated through. Makes 5 servings.

EACH SERVING *615 cal, 31 g fat, 116 mg chol, 531 mg sodium, 48 g carb, 4 g fiber, 33 g pro.*

PROSCIUTTO-
PROVOLONE STUFFED
CHICKEN BREASTS

Prosciutto-Provolone Stuffed Chicken Breasts

PREP 45 minutes
BAKE 12 minutes at 400°F

- 4 boneless, skinless chicken breast halves
- 8 thin slices prosciutto
- 8 slices provolone cheese
- ½ cup lightly packed fresh basil leaves
- ¼ cup olive oil
- 8 ounces dried fettuccine or linguine
- 1 tablespoon butter
- 4 cloves garlic, chopped
- 1 cup grated Parmesan cheese

1. Preheat oven to 400°F. Place each chicken breast half between two pieces of plastic wrap. Using the flat side of a meat mallet, pound chicken lightly, from the center to edges, to about ⅛-inch-thick rectangles. Remove plastic wrap. Sprinkle both sides with salt and pepper.
2. Lay two slices of the prosciutto, two slices of the provolone cheese, and a few basil leaves on each chicken rectangle. Fold in sides; roll up from lower edge, pressing to seal in the filling. Secure each with a wooden toothpick.
3. In a large cast-iron or oven-going skillet heat 2 tablespoons of the oil over medium-high heat. Cook chicken rolls about 6 minutes or until golden brown, turning to brown all sides. Transfer skillet to the oven and bake, uncovered, for 12 minutes or until chicken is no longer pink (170°F).
4. Meanwhile, cook pasta in lightly salted boiling water according to package directions; drain. Return pasta to hot pan; cover and keep warm.
5. Remove chicken from skillet; keep warm. In the same skillet add the remaining 2 tablespoons of oil, the butter, and garlic. Cook and stir over medium heat for 1 minute. Remove skillet from heat. Add the drained pasta; toss to coat. Sprinkle with ½ cup of the Parmesan cheese; toss to combine.
6. To serve, remove toothpicks from chicken. Cut each roll into 2 slices; arrange on the pasta. Serve with the remaining ½ cup Parmesan cheese on the side. Makes 4 servings.

EACH SERVING *793 cal, 39 g fat, 127 mg chol, 1,246 mg sodium, 45 g carb, 2 g fiber, 62 g pro.*

CHICKEN AND OLIVES

Chicken and Olives

START TO FINISH 30 minutes

- 12 to 16 ounces dried pasta
- 1 pound skinless, boneless chicken breast halves, cut into 1-inch pieces
- 1 large onion, cut into thin wedges
- 2 cloves garlic, minced
- 2 tablespoons olive oil
- 1 28-ounce can Italian-style whole peeled tomatoes in puree
- ½ teaspoon coarsely ground black pepper
- ¼ teaspoon salt
- ½ cup whipping cream
- 1½ cups large pimento-stuffed green olives and/or pitted Kalamata olives, sliced
- ½ cup slivered fresh basil
- ¼ cup grated Parmesan cheese

1. Cook pasta according package directions; drain. Cover and keep warm.
2. In a large skillet cook chicken, onion, and garlic in hot oil over medium-high heat for 5 minutes or until chicken is no longer pink, stirring occasionally. Meanwhile, place half the tomatoes in a blender or food processor. Cover and blend or process until smooth. Snip the remaining tomatoes into bite-size pieces.
3. Stir pureed tomatoes, tomato pieces in puree, pepper, and salt into chicken mixture. Bring to boiling; reduce heat. Boil gently, uncovered, for 2 minutes. Stir in cream. Boil gently, uncovered, for 3 minutes more, stirring occasionally. Stir in olives; heat through.
4. Add chicken mixture, basil, and cheese to hot cooked pasta; toss gently to combine. Makes 6 servings.

EACH SERVING *499 cal, 20 g fat, 74 mg chol, 891 mg sodium, 53 g carb, 5 g fiber, 28 g pro.*

Sweet-and-Sour Baked Chicken

PREP 25 minutes
BAKE 30 minutes at 350°F

 4 skinless, boneless chicken breast halves
    Salt and black pepper
 1 tablespoon vegetable oil
 1 8-ounce can pineapple chunks (juice pack), undrained
 ½ cup jellied cranberry sauce
 2 tablespoons cornstarch
 2 tablespoons packed brown sugar
 2 tablespoons rice vinegar or cider vinegar
 2 tablespoons frozen orange juice concentrate, thawed
 2 tablespoons dry sherry, chicken broth, or water
 2 tablespoons soy sauce
 ¼ teaspoon ground ginger
 1 medium green sweet pepper, cut into bite-size strips

1. Preheat oven to 350°F. Lightly sprinkle chicken with salt and black pepper. In a large skillet heat oil over medium-high heat. Add chicken; cook about 4 minutes or until browned, turning once. Transfer chicken to an ungreased 2-quart baking dish. Drain pineapple, reserving ⅓ cup juice. Spoon pineapple chunks evenly over chicken; set aside.

2. For sauce, in a medium saucepan whisk together the reserved ⅓ cup pineapple juice, cranberry sauce, cornstarch, brown sugar, vinegar, orange juice concentrate, sherry, soy sauce, and ginger. Cook and stir over medium heat until thickened and bubbly. Pour over chicken and pineapple in dish.

3. Bake, covered, for 25 minutes. Add sweet peppers, stirring gently to coat with sauce. Bake, uncovered, about 5 minutes more or until chicken is no longer pink (170°F). Makes 4 servings.

EACH SERVING *354 cal, 5 g fat, 82 mg chol, 669 mg sodium, 37 g carb, 2 g fiber, 34 g pro.*

CHICKEN AND PASTA PRIMAVERA

Chicken and Pasta Primavera

START TO FINISH 25 minutes

- 1 9-ounce package refrigerated spinach or plain fettuccine
- 1 cup thinly sliced carrots
- 1 medium zucchini, halved lengthwise and thinly sliced
- ¾ cup frozen whole kernel corn
- 3 cups shredded cooked chicken
- 1½ cups chicken broth
- 4 teaspoons cornstarch
- 2 teaspoons finely shredded lemon peel
- 1 teaspoon dried basil, crushed
- ½ cup sour cream
- 2 tablespoons Dijon mustard
   Finely shredded Parmesan cheese

1. Cook pasta according to package directions, adding carrots, zucchini, and corn to the water with pasta; drain. Return pasta and vegetables to pan; add chicken. (If chicken has been refrigerated, place it in a colander. Pour pasta, vegetables, and cooking liquid over chicken to warm it; drain and return to pan.)
2. Meanwhile, in a medium saucepan stir together broth, cornstarch, lemon peel, and basil. Cook and stir over medium heat until thickened and bubbly. Cook and stir for 2 minutes more. Remove from heat. Stir in

CHICKEN LINGUINE WITH PESTO SAUCE

sour cream and mustard. Pour over pasta mixture, toss gently to combine. Sprinkle with cheese. Serve immediately. Makes 6 servings.

EACH SERVING *334 cal, 10 g fat, 98 mg chol, 547 mg sodium, 34 g carb, 3 g fiber, 27 g pro.*

Chicken Linguine with Pesto Sauce

START TO FINISH 20 minutes

- 8 ounces dried linguine
- 1 10-ounce package frozen broccoli, cauliflower, and carrots
- 1 10-ounce container refrigerated Alfredo pasta sauce or 1 cup bottled Alfredo sauce
- ⅓ cup purchased basil pesto
- ¼ cup milk
- 1½ cups chopped deli-roasted chicken
   Milk (optional)
   Grated Parmesan cheese

1. In a 4- or 5-quart Dutch oven cook pasta according to package directions, adding vegetables during the last 5 minutes of cooking; drain. Return pasta and vegetables to Dutch oven.
2. While pasta is cooking, in a small bowl combine Alfredo sauce, pesto, and the ¼ cup milk; set aside.
3. Add chicken to pasta and vegetables in Dutch oven. Add sauce mixture, tossing gently to combine. Heat through over medium-low heat. If desired, stir in additional milk to reach desired consistency. Divide among 4 dinner plates. Sprinkle Parmesan cheese over each serving. Makes 4 servings.

EACH SERVING *801 cal, 48 g fat, 109 mg chol, 546 mg sodium, 54 g carb, 3 g fiber, 37 g pro.*

EASY CHICKEN
AND DUMPLINGS

Easy Chicken and Dumplings

START TO FINISH 40 minutes

- 1 2- to 2½-pound deli-roasted chicken
- 1 16-ounce package frozen mixed vegetables
- 1¼ cups reduced-sodium chicken broth or water
- 1 10.75-ounce can reduced-fat, reduced-sodium condensed cream of chicken soup
- ½ teaspoon dried Italian seasoning, crushed
- ⅛ teaspoon black pepper
- 1 16.3-ounce can flaky layers buttermilk refrigerated biscuits

1. Remove and discard skin from chicken. Pull meat from bones, discard bones. Chop or shred meat.
2. In a large saucepan combine chicken, vegetables, broth, soup, Italian seasoning, and pepper. Bring to boiling; reduce heat. Cover and simmer about 15 minutes or until vegetables are tender.
3. Meanwhile, bake biscuits according to package directions.
4. To serve, split biscuits. Spoon chicken mixture on biscuit half; top with a second half. Makes 8 servings.

EACH SERVING *650 cal, 30 g fat, 107 mg chol, 1,399 mg sodium, 57 g carb, 5 g fiber, 42 g pro.*

Tetrazzini Primavera

PREP 40 minutes BAKE 35 minutes at 350°F STAND 5 minutes

Nonstick cooking spray
- 8 ounces dried whole wheat linguine or spaghetti, broken in half
- 1 pound broccoli, trimmed and cut into 1-inch pieces
- 2 tablespoons butter
- 3 medium red and/or yellow sweet peppers, stemmed, seeded, and cut into 1-inch pieces
- 2 cloves garlic, minced
- ¼ cup all-purpose flour
- ¼ teaspoon salt
- ⅛ teaspoon black pepper
- 1 14.5-ounce can reduced-sodium chicken broth
- ¾ cup fat-free milk
- ½ cup light sour cream
- 3 cups shredded cooked turkey or chicken
- ¾ cup shredded white cheddar cheese
- 1 cup soft bread crumbs
- 1 tablespoon snipped fresh parsley
- 1 teaspoon finely shredded lemon peel
- 1 tablespoon olive oil

1. Preheat oven to 350°F. Coat a 3-quart baking dish with cooking spray.
2. In a Dutch oven cook linguine according to package directions, adding broccoli the last 2 minutes of cooking time. Drain. Return linguine and broccoli to Dutch oven.
3. Meanwhile, for sauce, in a large skillet melt butter over medium heat. Add sweet peppers and garlic; cook about 5 minutes or just until peppers are tender, stirring occasionally. Stir in flour, salt, and black pepper until combined. Add broth and milk all at once. Cook and stir until thickened and bubbly. Stir in sour cream.
4. Add sauce, turkey, and cheese to linguine mixture; toss to combine. Spoon into prepared casserole. Bake, covered, for 25 minutes. Meanwhile, for bread crumb topping, in a small bowl toss together soft bread crumbs, parsley, lemon peel, and olive oil.
5. Sprinkle topping over casserole. Bake, uncovered, for 10 minutes or until topping is lightly browned. Makes 6 servings.

EACH SERVING *473 cal, 17 g fat, 84 mg chol, 515 mg sodium, 46 g carb, 6 g fiber, 35 g pro.*

Chicken with Orzo

START TO FINISH 15 minutes

- 8 ounces dried orzo pasta
- 2 cups shredded fresh spinach leaves
- ½ cup crumbled feta cheese
- 1 teaspoon finely shredded lemon peel
- 1 2- to 2½-pound hot deli-roasted chicken, cut into serving-size pieces
- 1 medium tomato, cut into wedges

1. Cook orzo according to package directions; drain. Return orzo to saucepan.
2. Add spinach, half the feta cheese, and the lemon peel to orzo in saucepan, tossing to mix. Divide orzo mixture among four dinner plates. Arrange chicken pieces and tomato wedges on orzo mixture. Sprinkle with remaining feta cheese. Makes 4 servings.

EACH SERVING *528 cal, 19 g fat, 112 mg chol, 267 mg sodium, 45 g carb, 3 g fiber, 41 g pro.*

Kalamata-Lemon Chicken

PREP 10 minutes
BAKE 35 minutes at 400°F

- 1 tablespoon olive oil
- 1 pound skinless, boneless chicken thighs
- 1 14.5-ounce can chicken broth
- ⅔ cup dried orzo
- ½ cup drained pitted Kalamata olives
- ½ lemon, cut into wedges or chunks
- 1 tablespoon lemon juice
- 1 teaspoon dried Greek seasoning or dried oregano, crushed
- ¼ teaspoon salt
- ¼ teaspoon black pepper
  Hot chicken broth (optional)
  Fresh snipped oregano (optional)

1. Preheat oven to 400°F. In a 4-quart Dutch oven heat oil over medium-high heat. Add chicken; cook about 5 minutes or until lightly browned, turning once. Stir in broth, orzo, olives, lemon wedges, lemon juice, Greek seasoning, salt, and pepper. Transfer mixture to a 2-quart baking dish.
2. Bake, covered, about 35 minutes or until chicken is tender and no longer pink (180°F). If desired, serve in shallow bowls with additional hot broth and top with fresh oregano. Makes 4 servings.

EACH SERVING *304 cal, 10 g fat, 95 mg chol, 830 mg sodium, 25 g carb, 2 g fiber, 27 g pro.*

Spicy Egg-Stuffed Peppers

PREP 35 minutes
BAKE 10 minutes at 325°F

- 4 medium yellow, red, and/or green sweet peppers and/or medium fresh poblano chile peppers
- 2 teaspoons olive oil
- 1 cup chopped zucchini
- ½ cup chopped onion
- 1 3-ounce link cooked habenero-chile chicken sausage or sweet Italian chicken sausage* or 3 ounces cooked smoked turkey sausage,* chopped

SPICY EGG-STUFFED PEPPERS

- 4 eggs, beaten
- 2 tablespoons fat-free milk
- ¼ cup shredded Monterey Jack cheese

1. Preheat oven to 325°F. Halve peppers lengthwise, leaving stems intact. Remove and discard ribs and seeds. In a large saucepan or pot cook peppers in a large amount of boiling water for 3 minutes or just until tender. Invert pepper halves on paper towels to drain.
2. In a large skillet heat oil over medium heat. Add zucchini, onion, and chopped sausage; cook about 3 minutes or just until zucchini is tender, stirring occasionally. Remove sausage mixture from skillet; set aside.
3. In a medium bowl whisk together eggs and milk. Add egg mixture to hot skillet. Cook over medium heat, without stirring, until mixture begins to set on the bottom and around the edges. With a spatula or large spoon, lift and fold the partially cooked egg mixture so the uncooked portion flows underneath. Continue cooking over medium heat for 2 minutes or until cooked through, yet still glossy and moist. Fold in sausage mixture.
4. In a 2-quart rectangular baking dish arrange peppers, open sides up. Spoon sausage-egg mixture into peppers. Sprinkle with cheese. Bake for 10 minutes or until cheese is melted and filling is heated through. Makes 4 servings.
*If using Italian chicken sausage or turkey sausage, add 1 fresh jalapeño, seeded and finely chopped (see tip, page 35) to skillet with fresh sausage.

EACH SERVING *197 cal, 11 g fat, 235 mg chol, 285 mg sodium, 11 g carb, 3 g fiber, 14 g pro.*

**TOMATO AND
OLIVE CHICKEN**

Tomato and Olive Chicken

PREP 20 minutes
BAKE 25 minutes at 400°F

- 3 pounds skinless, bone-in chicken thighs
  Salt and black pepper
- 1 tablespoon olive oil
- 1 cup chicken broth
- 1 cup dried orzo (rosamarina) pasta
- 8 roma tomatoes, halved and seeded
- ½ cup pitted Kalamata olives
  Fresh basil leaves

1. Preheat oven to 400°F. Lightly season chicken with salt and pepper. In a very large oven-going skillet heat oil over medium-high heat. Add chicken thighs, meaty sides down, and cook for 10 minutes or until browned, turning halfway through cooking. Remove chicken from skillet; discard pan drippings.
2. Add broth to skillet; bring to boiling. Stir in orzo. Return chicken to skillet, meaty sides up, and add tomatoes and olives.
3. Baked, covered, about 25 minutes or until chicken is no longer pink (180°F) and orzo is tender. Sprinkle with basil. Makes 4 servings.

EACH SERVING 796 cal, 46 g fat, 225 mg chol, 752 mg sodium, 40 g carb, 4 g fiber, 54 g pro.

Lemon-Herb Chicken with Ricotta Salata

PREP 20 minutes
COOK 4½ hours (low)

- 2 teaspoons finely shredded lemon peel
- 1 teaspoon dried basil, crushed
- 1 teaspoon dried rosemary, crushed
- 2 cloves garlic, minced
- ½ teaspoon salt
- ¼ teaspoon black pepper
- 4 pounds chicken thighs and/or drumsticks, skinned
- ½ cup reduced-sodium chicken broth
- ½ cup crumbled ricotta salata
- 2 tablespoons coarsely snipped fresh parsley

QUICK CHICKEN TORTILLA BAKE

1. In a small bowl combine 1 teaspoon of the lemon peel, the basil, rosemary, garlic, salt, and pepper. Sprinkle mixture evenly over chicken; rub in with your fingers. Place chicken in a 3½- or 4-quart slow cooker. Pour broth over chicken.
2. Cover and cook on low-heat setting for 4½ to 5 hours. Transfer chicken to a serving platter.
3. Skim fat from cooking liquid. Spoon some of the cooking liquid over chicken; discard the remaining liquid. Sprinkle chicken with ricotta salata, parsley, and the remaining 1 teaspoon lemon peel. Makes 5 servings.

EACH SERVING 245 cal, 8 g fat, 132 mg chol, 617 mg sodium, 1 g carb, 0 g fiber, 40 g pro.

Quick Chicken Tortilla Bake

PREP 15 minutes
BAKE 45 minutes at 350°F

- 2 10.75-ounce cans reduced-fat and reduced-sodium condensed cream of chicken soup
- 1 10-ounce can diced tomatoes with green chiles, undrained
- 12 6- or 7-inch corn tortillas, cut into narrow bite-size strips
- 3 cups cubed cooked chicken
- 1 cup shredded taco cheese

1. Preheat oven to 350°F. In a medium bowl combine soup and undrained tomatoes; set aside. Sprinkle one-third of the tortilla strips in an ungreased 3-quart baking dish. Layer half the chicken over the tortilla strips; evenly spoon half the soup mixture over top. Repeat layers. Sprinkle with the remaining tortilla strips.
2. Bake, covered, about 40 minutes or until bubbly around edges and center is hot. Uncover; sprinkle with cheese. Bake about 5 minutes more or until cheese is melted. Makes 8 servings.

EACH SERVING 291 cal, 10 g fat, 64 mg chol, 658 mg sodium, 28 g carb, 2 g fiber, 22 g pro.

SMOKIN'
TETRAZZINI

Smokin' Tetrazzini

PREP 30 minutes
BAKE 30 minutes at 350°F
STAND 5 minutes

- 12 ounces spinach or whole wheat fettuccine or linguine
- ¾ cup dried tomatoes (not oil-packed), snipped
- 8 ounces sliced fresh mushrooms
- 2 medium yellow sweet peppers, cut in bite-size strips
- ½ cup chopped onion
- 2 tablespoons olive oil
- 2 tablespoons all-purpose flour
- 1⅓ cups milk
- 2 cups smoked Gouda or smoked cheddar cheese, shredded
- 2 cups shredded roasted turkey
- 2 tablespoons sliced almonds, toasted (see tip, page 31)

1. Preheat oven to 350°F. Grease a 3-quart baking dish; set aside.
2. Cook pasta according to package directions, adding dried tomatoes to boiling water with pasta; drain.
3. For sauce, in a large skillet cook mushrooms, sweet peppers, and onion in hot oil until tender. Stir in flour. Add milk and 1 cup *water* all at once. Cook and stir until slightly thickened and bubbly. Gradually stir in cheese until melted. Season with *salt* and *pepper*.

4. In a large bowl combine pasta mixture, turkey, and sauce. Spoon into prepared dish. Sprinkle with almonds. Bake, covered, 30 minutes or until heated through. Let stand 5 minutes before serving. Makes 6 servings.
EACH SERVING *540 cal, 19 g fat, 70 mg chol, 811 mg sodium, 59 g carb, 4 g fiber, 33 g pro.*

Chicken Alfredo Casserole

PREP 30 minutes
BAKE 25 minutes at 350°F

- 1 19-ounce package frozen cheese-filled tortellini
- 3 cloves garlic, minced
- 1 tablespoon olive oil
- 1 pound skinless, boneless chicken breast halves, cubed
- 1 cup pepperoni, chopped
- ¾ cup oil-packed dried tomatoes, drained and chopped
- 1 15- to 16-ounce jar Alfredo pasta sauce
- ½ cup shredded Italian cheese blend
  Chopped fresh parsley (optional)

1. Preheat oven to 350°F. Cook tortellini according to package directions; drain.
2. Meanwhile, in a large skillet cook garlic in hot oil 15 seconds; add chicken. Cook, stirring occasionally, 3 minutes or until no pink remains. Stir in pepperoni and tomatoes; cook 2 minutes. Add Alfredo sauce; heat through.
3. In a large bowl combine tortellini and chicken mixture; transfer to a 2-quart baking dish Sprinkle with cheese. Bake, covered, 25 minutes or until heated through. Sprinkle with parsley. Makes 6 servings.
EACH SERVING *588 cal, 32 g fat, 130 mg chol, 1,059 mg sodium, 42 g carb, 2 g fiber, 36 g pro.*

Chicken, Spinach, and Rice Casserole

PREP 15 minutes
BAKE 1¼ hours at 375°F

  Nonstick cooking spray
- 1 10-ounce package frozen chopped spinach, thawed and well drained
- ½ an 8-ounce tub cream cheese spread with chives and onion
- 1 10.75-ounce can condensed cream of chicken soup
- 1 cup milk
- ¼ cup snipped fresh oregano
- ¼ cup grated Parmesan cheese
- 2 cloves garlic, minced
- ¼ teaspoon crushed red pepper
- 1 cup long grain rice
- 6 small bone-in chicken breast halves, skinned
  Salt and black pepper

1. Preheat oven to 375°F. Lightly coat a 3-quart baking dish with cooking spray. In a bowl combine spinach and cream cheese; spread in prepared dish. In another bowl combine soup, milk, 2 tablespoons of the oregano, 2 tablespoons of the cheese, garlic, and crushed red pepper; reserve ¼ cup of mixture. Stir rice into remaining soup mixture, then spoon on top of spinach. Place chicken, bone sides down, in dish. Season with salt and pepper. Spoon reserved soup mixture over chicken.
2. Cover tightly with foil and bake 1¼ hours or until rice is tender and chicken is no longer pink. Sprinkle with remaining oregano and Parmesan before serving. Makes 6 servings.
EACH SERVING *470 cal, 13 g fat, 137 mg chol, 743 mg sodium, 33 g carb, 2 g fiber, 51 g pro.*

Thai Chicken Tacos

PREP 30 minutes MARINATE 1 hour

- 1 lime, halved
- 1 pound skinless, boneless chicken breasts or tenders, cut into ½- to ¾-inch pieces
- ¼ cup chopped fresh cilantro
- 1 large shallot, finely chopped
- 3 cloves garlic, minced
- 1 tablespoon fish sauce
- 2 teaspoons reduced-sodium soy sauce
- ½ to 1 teaspoon crushed red pepper
- ½ to 1 teaspoon hot chili sauce (such as Sriracha)
- 2 tablespoons vegetable oil
- 16 corn tortillas, heated
- 1 recipe Cabbage Slaw

1. Juice 1 lime half (about 1 tablespoon); cut remaining half in wedges. In a large bowl stir together chicken, cilantro, shallot, garlic, the 1 tablespoon lime juice, fish sauce, soy sauce, pepper, and chili sauce. Cover; marinate in the refrigerator 1 hour.
2. In a large skillet cook chicken mixture in hot oil over medium-high heat about 5 minutes or until chicken is cooked thoroughly, stirring occasionally.
3. To serve, layer 2 tortillas. Top with chicken and Cabbage Slaw. Serve with remaining slaw and lime wedges. Makes 4 servings.
Cabbage Slaw In a large bowl combine 2 cups shredded napa cabbage, ½ cup shredded carrot, ½ cup sliced green onions, ⅓ cup sliced radishes, ¼ cup chopped fresh cilantro, and ¼ cup coarsely chopped peanuts (optional). Add ¼ cup rice vinegar; toss.
EACH SERVING *454 cal, 11 g fat, 66 mg chol, 596 mg sodium, 55 g carb, 9 g fiber, 34 g pro.*

Smoky Chicken and Cheesy Potato Casserole

PREP 20 minutes
BAKE 40 minutes at 350°F

- 1 10.75-ounce can condensed cream of chicken with herbs soup
- 1 8-ounce carton sour cream
- 1½ cups shredded smoked cheddar cheese

SMOKY CHICKEN AND CHEESY POTATO CASSEROLE

- 1 28-ounce package loose-pack frozen diced hash brown potatoes with onion and peppers, thawed
- 1 pound smoked or roasted chicken or turkey, cut into bite-size strips
- 1 cup crushed croutons
- 1 tablespoon butter, melted

1. Preheat oven to 350°F. In a large bowl combine soup, sour cream, and cheese. Stir in frozen potatoes and chicken. Transfer to a lightly greased 3-quart baking dish. In a small bowl combine crushed croutons and melted butter. Sprinkle over potato mixture in dish.
2. Bake, uncovered, for 40 minutes or until heated through. Makes 6 servings.
EACH SERVING *461 cal, 24 g fat, 89 mg chol, 1,468 mg sodium, 36 g carb, 3 g fiber, 27 g pro.*

Chicken and Noodles

START TO FINISH 45 minutes

- 1 12-ounce package frozen noodles
- 3 cups reduced-sodium chicken broth

- 2 cups sliced carrots
- 1 cup chopped onion
- ½ cup sliced celery
- 2 cups milk
- 1 cup frozen peas
- 3 tablespoons all-purpose flour
- ½ teaspoon salt
- ⅛ teaspoon black pepper
- 2 cups chopped cooked chicken
  Coarsely ground black pepper (optional)

1. Preheat oven to 350°F. In a 4-quart Dutch oven combine noodles, chicken broth, carrots, onion, and celery. Bring to boiling; reduce heat. Cover and simmer about 20 minutes or until noodles and vegetables are tender. Stir in 1½ cups of the milk and the peas.
2. In a small bowl stir together the remaining ½ cup milk, the flour, salt, and ⅛ teaspoon pepper. Whisk until smooth; stir into noodle mixture. Stir in chicken. Cook and stir until thickened and bubbly. Cook and stir for 1 minute more. If desired, season with coarsely ground pepper. Makes 8 servings.
EACH SERVING *269 cal, 5 g fat, 86 mg chol, 468 mg sodium, 36 g carb, 3 g fiber, 19 g pro.*

CHUCKWAGON CHICKEN SHEPHERD'S PIE

1. Preheat oven to 350°F. Heat mashed potatoes according to package directions. Stir in 2 tablespoons of the parsley; set aside.

2. Remove chicken from bones, discarding skin and bones. Using forks, pull meat apart into shreds. In a large bowl stir together chicken, beans, corn, salsa, and the remaining 2 tablespoons parsley. Spoon into a 3-quart baking dish. Spoon mashed potatoes over chicken mixture; spread evenly.

3. Bake, uncovered, for 30 minutes or until heated through. Makes 6 servings.

EACH SERVING *437 cal, 15 g fat, 83 mg chol, 1,478 mg sodium, 55 g carb, 8 g fiber, 28 g pro.*

Garlic Parmesan Chicken and Noodles

PREP 30 minutes
BAKE 5 minutes at 450°F

6 ounces extra-wide egg noodles
1 2- to 2¼-pound purchased roasted chicken
1 cup frozen peas
4 cloves garlic, minced
1¾ cups whole milk or light cream
½ slice white or wheat bread
¾ cup shredded Parmesan cheese
Snipped fresh thyme (optional)

1. Preheat oven to 450°F. In a Dutch oven bring 6 cups salted water to boiling; add noodles. Cook 10 minutes or until tender; drain.

2. Meanwhile, remove chicken from bones. Discard skin and bones; shred chicken. In saucepan combine chicken, peas, garlic, and milk; heat through. Cover and keep warm.

3. In a blender or food processor process bread into coarse crumbs. Transfer to a small bowl; add ¼ cup of the Parmesan and 2 tablespoons melted butter.

4. Stir noodles and remaining Parmesan into hot chicken mixture. Heat and stir until bubbly. Divide among 4 individual casserole dishes. Top each with some of the bread crumb mixture. Bake for 5 minutes or until top begins to brown. Top with fresh thyme. Makes 4 servings.

EACH SERVING *701 cal, 37 g fat, 222 mg chol, 1,388 mg sodium, 45 g carb, 3 g fiber, 50 g pro.*

Spinach and Chicken Pie

PREP 35 minutes
BAKE 45 minutes at 375°F

Nonstick cooking spray
1¼ pounds uncooked ground chicken
½ cup chopped onion (1 medium)
1 tablespoon butter or margarine
2 10-ounce packages frozen chopped spinach, thawed and squeezed dry
½ teaspoon black pepper
¼ teaspoon salt
¼ teaspoon ground nutmeg
⅛ teaspoon crushed red pepper
2 eggs, lightly beaten
¾ cups crumbled feta cheese
1½ teaspoons snipped fresh oregano
8 sheets frozen phyllo dough, thawed

1. Preheat oven to 375°F. Lightly coat a 2-quart baking dish with cooking spray; set aside. In a skillet cook chicken and onion in hot butter over medium-high heat about 8 minutes or until chicken is browned and onion is tender. Drain. Stir spinach, black pepper, salt, nutmeg, and crushed red pepper into chicken mixture. Cook and stir for 5 minutes; spoon into a bowl. Stir in eggs, cheese, and oregano.

2. Unfold phyllo dough. Using a sharp knife, cut a 1-inch strip off one short end of phyllo stack; discard. Remove 1 sheet of phyllo dough. (Cover remaining phyllo dough with plastic wrap to prevent drying out.) Place the phyllo sheet in baking dish. Lightly coat with cooking spray. Top with 3 more sheets, coating each with cooking spray. Spread chicken mixture on phyllo in baking dish. Top with remaining 4 phyllo sheets, coating each with cooking spray. Cut the top layer of phyllo sheets into 4 portions.

3. Bake, uncovered, about 45 minutes or until heated through and top is browned. Recut along scored lines. Makes 4 servings.

EACH SERVING *530 cal, 29 g fat, 273 mg chol, 1,024 mg sodium, 29 g carb, 4 g fiber, 41 g pro.*

Chuckwagon Chicken Shepherd's Pie

PREP 25 minutes
BAKE 30 minutes at 350°F

1 24-ounce package refrigerated mashed potatoes
¼ cup snipped fresh parsley
1 2¼- to 2½-pound deli-roasted chicken
1 28-ounce can baked beans
1 11-ounce can whole kernel corn with sweet peppers, drained
½ cup salsa

SPANISH-STYLE STRATA

BUFFALO CHICKEN COBB

The Original Chicken à la King

START TO FINISH 25 minutes

1 tablespoon butter
½ cup thinly sliced mushrooms
2 tablespoons finely chopped green sweet pepper
1 tablespoon all-purpose flour
¼ teaspoon salt
1 cup half-and-half or light cream
1 tablespoon butter, softened
1 egg yolk
1½ teaspoons lemon juice
½ teaspoon onion juice (optional)
¼ teaspoon paprika
1½ cups chopped cooked chicken
1 tablespoon diced pimiento, drained
1½ teaspoons sherry
4 baked pastry shells

1. In a large skillet melt 1 tablespoon butter over medium heat. Add mushrooms and sweet pepper; cook until tender. Stir in the flour and salt. Add half-and-half all at once; cook and stir until thickened and bubbly.
2. Stir together 1 tablespoon softened butter and egg yolk. Add the lemon juice, onion juice (if using), and paprika. Stir about ½ cup of the half-and-half mixture into the egg mixture; add to the half-and-half mixture in the skillet. Cook and stir over medium heat until bubbly. Stir in chicken, pimiento, and sherry; heat through. Serve in pastry shells. Makes 4 servings.
EACH SERVING *297 cal, 19 g fat, 163 mg chol, 346 mg sodium, 12 g carb, 1 g fiber, 20 g pro.*

Spanish-Style Strata

PREP 40 minutes   CHILL 1 hour
BAKE 55 minutes at 325°F
STAND 10 minutes

Nonstick cooking spray
7 cups 1-inch cubes crusty country bread
16 ounces cooked chicken sausage links, cut into ½-inch pieces
1 14.5-ounce can diced tomatoes with Italian herbs, drained
¼ cup chopped roasted red sweet peppers, drained
¼ cup sliced green onions
¼ cup sliced pitted green olives
1 cup shredded Manchego cheese
6 eggs, beaten
3 cups milk
½ teaspoon paprika
½ teaspoon dried oregano, crushed
½ teaspoon black pepper
Snipped fresh parsley (optional)

1. Lightly coat a 3-quart baking dish with cooking spray. Spread half the bread cubes in the dish. In a large bowl combine the sausage pieces, tomatoes, roasted sweet peppers, green onions, and olives. Spoon half the sausage mixture over bread cubes. Sprinkle with half the cheese. Top with the remaining bread cubes, sausage mixture, and cheese.
2. In a large bowl whisk together eggs, milk, paprika, oregano, and black pepper. Pour evenly over the layers in dish. Cover and chill for 1 to 24 hours.
3. Preheat oven to 325°F. Bake, covered, for 30 minutes. Uncover and bake for 25 minutes more or until the internal temperature registers 170°F on an instant-read thermometer. Let stand for 10 minutes before serving. If desired, sprinkle with parsley. Makes 8 servings.
EACH SERVING *362 cal, 13 g fat, 223 mg chol, 1,183 mg sodium, 33 g carb, 2 g fiber, 26 g pro.*

Buffalo Chicken Cobb

START TO FINISH 25 minutes

1 25.5-ounce package frozen Buffalo-style boneless chicken wings
2 hearts of romaine lettuce, halved or quartered
1½ cups sliced celery and/or carrots
½ cup light mayonnaise
¼ cup crumbled blue cheese
¼ teaspoon black pepper
2 small lemons

1. Prepare chicken wings according to package directions.
2. Meanwhile, line a platter or four plates with romaine. Top with celery; set aside. In a small bowl stir together mayonnaise, blue cheese, and pepper. Squeeze juice from half a lemon (about 1½ tablespoons) into mayonnaise mixture; stir to combine.
3. Slice heated chicken. Arrange chicken on romaine. Cut remaining lemon into halves or wedges; serve with salad. Pass dressing. Makes 4 servings.
EACH SERVING *389 cal, 16 g fat, 157 mg chol, 1,359 mg sodium, 14 g carb, 6 g fiber, 48 g pro.*

JERK CHICKEN AND SLAW

OPEN-FACE CHICKEN SALAD SANDWICHES

Spring Chicken Stew

START TO FINISH **30 minutes**

- 1 lemon
- 1¼ pounds skinless, boneless chicken thighs
  Salt and black pepper
- 1 tablespoon olive oil
- 8 ounces baby carrots with tops, scrubbed, trimmed, and halved lengthwise
- 1 12-ounce jar chicken gravy
- 1 tablespoon Dijon mustard
- 2 heads baby bok choy, quartered
  Fresh lemon thyme (optional)

1. Finely shred peel from lemon; set peel aside. Juice lemon and set juice aside. Lightly season chicken with salt and pepper.
2. In a Dutch oven heat olive oil over medium-high heat; add chicken. Cook 2 minutes or until chicken is browned, turning occasionally.
3. Add carrots, gravy, and 1½ cups *water* to Dutch oven. Stir in mustard. Bring to boiling. Place bok choy on top. Reduce heat. Cover and simmer 10 minutes or just until chicken is done and vegetables are tender. Add lemon juice to taste.
4. Ladle into bowls. Top with lemon peel and lemon thyme. Makes 4 servings.
EACH SERVING *273 cal, 12 g fat, 117 mg chol, 909 mg sodium, 13 g carb, 3 g fiber, 31 g pro.*

Open-Face Chicken Salad Sandwiches

START TO FINISH **25 minutes**

- 2 tablespoons olive oil
- 14 ounces chicken tenders
- 2 cups seedless red grapes, whole and/or halved
- 6 cups fresh baby spinach
- 2 tablespoons red wine vinegar
- 1 18-inch loaf baguette-style French bread
- 4 ounces provolone cheese, thinly sliced

1. Preheat broiler. Line a 15×10×1-inch baking pan with foil; lightly brush with some olive oil. Place chicken and grapes in a single layer in pan; drizzle remaining oil; lightly sprinkle with *salt* and *pepper*. Broil 2 to 3 inches from heat for 10 minutes or until chicken is cooked through and begins to brown.
2. In a large bowl toss together spinach, chicken, grapes, pan juices, and vinegar. Cut baguette into 4 portions, slice open, then place on baking sheet. Top with cheese; broil 2 minutes or until cheese is melted. Layer chicken salad on bread. Makes 4 servings.
EACH SERVING *315 cal, 15 g fat, 66 mg chol, 574 mg sodium, 25 g carb, 1 g fiber, 20 g pro.*

Jerk Chicken and Slaw

START TO FINISH **20 minutes**

- 3 heads baby bok choy, trimmed and thinly sliced
- 2 cups shredded red cabbage
- ½ a peeled, cored fresh pineapple, chopped
- 2 tablespoons cider vinegar
- 4 teaspoons packed brown sugar
- 2 teaspoons all-purpose flour
- 2 teaspoons jerk seasoning
- 4 small skinless, boneless chicken breast halves

1. For slaw, in a large bowl combine bok choy, cabbage, and pineapple. Combine cider vinegar and 2 teaspoons of the brown sugar. Drizzle over slaw; toss to coat. Set aside.
2. In a large resealable plastic bag combine the remaining 2 teaspoon brown sugar, the flour, and jerk seasoning. Add chicken; shake well to coat. Cook chicken on a lightly greased grill pan or very large heavy skillet over medium heat for 6 to 8 minutes, turning once, or until no pink remains (170°F). Remove chicken to cutting board. Slice chicken and serve with pineapple slaw. Makes 4 servings.
EACH SERVING *205 cal, 2 g fat, 66 mg chol, 318 mg sodium, 19 g carb, 3 g fiber, 29 g pro.*

SPRING CHICKEN STEW

Curried Chicken Stew

PREP 20 minutes COOK 7 hours
(low) or 3½ hours (high)

    8 bone-in chicken thighs (2½ to
       3 pounds)
    2 teaspoons olive oil
    6 carrots, cut in 2-inch chunks
    1 medium sweet onion, cut in
       narrow wedges
    1 cup unsweetened coconut milk
    ¼ cup mild (or hot) curry paste
       Chopped pistachios, golden
       raisins, cilantro, and/or crushed
       red pepper (optional)

1. Trim excess skin and fat from
chicken. In a very large skillet cook
chicken, skin sides down, in hot olive
oil for 8 minutes or until browned. (Do
not turn thighs.) Remove from heat;
drain and discard fat.
2. In a 3½- or 4-quart slow cooker
combine carrots and onion. In a bowl
whisk together half the coconut milk
and the curry paste; pour over carrots
and onion (refrigerate remaining
coconut milk). Place chicken, skin
sides up, on vegetables. Cover. Cook
on low-heat setting for 7 to 8 hours or
on high-heat setting for 3½ to 4 hours.
Remove chicken. Skim off excess fat,
then stir in remaining coconut milk.
Ladle vegetables into bowls. Sprinkle
servings with chicken. Top servings
with pistachios, raisins, cilantro, and/or
crushed red pepper. Makes 4 servings.
EACH SERVING 850 cal, 63 g fat, 238 mg
chol, 1,314 mg sodium, 221 g carb, 5 g fiber,
52 g pro.

Sweet Potato-Topped
Chicken Stew

START TO FINISH 35 minutes

    1   17-ounce can sweet potatoes,
        drained
    1   tablespoon butter, melted
    2   tablespoon butter
    ½   cup chopped onion (1 medium)
    2   cups chopped cooked chicken or
        turkey
    1   10.75-ounce can condensed
        cream of mushroom soup
    1   10-ounce package frozen peas
        and carrots
    ½   teaspoon dried sage, crushed
    ½   teaspoon freshly ground black
        pepper

SWEET POTATO-TOPPED CHICKEN STEW

1. In a medium bowl mash sweet potatoes with an electric mixer on low to medium until smooth. Beat in the 1 tablespoon melted butter.

2. In a large skillet heat the 2 tablespoons butter over medium heat. Add onion; cook for 4 to 5 minutes or until tender. Stir in chicken, soup, peas and carrots, and sage. Cook and stir until bubbly.

3. Spoon mashed sweet potatoes into six mounds on chicken mixture. Simmer, covered, about 10 minutes or until heated through. Sprinkle with pepper. Makes 4 servings.

EACH SERVING *436 cal, 19 g fat, 88 mg chol, 815 mg sodium, 41 g carb, 6 g fiber, 25 g pro.*

Harvest Chili

PREP 20 minutes   COOK 30 minutes

- 2   tablespoons olive oil
- 1½   pounds cooked chicken-apple sausage links, cut into 1-inch pieces
- 2   cups chopped red onions (2 large)
- 3   cloves garlic, minced
- 1   large butternut squash, peeled, seeded, and cut into ¾-inch chunks (about 6 cups)
- 2   teaspoons chili powder
- ¼   teaspoon salt
- ⅛   teaspoon cayenne pepper
- 3   cups reduced-sodium chicken broth
- 3   medium Granny Smith apples, peeled, cored, and cut into ¾-inch slices

HARVEST CHILI

- 1   15- to 16-ounce can pinto beans, rinsed, drained, and slightly mashed
- 1   tablespoon snipped fresh sage or tiny sage leaves
       Golden Delicious or other apple, cut into rings

1. In a large Dutch oven heat 1 tablespoon of the oil over medium-high heat. Add sausage; cook 5 minutes or until browned; stir occasionally. Remove with slotted spoon.

2. In same pan cook onions and garlic 2 minutes, stirring occasionally, until nearly tender. Add squash; cook 5 minutes. Stir in chili powder, salt, and cayenne; cook 1 minute. Return sausage to pan. Add broth; bring to boiling, then reduce heat. Simmer, covered, 8 minutes.

3. Meanwhile, in a large skillet heat remaining oil over medium-high. Cook apples 4 minutes, stirring occasionally, until lightly browned. Transfer apples along with beans to chili. Simmer 3 minutes or until apples are tender. Top with sage and apple rings. Makes 8 servings.

EACH SERVING *356 cal, 11 g fat, 60 mg chol, 944 mg sodium, 48 g carb, 8 g fiber, 20 g pro.*

Chicken-Butternut Squash Soup

PREP 25 minutes
ROAST 20 minutes at 425°F
BAKE 7 minutes at 350°F

1¼ lb. butternut squash, peeled, seeded, and cut into ¾-inch pieces (4 cups)
1 small red onion, cut into ½-inch wedges
1 tablespoon curry powder
1 tablespoon olive oil
3 14.5-ounce cans reduced-sodium chicken broth
1 15- to 16-ounce can garbanzo beans (chickpeas), rinsed and drained
⅓ cup dried apricots, snipped
½ cup chopped walnuts
1 teaspoon olive oil
¼ teaspoon freshly grated or ground nutmeg
1 deli-roasted chicken, cut up
   Fresh cilantro leaves

1. Preheat oven to 425°F. In a shallow roasting pan toss squash and onion with curry powder and the 1 tablespoon oil. Roast, uncovered, 20 minutes or until tender. Reduce oven temperature to 350°F.
2. In 4-quart Dutch oven combine roasted vegetables, broth, beans, and apricots. Bring to boiling; reduce heat. Simmer, covered, for 10 minutes. Cool about 5 minutes. Transfer half the soup to food processor or blender. Cover; process or blend until smooth. Return to Dutch oven; heat through.
3. Meanwhile, in a bowl toss walnuts with 1 teaspoon oil and the nutmeg. Spread nuts on baking sheet. Bake 7 minutes or until golden and toasted. Reheat chicken if needed according to package directions.
4. To serve, top soup with nuts, chicken, and cilantro. Makes 6 servings.

EACH SERVING *577 cal, 35 g fat, 167 mg chol, 1,905 mg sodium, 30 g carb, 6 g fiber, 44 g pro.*

CHICKEN AND SAUSAGE GUMBO

Chicken and Sausage Gumbo

PREP 45 minutes
COOK 1 hour

1 cup all-purpose flour
⅔ cup vegetable oil
1 cup sliced celery
1 cup chopped green sweet pepper
½ cup chopped onion
2 cloves garlic, minced
8 ounces cooked smoked sausage, cut into 1-inch pieces
8 ounces andouille sausage, cut into ½-inch pieces
2 pounds meaty chicken pieces, skinned if desired (breast halves, thighs, and drumsticks)
5 cups water
1 teaspoon salt
¼ teaspoon cayenne pepper
¼ teaspoon black pepper
   Hot cooked rice (optional)

1. For roux, in a large heavy Dutch oven stir together flour and oil until smooth. Cook over medium-high heat for 5 minutes. Reduce heat to medium. Cook and stir for 10 minutes or until roux is reddish brown in color (the deeper the color, the richer and more flavorful the gumbo). Stir in celery, sweet pepper, onion, and garlic; cook for 5 minutes, stirring occasionally. Add sausages; cook until lightly browned.
2. Add chicken, the water, salt, cayenne pepper, and black pepper to gumbo. Bring to boiling; reduce heat. Cover and simmer about 1 hour or until chicken is tender and no longer pink (170°F for breasts; 180°F for thighs and drumsticks).
3. Skim off fat. Remove chicken; cool slightly. When chicken is cool enough to handle, remove meat from bones; discard bones. Coarsely chop chicken and return to gumbo in Dutch oven. Cook for 2 minutes or until chicken is heated through. If desired, serve with rice. Makes 8 servings.

EACH SERVING *460 cal, 34 g fat, 72 mg chol, 961 mg sodium, 12 g carb, 1 g fiber, 25 g pro.*

24-HOUR CHICKEN FIESTA SALAD

GREEK CHICKEN SALAD

Poached Chicken Salad Stack-Up

START TO FINISH 25 minutes

- 1 lemon
- 1 pound skinless, boneless chicken breast halves, cut into 2-inch pieces
- 1 cup chicken broth
- 4 cloves garlic, minced
- 1 teaspoon dried oregano
- 1 seedless cucumber
- 1 5-ounce container Greek-style honey-flavored yogurt
- 4 tomatoes, sliced
  Fresh oregano (optional)

1. Finely shred peel from lemon; juice lemon. In a saucepan combine peel, juice, chicken, broth, garlic, and oregano; bring to simmer over medium-high heat. Reduce heat and simmer, covered, 10 minutes or until no pink remains in chicken. Drain, reserving ⅓ cup cooking liquid.
2. Meanwhile, chop half the cucumber; slice remaining. For dressing, place reserved cooking liquid in bowl; whisk in yogurt. Remove half the dressing and set aside. Add chicken to bowl along with chopped cucumber; toss to coat.
3. Layer tomatoes, sliced cucumber, and chicken on plates. Drizzle with some of the reserved dressing. Season with *salt* and *black pepper*. Top with fresh oregano. Pass remaining dressing. Makes 4 servings.
EACH SERVING *196 cal, 3 g fat, 68 mg chol, 480 mg sodium, 13 g carb, 3 g fiber, 32 g pro.*

24-Hour Chicken Fiesta Salad

PREP 30 minutes CHILL 4 hours

- 1 cup mayonnaise or salad dressing
- 2 4-ounce cans chopped green chile peppers
- 1 tablespoon chili powder
- 2 cloves garlic, minced
- 8 cups torn iceberg lettuce
- 1 cup shredded Monterey Jack cheese with jalapeño peppers
- 1 cup black beans or pinto beans, rinsed and drained
- 6 cups chopped cooked chicken
- 2 medium tomatoes, cut into thin wedges
- 2 cups bite-size strips jicama or shredded carrot
- 1 cup sliced pitted ripe olives (optional)
- 1½ cups crushed tortilla chips (optional)

1. For dressing, in a medium bowl combine mayonnaise, green chiles, chili powder, and garlic; set aside.
2. Place lettuce in a very large salad bowl. Layer ingredients in the following order: cheese, beans, chicken, tomatoes, jicama, and, if desired, olives.

Top salad with dressing, sealing to edge of bowl. Cover tightly with plastic wrap. Chill for 4 to 24 hours. To serve, toss lightly to combine. If desired, sprinkle with crushed tortilla chips. Makes 8 servings.
EACH SERVING *444 cal, 32 g fat, 73 mg chol, 460 mg sodium, 17 g carb, 5 g fiber, 26 g pro.*

Greek Chicken Salad

START TO FINISH 20 minutes

- 1 2¼- to 2½-pound deli-roasted chicken
- 1 5-ounce package spring mix salad greens
- 2 small cucumbers, cut into spears
- 2 medium tomatoes, cut into wedges
- ⅔ cup bottled Greek salad dressing with feta cheese
  Cracked black pepper (optional)

1. Remove chicken from bones. Coarsely chop chicken; cover and set aside.
2. Divide salad greens, cucumber spears, and tomato wedges among 4 dinner plates or salad bowls. Arrange chicken on vegetables. Drizzle salad dressing. If desired, sprinkle with cracked black pepper. Makes 4 servings.
EACH SERVING *473 cal, 27 g fat, 136 mg chol, 433 mg sodium, 9 g carb, 9 g fiber, 46 g pro.*

MEDITERRANEAN
CHICKEN SALAD

1 tablespoon drained and finely
chopped oil-packed dried
tomatoes
Salt and black pepper
Croissants or sourdough bread

1. For dressing, in a small bowl stir together mayonnaise and mustards; set aside.
2. In a medium bowl combine chicken, celery, green onions, pine nuts, parsley, and tomatoes. Season to taste with salt and pepper. Pour dressing over salad; toss to coat. Cover and chill for 1 to 4 hours.
3. Serve chicken salad on croissants. Makes 4 servings.
EACH SERVING *556 cal, 34 g fat, 121 mg chol, 882 mg sodium, 29 g carb, 2 g fiber, 31 g pro.*

Warm Chicken Spinach Salad

START TO FINISH 20 minutes

4 skinless, boneless chicken breast halves
  Salt and black pepper
2 tablespoons canola oil
1½ cups sliced fresh mushrooms
1 10-ounce package prewashed fresh spinach
½ cup chopped walnuts, toasted if desired (see tip, page 31)
2 tablespoons finely shredded Parmesan cheese

1. Season chicken with *salt* and *black pepper*. In a very large skillet cook half the chicken in hot oil over medium heat for 8 minutes or until no longer pink (170°F), turning once. Repeat with remaining chicken. Remove chicken from skillet; keep warm.
2. Add mushrooms to skillet. Cook, stirring constantly, for 2 minutes. Add spinach to skillet. Cover and cook 1 minute or until spinach is just wilted, turning once. Stir in walnuts. Season to taste with additional salt and pepper. Transfer to a serving bowl and sprinkle with Parmesan cheese.
3. Serve chicken with spinach. Makes 4 servings.
EACH SERVING *347 cal, 19 g fat, 84 mg chol, 192 mg sodium, 6 g carb, 3 g fiber, 39 g pro.*

Mediterranean Chicken Salad

START TO FINISH 20 minutes

⅓ cup lemon juice
2 tablespoons snipped fresh mint
2 tablespoons snipped fresh basil
2 tablespoons olive oil
1 tablespoon honey
¼ teaspoon black pepper
5 cups shredded romaine lettuce
2 cups chopped cooked chicken breast
2 roma tomatoes, cut into wedges
1 15-ounce can garbanzo beans (chickpeas), rinsed and drained
2 tablespoons pitted Kalamata olives, quartered (optional)
2 tablespoons crumbled reduced-fat feta cheese
  Whole Kalamata olives (optional)

1. For dressing, in a screw-top jar combine lemon juice, mint, basil, oil, honey, and pepper. Cover and shake well.

2. Place lettuce on a large platter. Top with chicken, tomatoes, beans, the quartered olives (if using), and cheese. Drizzle with dressing. If desired, garnish each serving with whole olives. Makes 6 servings.
EACH SERVING *237 cal, 8 g fat, 41 mg chol, 292 mg sodium, 23 g carb, 5 g fiber, 20 g pro.*

Mustard Chicken Salad

PREP 25 minutes CHILL 1 hour

¼ cup mayonnaise
2 tablespoons creamy Dijon mustard blend
2 tablespoons coarse-grain brown mustard
2½ cups chopped cooked chicken or turkey
¼ cup finely chopped celery
¼ cup thinly sliced green onions
2 tablespoons pine nuts, toasted (see tip, page 31)
1 tablespoon snipped fresh parsley

**MUSTARD CHICKEN
SALAD**

**PAN-FRIED GARLIC STEAK ,
RECIPE PAGE 95**

beef & pork

STICK TO YOUR RIBS When supper calls for something substantial, satisfying, and absolutely sensational, you know where to turn—to the meat department. These recipes will satisfy even the heartiest of appetites.

CAPRESE PASTA
AND STEAK

PAN-FRIED
GARLIC STEAK

BEEF AND BEAN
STIR-FRY

Caprese Pasta and Steak

START TO FINISH 30 minutes

- 8 ounces dried large rigatoni
- ½ cup purchased basil pesto
- 1 pound flat iron or tri-tip steak, cut into 4 portions
- 4 roma tomatoes, sliced
- 4 ounces fresh mozzarella cheese, sliced
  Fresh basil leaves (optional)

1. Cook pasta according to package directions; drain and set aside.
2. Meanwhile, brush 2 tablespoons of the pesto on steaks. Heat a large heavy skillet over medium heat; add steaks. Cook about 10 minutes or to desired doneness, turning once.
3. Divide pasta among four plates. Top with steak, tomatoes, and cheese.
4. Place remaining pesto in a small microwave-safe bowl. Heat on high for 20 seconds or until hot, stirring once. Drizzle on pasta. Sprinkle with fresh basil. Makes 4 servings.
EACH SERVING *695 cal, 35 g fat, 94 mg chol, 486 mg sodium, 53 g carb, 3 g fiber, 40 g pro.*

Pan-Fried Garlic Steak

START TO FINISH 20 minutes

- 4 4- to 5-ounce beef ribeye (Delmonico) steaks, cut ½ inch thick
  Olive oil
  Salt and black pepper
- 6 cloves garlic, peeled and thinly sliced
- 2 tablespoons butter
- 1 15- to 19-ounce can cannellini beans (white kidney beans)
- ¼ cup snipped fresh parsley

1. Lightly drizzle steaks with olive oil; sprinkle with salt and black pepper.
2. Heat an extra-large heavy skillet over medium-high heat. Add steaks and reduce heat to medium. Cook steaks for 3 minutes per side or to desired doneness (145°F for medium-rare). Remove steaks from skillet; cover and keep warm. Add garlic slices to pan. Cook and stir 1 minute or until softened; remove from pan.
3. Add butter and beans to skillet; heat through. Add parsley and cook 1 minute more. Top steaks with garlic and serve with beans. Makes 4 servings.
EACH SERVING *326 cal, 18 g fat, 81 mg chol, 415 mg sodium, 16 g carb, 5 g fiber, 29 g pro.*

Beef and Bean Stir-Fry

START TO FINISH 20 minutes

- 2 tablespoons vegetable oil
- 1 pound boneless beef top loin steak, trimmed of fat and cut into thin strips
- 2 cloves garlic, minced
- 1 teaspoon chopped fresh ginger
- 2 carrots, thinly diagonally sliced
- 3½ cups broccoli florets (8 ounces)
- 6 green onions, cut into long thin strips
- ¼ cup orange juice concentrate, thawed, or orange juice
- 2 tablespoons reduced-sodium soy sauce
- ¼ teaspoon crushed red pepper
- 1 15-ounce can cannellini beans

1. In an extra-large skillet with flared sides or a large wok heat 1 tablespoon of the oil over medium-high heat. Cook and stir beef, garlic, and ginger about 2 minutes or until beef is browned. Remove from skillet. Heat remaining oil. Add carrots and broccoli; cook and stir 3 minutes. Add green onions; cook 1 minute more.
2. Add orange juice concentrate, soy sauce, and crushed red pepper; toss to coat. Add cooked beef and beans; cook until heated through. Makes 4 servings.
EACH SERVING *470 cal, 28 g fat, 76 mg chol, 557 mg sodium, 30 g carb, 8 g fiber, 31 g pro.*

GINGER-BEEF LETTUCE WRAP

vegetables. Add half the beef to wok. Stir-fry 2 minutes or until beef is slightly pink in center. Remove beef. Repeat with remaining beef. Return all to wok, away from center. Stir marinade mixture; add to center of wok. Cook until bubbly. Toss with beef and vegetables to coat. Remove from heat.
4. Serve beef and vegetables with lettuce leaves; top with cilantro. Wrap leaves around filling. Make 4 servings.

EACH SERVING 258 cal, 11 g fat, 46 mg chol, 517 mg sodium, 12 g carb, 2 g fiber, 27 g pro.

Wine-Glazed Steak
START TO FINISH 30 minutes

- 2 boneless beef top sirloin steaks, cut ½ to ¾ inch thick
- 4 teaspoons olive oil
- 2 cups sliced fresh mushrooms
- 4 cloves garlic, minced
- ¼ teaspoon crushed red pepper
- ½ cup dry red wine or low-calorie cranberry juice*
- ¼ cup balsamic vinegar
- 2 tablespoons reduced-sodium soy sauce
- 2 teaspoons honey*

1. Trim fat from steak; cut steak into two equal portions. In a very large skillet heat oil over medium-high heat. Add steaks. Reduce heat to medium; cook for 10 minutes or until desired doneness (145°F for medium-rare or 160°F for medium doneness), turning steaks occasionally. If steaks brown too quickly, reduce heat to medium-low. Transfer steaks to a serving platter; keep warm.
2. Add mushrooms, garlic, and crushed red pepper to skillet; cook and stir for 2 minutes. Remove skillet from heat. Carefully add wine. Return to heat. Boil gently, uncovered, for 3 minutes or until most of the liquid is evaporated. Add balsamic vinegar, soy sauce, and honey; return to simmering. Cook and stir about 2 minutes or until slightly thickened. Spoon over steaks. Makes 4 servings.
*If using the cranberry option omit the honey.

EACH SERVING 267 cal, 9 g fat, 48 mg chol, 336 mg sodium, 11 g carb, 1 g fiber, 28 g pro.

Ginger-Beef Lettuce Wraps
PREP 20 minutes FREEZE 30 minutes
MARINATE 4 hours COOK 7 minutes

- 1 pound beef flank steak or boneless beef top round steak
- 1 medium yellow or green sweet pepper, seeded, cut into bite-size strips
- 1 small zucchini, trimmed and cut into thin bite-size strips
- ½ medium red onion, cut into thin wedges
- ⅓ cup ginger beer or ginger ale
- 3 tablespoons reduced-sodium soy sauce
- 2 cloves garlic, minced
- ½ teaspoon cornstarch
- 2 teaspoons canola oil
- 2 tablespoons finely chopped fresh ginger
- 12 Bibb or leaf lettuce leaves (about 2 heads)
- ¼ cup fresh cilantro leaves

1. Trim fat from beef. For easy slicing, wrap and freeze beef 30 minutes or until firm. Thinly slice beef across grain; place slices in resealable plastic bag. In a second resealable plastic bag combine sweet pepper, zucchini, and onion.
2. For marinade, in a bowl combine ginger beer, soy sauce, and garlic. Divide marinade between beef and vegetables. Seal bags; turn to coat each. Refrigerate 4 to 6 hours, turning bags occasionally. Drain marinades into bowl. Stir in cornstarch; set aside.
3. Heat oil in a large nonstick wok or an extra-large nonstick skillet over medium-high heat. Add ginger; stir-fry 15 seconds. Add vegetables; stir-fry 3 minutes or until crisp-tender. Remove

WINE-GLAZED
STEAK

**FRIZZLED EGGS OVER
GARLIC STEAK AND
MUSHROOM HASH**

Frizzled Eggs over Garlic Steak and Mushroom Hash

START TO FINISH 30 minutes

- 2 tablespoons vegetable oil
- 2 cups frozen diced hash brown potatoes with onions and peppers
- 1 8-ounce package sliced fresh mushrooms
- 4 3- to 4-ounce thin breakfast steaks
  Salt and black pepper
- 4 to 6 cloves garlic, thinly sliced
- 4 eggs
  Fresh tarragon (optional)

1. In an extra-large skillet heat 1 tablespoon oil. Cook potatoes and mushrooms, covered, over medium-high heat for 10 minutes. Stir occasionally. Remove from skillet; cover to keep warm.
2. Sprinkle steaks with salt and pepper. Heat remaining oil in skillet. Cook steaks and garlic for 3 minutes, turning once, until desired doneness. Remove from skillet; cover to keep warm.
3. Add each egg to the hot skillet; sprinkle with salt and pepper. Cook to desired doneness. Place potatoes, steaks, and eggs on plates. Sprinkle with fresh tarragon. Makes 4 servings.
EACH SERVING 324 cal, 15 g fat, 258 mg chol, 397 mg sodium, 17 g carb, 2 g fiber, 29 g pro.

Fontina-Stuffed Tenderloin Steaks

PREP 25 minutes
ROAST 12 minutes at 400°F

- 4 6-ounce beef tenderloin steaks
- 1 cup shredded fontina cheese
- 2 tablespoons finely chopped oil-packed dried tomatoes
- 2 teaspoons snipped fresh parsley
- 1 teaspoon fresh thyme leaves
- 2 small cloves garlic, minced
- 2 thin slices prosciutto, halved
  Kosher salt and black pepper
- 2 tablespoons olive oil

1. Preheat oven to 400°F. Trim fat from steaks. Make a pocket in each steak by cutting horizontally from one side almost to the opposite side. Set aside.

2. For filling, in a small bowl combine cheese, dried tomatoes, 1 teaspoon parsley, thyme, and garlic. Divide filling among prosciutto halves; loosely roll up prosciutto around filling. Insert prosciutto bundles into pockets in steaks; secure with wooden toothpicks. Sprinkle steaks with salt and pepper.
3. In a medium skillet cook steaks in hot oil over medium-high heat until browned on both sides. Place steaks on a rack in a shallow baking pan. Roast for 12 to 15 minutes for medium-rare (145°F) to medium (160°F). Remove and discard toothpicks. Makes 4 servings.
EACH SERVING 623 cal, 49 g fat , 145 mg chol, 688 mg sodium, 2 g carb, 0 g fiber, 43 g pro.

Garlic Steaks with Nectarine Relish

PREP 20 minutes
MARINATE 30 minutes
GRILL 4 minutes

- 2 boneless beef top loin steaks, cut 1 inch thick
- 6 cloves garlic, thinly sliced
- ¼ teaspoon salt
- ¼ teaspoon black pepper
- 2 medium onions, coarsely chopped
- 2 teaspoons olive oil
- 2 tablespoons cider vinegar
- 2 teaspoons honey
- 2 small nectarines, pitted and chopped
- 2 teaspoon snipped fresh mint

1. Trim fat from steak. With the tip of a paring knife, make small slits in steak; insert half the garlic into slits. Wrap steak in plastic wrap; chill 30 minutes. Sprinkle with salt and pepper.
2. Meanwhile, for relish, in a large nonstick skillet cook onions and remaining garlic in hot oil over medium heat 5 minutes or until onions are golden, stirring occasionally. Stir in vinegar and honey. Stir in nectarine and snipped mint; heat through.
3. For a charcoal grill, place steaks on grill rack directly over medium coals. Grill 10 to 12 minutes for medium-rare (145°F)or 12 to 15 minutes for medium (160°F), turning once halfway through grilling. (If using a gas grill, preheat grill. Reduce temperature to medium. Place steak on grill rack over heat; cover and grill as above.) Cut each steak in half. Serve steaks with relish. Makes 4 servings.
EACH SERVING 274 cal, 13 g fat, 60 mg chol, 200 mg sodium, 15 g carb, 2 g fiber, 24 g pro.

GARLIC STEAKS WITH NECTARINE RELISH

SIRLOIN
STROGANOFF

Sirloin Stroganoff

START TO FINISH 40 minutes

- 1 20-ounce package refrigerated red potato wedges
- 1 cup chopped onion
- 3 cloves garlic, minced
- 2 tablespoons butter
- 12 ounces boneless beef sirloin steak, thinly sliced into bite-size strips
- 4 small apples, halved and cored
- 1 cup apple cider
- 1 8-ounce carton sour cream
- ¼ teaspoon salt
- ¼ teaspoon black pepper

1. In an extra-large skillet cook potatoes, onion, and garlic in hot butter over medium-high heat 8 minutes or until tender. Transfer to a serving platter; cover to keep warm. Add beef to skillet (add 1 tablespoon cooking oil if necessary). Cook and stir 3 minutes or to desired doneness; add to potatoes, reserving drippings in skillet. Cover; keep warm.
2. In same skillet cook apples, cut sides down, 2 minutes or until browned. Stir in apple cider. Bring to boiling; reduce heat. Simmer, covered, 4 minutes or until apples are tender; remove from skillet with a slotted spoon. Cover; keep warm.
3. Remove skillet from heat. For sauce, whisk sour cream, salt, and pepper into juices in skillet until smooth. Spoon sauce over steak, potatoes, and apples. Makes 4 servings.
EACH SERVING *538 cal, 25 g fat, 82 mg chol, 359 mg sodium, 51 g carb, 5 g fiber, 22 g pro.*

Roast Beef Panini

PREP 25 minutes COOK 3 minutes

- 2 tablespoons light mayonnaise
- 1 tablespoon prepared horseradish
- 1 teaspoon Dijon mustard
- ⅛ teaspoon caraway seeds
  Nonstick cooking spray
- 8 slices marble rye, rye, or pumpernickel bread
- 8 ounces cooked roast beef, sliced
- 1 cup watercress or baby arugula
- 2 slices Havarti cheese, halved
- ¼ cup thinly sliced red onion

ROAST BEEF PANINI

1. For the horseradish spread, in a bowl combine mayonnaise, horseradish, mustard, and caraway seeds. Set aside.
2. Lightly coat a panini maker or griddle with nonstick cooking spray. Preheat panini maker or griddle over medium heat.
3. On one side of the bread slices spread horseradish spread. On 4 of the slices place roast beef, watercress, cheese, and red onion. Top with remaining bread slices, spread sides down.
4. Cook panini 3 minutes in the panini maker or 5 minutes on a griddle, weighting with a skillet and turning once halfway through cooking time. Makes 4 servings.
EACH SERVING *333 cal, 11 g fat, 60 mg chol, 615 mg sodium, 32 g carb, 4 g fiber, 24 g pro.*

Beef and Carrot Ragu

PREP 25 minutes COOK 6 hours (low) or 3 hours (high)

- 1 to 1½ pounds boneless beef short ribs
  Salt and black pepper
- 10 cloves garlic

- 1 8-ounce package peeled fresh baby-cut carrots, chopped
- 1 pound roma tomatoes, chopped
- ½ 6-ounce can tomato paste with basil, garlic, and oregano
- ½ cup water or red wine
  Fresh basil leaves (optional)

1. Trim excess fat from rib meat. Cut beef into chunks, then sprinkle lightly with salt and pepper. Place beef in a 3½- or 4-quart slow cooker.
2. Smash garlic cloves with the flat side of a chef's knife or meat mallet. Separate and discard skins from garlic. Place smashed garlic on beef. Add carrots and tomatoes to slow cooker.
3. In a medium bowl whisk together tomato paste and water or wine. Pour over meat and vegetables. Cover and cook on low-heat setting for 6 to 8 hours or on high-heat setting for 3 to 4 hours.
3. Stir well before serving. If desired, top with fresh basil leaves. Makes 4 servings.
EACH SERVING *509 cal, 42 g fat, 86 mg chol, 568 mg sodium, 15 g carb, 4 g fiber, 19 g pro.*

ALFREDO BEEF SANDWICHES

Philly Steak Sandwiches

PREP 20 minutes BROIL 17 minutes

- 1 12-ounce boneless beef top sirloin steak, cut 1 inch thick
- ½ teaspoon garlic-pepper seasoning
  Nonstick cooking spray
- 2 medium red and/or green sweet peppers, seeded and cut into thin strips
- 1 large onion, thinly sliced and separated into rings
- 4 whole wheat frankfurter buns, split
- ½ cup shredded reduced-fat cheddar

1. Preheat broiler. Trim fat from steak. Sprinkle steak with garlic-pepper seasoning. Place seasoned steak on the unheated rack of a broiler pan. Broil 3 to 4 inches from heat until desired doneness. Allow 15 minutes for medium-rare (145°F) or 20 minutes for medium (160°F).
2. Meanwhile, coat an extra-large nonstick skillet with cooking spray. Preheat skillet over medium heat. Add sweet peppers and onion. Cover and cook for 5 minutes. Uncover and cook about 5 minutes or just until tender, stirring occasionally.
3. Place split buns on a large baking sheet. Broil 4 to 5 inches from heat for 1 minute or until lightly toasted. Remove bun tops from baking sheet; set aside. Slice steak into bite-size strips. Divide steak strips and sweet pepper mixture among bun bottoms. Sprinkle with cheese. Broil 4 to 5 inches from the heat for 1 minute or until cheese is melted. Top with bun tops. Makes 4 servings.
EACH SERVING *295 cal, 8 g fat, 46 mg chol, 416 mg sodium, 29 g carb, 4 g fiber, 27 g pro.*

Alfredo Beef Sandwiches

PREP 20 minutes
BAKE 21 minutes at 350°F

- 1 egg lightly beaten
- ½ cup fine dry bread crumbs
- ½ teaspoon garlic salt
- ¼ teaspoon black pepper
- 1 pound lean ground beef
- 6 hoagie buns
- 1 16-ounce jar Alfredo or marinara pasta sauce
- 6 ounces provolone cheese

1. Preheat oven to 350°F. In a large bowl combine egg, bread crumbs, garlic salt, and pepper. Add ground beef; mix well. Shape mixture into twenty-four 1¼-inch meatballs. Arrange in a 2-quart baking pan. Bake, uncovered, for 15 minutes.
2. Split hoagie buns nearly all the way through, leaving one long side attached. Spread 2 tablespoons of the Alfredo sauce on the bottom of each bun. Fill buns with meatballs and cheese.
3. Place sandwiches on a baking sheet. Bake, uncovered, for 6 minutes or until buns are toasted and cheese is melted. Meanwhile, heat the remaining Alfredo sauce and serve with sandwiches for dipping. Makes 6 servings.
EACH SERVING *733 cal, 41 g fat, 152 mg chol, 1,405 mg sodium, 57 g carb, 2 g fiber, 33 g pro.*

GRILLED STEAK
WITH CHEDDAR
CRISPS

MINI MEAT LOAVES WITH GREEN BEANS

MEAT AND POTATO LOAVES

Grilled Steak with Cheddar Crisps

START TO FINISH 30 minutes

- 1 cup fresh raspberries
- 1 tablespoon Dijon mustard
- ¼ cup cider vinegar
- 2 teaspoons sugar
- ¼ cup olive oil
- 1 12-ounce flank steak
- 2 cups refrigerated shredded hash brown potatoes
- 1 cup smoked cheddar cheese (4 ounces)
- 1 head romaine lettuce

1. Preheat broiler. For dressing, in a small bowl mash 8 berries. Stir in mustard, vinegar, and sugar. Whisk in the ¼ cup olive oil; set aside.
2. Lightly sprinkle the steak with *salt* and *black pepper*, then lightly brush with olive oil. Heat grill pan over medium-high heat. Cook steak 12 to 14 minutes, turning once. Slice steak into strips.
3. Meanwhile, generously grease a 3-quart baking dish. Toss together potatoes and cheese; spread in pan. Broil 3 to 4 inches from heat for 6 minutes or until golden brown and crisp. Remove from pan; cut into fourths.
4. Remove core from lettuce; cut crosswise into fourths. Serve with steak, potatoes, and remaining whole berries. Pass dressing. Makes 4 servings.
EACH SERVING *479 cal, 29 g fat, 60 mg chol, 514 mg sodium, 25 g carb, 5 g fiber, 28 g pro.*

Mini Meat Loaves with Green Beans

PREP 10 minutes

BAKE 15 minutes at 450°F

- 1 egg, lightly beaten
- 1 cup purchased pasta sauce
- ½ cup fine dry bread crumbs
- ¼ cup fresh basil leaves, chopped
- 1 pound lean ground beef
- 1 cup shredded mozzarella cheese (4 ounces)
- 1 12-ounce package fresh green beans, trimmed
- 1 tablespoon olive oil

1. Preheat oven to 450°F. Bring a medium saucepan of salted water to boiling.
2. Meanwhile, in a large bowl combine egg, ½ cup of the pasta sauce, bread crumbs, 2 tablespoons of the basil, and ¼ teaspoon *salt*. Add beef and ½ cup of the cheese; mix well. Divide beef mixture into four equal portions. Shape each portion into a 5½×2-inch oval. Place on a 15×10×1-inch baking pan. Spoon on remaining pasta sauce and sprinkle with remaining cheese. Bake 15 minutes or until internal temperature registers 160°F.
3. Meanwhile, cook green beans in boiling salted water for 10 minutes. Drain; toss with 1 tablespoon olive oil. Serve with meat loaves. Sprinkle all with remaining basil leaves. Makes 4 servings.
EACH SERVING *496 cal, 29 g fat, 145 mg chol, 742 mg sodium, 25 g carb, 5 g fiber, 34 g pro.*

Meat and Potato Loaves

PREP 25 minutes

BAKE 35 minutes at 350°F

- 1 egg, beaten
- ⅓ cup fine dry bread crumbs
- ¼ cup finely chopped onion
- ¼ cup beef broth
- ¼ teaspoon salt
- ¼ teaspoon black pepper
- 1 pound ground beef
- 1¼ cups frozen shredded hash brown potatoes, thawed
- 1 cup shredded Mexican cheese blend
- ¾ cup chunky salsa

1. Preheat oven to 350°F. In a large bowl combine egg, bread crumbs, onion, broth, salt, and pepper. Add ground beef; mix well. Divide into 8 portions. On foil pat each portion of meat into a 5-inch square.
2. In a medium bowl combine potatoes, ½ cup of the cheese, and ¼ cup of the salsa. Place one-fourth of the potato mixture in the center of each square, leaving a 1-inch border all around. Top each with a second square; press to seal edges. Place loaves, seam sides down, in a 3-quart baking dish.
3. Bake, uncovered, for 30 minutes or until an instant-read thermometer inserted in centers registers 160°F. Top with remaining salsa and cheese; bake 5 minutes more. Makes 4 servings.
EACH SERVING *612 cal, 45 g fat, 166 mg chol, 863 mg sodium, 23 g carb, 2 g fiber, 27 g pro.*

MEXICAN BEEF BAKE WITH CILANTRO-LIME CREAM

5. Meanwhile, for Cilantro-Lime Cream, in a small bowl stir together sour cream, 2 tablespoons of the green onions, cilantro, and lime peel. Serve beef bake with cilantro lime cream, the remaining 1 tablespoon green onions, and, if desired, lime wedges. Makes 6 servings.

EACH SERVING 283 cal, 10 g fat, 45 mg chol, 520 mg sodium, 29 g carb, 7 g fiber, 23 g pro.

Baked Penne with Meat Sauce

PREP 30 minutes
BAKE 25 minutes at 350°F

  8 ounces dried penne pasta
  1 pound lean ground beef
 ½ cup chopped onion
  1 14.5-ounce can diced tomatoes, undrained
 ½ 6-ounce can Italian-style tomato paste
 ⅓ cup dry red wine or tomato juice
 ⅓ cup water
 ½ teaspoon sugar
 ½ teaspoon dried oregano, crushed
 ¼ teaspoon salt
 ¼ teaspoon black pepper
 ¼ cup sliced pitted ripe olives
  1 cup shredded reduced-fat mozzarella cheese

1. Preheat oven to 350°F. Cook pasta according to package directions; drain.
2. Meanwhile, in a large skillet cook ground beef and onion over medium heat until meat is browned, stirring to break up meat as it cooks. Drain off fat. Stir undrained tomatoes, tomato paste, wine, water, sugar, dried oregano (if using), salt, and pepper into meat in skillet. Bring to boiling; reduce heat. Simmer, covered, for 10 minutes. Stir in pasta and olives. Spoon into a 3-quart rectangular baking dish.
3. Cover with foil. Bake for 20 minutes or until heated through. Sprinkle with mozzarella cheese. Bake, uncovered, about 5 minutes more or until cheese is melted. Makes 6 servings.

EACH SERVING 342 cal, 10 g fat, 51 mg chol, 465 mg sodium, 37 g carb, 2 g fiber, 22 g pro.

Mexican Beef Bake with Cilantro-Lime Cream

PREP 25 minutes
BAKE 33 minutes at 350°F

  4 ounces packaged dried multigrain rotini macaroni
 12 ounces extra-lean ground beef
  2 cloves garlic, minced
  1 15-ounce can black beans or pinto beans, rinsed and drained
  1 14.5-ounce can no-salt-added diced tomatoes, undrained
 ¾ cup bottled picante sauce or salsa
  1 teaspoon dried oregano, crushed
 ½ teaspoon ground cumin
 ½ teaspoon chili powder
 ½ cup shredded reduced-fat Colby and Monterey Jack cheese
 ⅓ cup light sour cream
  3 tablespoons sliced green onions
  2 teaspoons coarsely snipped fresh cilantro
 ½ teaspoon finely shredded lime peel
     Lime wedges (optional)

1. Preheat oven to 350°F. In a large saucepan cook pasta according to package directions; drain. Return pasta to hot saucepan; set aside.
2. Meanwhile, in a large skillet cook ground beef over medium heat and garlic until meat is browned, stirring with a wooden spoon to break up meat as it cooks. Drain off fat.
3. Stir cooked beef into pasta in saucepan. Stir in beans, tomatoes, picante sauce, oregano, cumin, and chili powder. Transfer mixture to an ungreased 1½- or 2-quart baking dish.
4. Bake, covered, about 30 minutes or until heated through. Sprinkle with cheese. Bake, uncovered, about 3 minutes or until cheese is melted.

**BAKED PENNE
WITH MEAT SAUCE**

BEEF AND NOODLE
CASEROLE

CHEESY ITALIAN
MEATBALL
CASSEROLE

Beef and Noodle Casserole

PREP 20 minutes BAKE 25 minutes at 350°F STAND 5 minutes

- 1 4.6-ounce packages vermicelli with garlic and olive oil
- 1 pounds lean ground beef
- ½ cup shredded carrots
- ½ 8-ounce tub cream cheese spread with chive and onion
- ½ cup milk
   Small fresh basil leaves (optional)

1. Preheat oven to 350°F. Grease a 2-quart baking dish; set aside. Prepare vermicelli according to package directions (including standing time).
2. Meanwhile, in a large skillet cook ground beef over medium heat until brown. Drain off fat. Stir in carrots, cream cheese, and milk. Stir in cooked vermicelli and, if desired, a few basil leaves. Transfer mixture to the prepared dish.
3. Bake, uncovered, for 25 minutes or until heated through, stirring once halfway through baking. Let stand for 5 minutes before serving. Makes 4 servings.
EACH SERVING 369 cal, 23 g fat, 104 mg chol, 359 mg sodium, 11 g carb, 1 g fiber, 26 g pro.

Cheesy Italian Meatball Casserole

PREP 30 minutes
BAKE 45 minutes at 350°F

- 8 ounces packaged dried ziti or penne pasta
- 1 15-ounce jar tomato pasta sauce
- ½ 16-ounce package frozen cooked Italian-style meatballs, thawed
- 1 8-ounce can Italian-style tomato sauce
- ½ 15-ounce carton ricotta cheese
- ¼ cup grated Parmesan cheese
- 1 cup shredded mozzarella cheese (4 ounces)

1. Preheat oven to 350°F. Cook pasta according to package directions; drain. Return to pan. Stir in pasta sauce, meatballs, and tomato sauce. Transfer to a 2-quart baking dish. Cover dish with foil. Bake for 30 minutes.
2. Meanwhile, in a small bowl combine ricotta and Parmesan cheeses. Remove foil from baking dish. Spoon cheese mixture in mounds on top of pasta mixture. Cover loosely; bake about 10 minutes more or until heated through. Top with mozzarella cheese and bake, uncovered, for 5 minutes more or until cheese is melted. Makes 4 servings.
EACH SERVING 636 cal, 30 g fat, 91 mg chol, 1,371 mg sodium, 59 g carb, 6 g fiber, 32 g pro.

Meatballs with Mustard and Mushroom Sauce

START TO FINISH 20 minutes

- 2 tablespoons olive oil
- 2 cups sliced fresh mushrooms
- 1 tablespoons Dijon mustard
- 2 tablespoons all-purpose flour
- 1 14.5-ounce can beef broth
- ½ 16-ounce package frozen cooked Italian-style meatballs
- 2 cups packaged refrigerated diced potatoes
- 1½ cups cherry tomatoes, halved
- 2 tablespoons snipped fresh parsley (optional)

1. In an extra-large large skillet heat oil over medium heat. Add mushrooms; cook until tender. Stir in mustard and flour. Gradually stir in beef broth. Bring to boiling. Stir in meatballs and potatoes; reduce heat. Simmer, covered, for 10 minutes, stirring occasionally.
2. Add tomatoes; cook just until heated through. If desired, garnish with parsley. Makes 4 servings.
EACH SERVING 510 cal, 33 g fat, 73 mg chol, 1,341 mg sodium, 30 g carb, 6 g fiber, 25 g pro.

MEATBALLS WITH
MUSTARD AND
MUSHROOM SAUCE

**BEEF AND PASTA
SKILLET**

Baked Beef Ravioli

PREP 20 minutes
BAKE 20 minutes at 375°F

- 2   9-ounce packages refrigerated cheese-filled ravioli
- 1½ pounds ground beef
- 1   cup chopped onion
- 6   cloves garlic, minced
- 1   14.5-ounce can diced tomatoes, undrained
- 1   10.75-ounce can condensed tomato soup
- 1   teaspoon dried basil, crushed
- 1   teaspoon dried oregano, crushed
- 1½ cups shredded mozzarella cheese
- ½   cup finely shredded Parmesan cheese

1. Preheat oven to 375°F. Cook ravioli according to package directions; drain. Return to pan; cover and keep warm.
2. Meanwhile, in a large skillet cook ground beef, onion, and garlic over medium heat until meat is browned and onion is tender. Drain off fat. Stir in tomatoes, soup, basil, and oregano. Gently stir in cooked ravioli.
3. Transfer mixture to an ungreased 3-quart baking dish. Sprinkle with mozzarella cheese and Parmesan cheese. Bake, uncovered, about 20 minutes or until heated through. Makes 8 servings.

EACH SERVING 503 cal, 20 g fat, 113 mg chol, 854 mg sodium, 40 g carb, 3 g fiber, 40 g pro.

Spaghetti with Bolognese Sauce

PREP 25 minutes   COOK 30 minutes

- 1½ pounds ground beef
- 1   cup chopped onion (1 large)
- 1   cup chopped carrots (2 medium)
- 3   cloves garlic
- 1   cup half-and-half or milk
- 1   cup chicken broth
- 1   tablespoon white wine vinegar
- 1   28-ounce can crushed tomatoes
- 1   6-ounce can tomato paste
- 2   teaspoons Italian seasoning, crushed

SPAGHETTI WITH BOLOGNESE SAUCE

- 1   teaspoon black pepper
- ½   teaspoon salt
- 1   14- to 16-ounce package dried whole wheat or regular spaghetti
      Grated Parmesan (optional)
      Fresh oregano (optional)

1. For sauce, in an extra-large skillet cook beef, onion, carrots, and garlic until meat is browned, stirring occasionally. Drain off fat.
2. Add half-and-half. Bring to boiling. Reduce heat; simmer, uncovered, for 5 minutes or until half-and-half is nearly evaporated. Stir in broth, then vinegar. Return to boiling. Reduce heat; simmer, uncovered, 15 minutes or until liquid is nearly evaporated. Stir in crushed tomatoes, tomato paste, seasoning, pepper, and salt. Bring to boiling. Reduce heat; simmer uncovered, 5 minutes or until thickened.
3. Meanwhile, cook spaghetti according to package directions with 1 tablespoon salt added to water. Drain. Serve sauce with spaghetti. If desired, sprinkle with cheese and oregano. Makes 8 servings.

EACH SERVING 474 cal, 18 g fat, 69 mg chol, 645 mg sodium, 53 g carb, 6 g fiber, 26 g pro.

Beef and Pasta Skillet

START TO FINISH 35 minutes

- 4   ounces packaged dried campanelle, cellentani, or penne
- 4   ounces lean ground beef or bulk hot or sweet Italian sausage
- 1   medium onion, cut into thin wedges
- 1   26-ounce jar garlic pasta sauce
- ⅔   cup bottled roasted red sweet peppers, cut into bite-size strips
- ¼   cup pitted Kalamata olives, quartered
- 1   cup shredded Italian cheese blend

1. In a large saucepan cook pasta according to package directions; drain.
2. In a large skillet cook ground beef and onion until meat is browned and onion is tender; drain off fat. Stir in pasta sauce, sweet peppers, and olives. Bring to boiling. Stir in pasta to coat. Top with cheese. Makes 4 servings.

EACH SERVING 512 cal, 18 g fat, 59 mg chol, 1,215 mg sodium, 59 g carb, 8 g fiber, 28 g pro.

ITALIAN-STYLE
MEATBALLS AND PASTA

CREAMY MEATBALL
CASSEROLE

Italian-Style Meatballs and Pasta

PREP 25 minutes BAKE 25 minutes
at 350°F

8	ounces dried mafalda pasta
2	14.5-ounce cans Italian-style stewed tomatoes, undrained
2	8-ounce cans tomato sauce
½	cup dry red wine
¼	cup dry onion soup mix
1	teaspoon dried oregano, crushed
⅛	teaspoon black pepper
32	frozen Italian-style cooked meatballs
1	cup shredded mozzarella cheese

1. Preheat oven to 350°F. Cook mafalda according to package directions; drain and set aside. In a large saucepan combine undrained stewed tomatoes, tomato sauce, red wine, dry onion soup mix, oregano, and pepper. Stir in meatballs. Bring mixture to boiling over medium heat. Stir in pasta.
2. Spoon mixture into an ungreased 3-quart baking dish. Bake, covered, for 20 minutes. Sprinkle with cheese. Bake, uncovered, about 5 minutes more or until cheese is melted. Makes 8 servings.

EACH SERVING *389 cal, 16 g fat, 45 mg chol, 1,308 mg sodium, 39 g carb, 4 g fiber, 18 g pro.*

Creamy Meatball Casserole

PREP 15 minutes
BAKE 1 hour at 350°F

1	10.75-ounce can condensed cream of mushroom soup or cream of onion soup
1	cup milk
½	cup sour cream
½	teaspoon salt
⅛	teaspoon black pepper
1	20-ounce package refrigerated red-skin potato wedges
1	16-ounce package frozen cooked meatballs
1	16-ounce package frozen stir-fry vegetables (any combination)

1. Preheat oven to 350°F. In a large bowl, combine soup, milk, sour cream, salt, and pepper. Stir in potatoes, meatballs, and frozen vegetables.
2. Transfer mixture to an ungreased 3-quart baking dish. Bake, covered, about 1 hour or until heated through. Makes 6 servings.

EACH SERVING *423 cal, 28 g fat, 37 mg chol, 1,291 mg sodium, 28 g carb, 6 g fiber, 17 g pro.*

Guadalupe Beef Pie

PREP 30 minutes
BAKE 30 minutes at 375°F

2¼	cups packaged biscuit mix
½	cup cold water
16	ounces ground beef
1	8-ounce carton sour cream
1	cup shredded cheddar cheese
⅔	cup mayonnaise
2	tablespoons chopped onion
2	medium tomatoes, thinly sliced
¾	cup chopped green sweet pepper Pimiento-stuffed green olives, halved (optional)

1. Preheat oven to 375°F. Grease a 3-quart baking dish; set aside. For crust, in a medium bowl combine biscuit mix and cold water, stirring with a fork until biscuit mix is moistened and a soft dough has formed. Press dough onto the bottom and ½ inch up the sides of the prepared baking dish. Bake, uncovered, about 12 minutes or until lightly browned.
2. Meanwhile, in a large skillet cook ground beef over medium heat until brown. Drain off fat. In a medium bowl, combine sour cream, cheese, mayonnaise, and onion.
3. Sprinkle cooked meat over baked crust. Layer tomatoes over meat then sprinkle with sweet pepper. Spread sour cream mixture over ingredients in dish.
4. Bake, uncovered, about 30 minutes or until bubbly around edges. If desired, top with olives. Makes 8 servings.

EACH SERVING *516 cal, 43 g fat, 75 mg chol, 653 mg sodium, 26 g carb, 1 g fiber, 17 g pro.*

GUADALUPE
BEEF PIE

Shortcut Lasagna

PREP 30 minutes BAKE 40 minutes
at 350°F STAND 5 minutes

- 8 ounces ground beef
- 8 ounces bulk Italian sausage
- 1 26-ounce jar tomato-basil pasta sauce
- 1 egg
- 1 15-ounce carton low-fat ricotta cheese or cream-style cottage cheese
- 1 2.25-ounce can sliced pitted ripe olives
- 9 no-boil lasagna noodles
- 8 ounces mozzarella cheese
- ¼ cup grated Parmesan cheese

1. Preheat oven to 350°F. In a large saucepan cook beef and sausage over medium heat until browned, stirring to break up meat as it cooks. Drain off fat. Stir pasta sauce into meat in saucepan; bring to boiling.
2. Meanwhile, in a medium bowl slightly beat egg with a fork. Stir in ricotta cheese and olives.
3. To assemble lasagna, spread about 1 cup of the hot meat mixture into a 3-quart baking dish. Cover with 3 of the uncooked lasagna noodles, breaking noodles as necessary to fit and making sure that noodles do not touch the edge of the dish. Cover with one-third of the ricotta mixture, one-third of the remaining meat mixture, and one-third of the mozzarella cheese. Repeat with two more layers of noodles, meat mixture, ricotta cheese mixture, and mozzarella cheese. (Make sure noodles are covered with sauce.) Sprinkle with Parmesan cheese.
4. Cover with foil. Bake for 30 minutes. Uncover. Bake for 10 minutes more or until cheese is golden brown and noodles are tender. Let stand for 5 minutes before serving. Makes 8 servings.

EACH SERVING 492 cal, 26 g fat, 109 mg chol, 987 mg sodium, 34 g carb, 2 g fiber, 31 g pro.

Eight-Layer Casserole

PREP 30 minutes BAKE 55 minutes
at 350°F STAND 10 minutes

- 6 ounces dried medium noodles
- 1 pound ground beef
- 1 16-ounce can tomato sauce
- 1 teaspoon dried basil, crushed
- ½ teaspoon sugar
- ½ teaspoon garlic powder
- ¼ teaspoon salt
- ¼ teaspoon black pepper
- 1 8-ounce carton sour cream
- 1 8-ounce package cream cheese, softened
- ½ cup milk
- ⅓ cup onion, chopped
- 1 10-ounce package frozen chopped spinach, thawed and well drained
- 1 cup shredded cheddar cheese

1. Preheat oven to 350°F. Grease a 2-quart baking dish; set aside. Cook noodles according to package directions; drain.
2. Meanwhile, in a large skillet cook ground beef over medium heat until brown. Drain off fat. Stir in tomato sauce, basil, sugar, garlic powder, salt, and pepper. Bring to boiling; reduce heat. Simmer, uncovered, for 5 minutes.
3. In a medium mixing bowl combine sour cream and cream cheese. Beat with an electric mixer on medium until smooth. Stir in milk and onion.
4. Place half the cooked noodles in the prepared dish. Top with half of the meat mixture, half the cream cheese mixture, and all the spinach. Top with the remaining meat mixture and noodles. Cover and chill the remaining cream cheese mixture until needed.
5. Cover casserole with lightly greased foil. Bake about 45 minutes or until heated through. Spread with the remaining cream cheese mixture; sprinkle with cheddar cheese. Bake, uncovered, about 10 minutes more or until cheese is melted. Let stand for 10 minutes before serving. Makes 8 servings.

EACH SERVING 472 cal, 30 g fat, 127 mg chol, 683 mg sodium, 25 g carb, 3 g fiber, 27 g pro.

CAJUN STEAK
SANDWICHES WITH
SWEET POTATO FRIES

Tamale Pies

PREP 15 minutes
BAKE 15 minutes at 350°F

- 1 pound ground beef
- 1 pound tomatoes, chopped
- ½ cup pitted olives (such as green, ripe, Kalamata, and/or niçoise), coarsely chopped
- ¼ cup water
- ½ teaspoon salt
- ½ teaspoon black pepper
- 1 8½-ounce package corn muffin mix
- ½ cup shredded cheddar cheese (2 ounces)
  Pitted olives, coarsely chopped tomatoes, and cilantro leaves (optional)

1. Preheat oven to 425°F. In very large skillet cook beef until browned. Drain off fat. Add chopped tomatoes, olives, the water, salt, and pepper. Cook, stirring occasionally, until heated through.
2. Prepare corn muffin mix according to package directions. Divide hot ground beef among four 12- to 16-ounce ovenproof dishes. Top with muffin mix; sprinkle with cheddar cheese.

3. Bake 15 minutes or until topping is lightly golden and cooked through. If desired, top with olives, tomatoes, and cilantro. Makes 4 servings.
EACH SERVING 384 cal, 11 g fat, 75 mg chol, 1,574 mg sodium, 65 g carb, 10 g fiber, 14 g pro.

Cajun Steak Sandwiches with Sweet Potato Fries

START TO FINISH 28 minutes

- 1 20-ounce package frozen french-fried sweet potatoes
- 2 8-ounce trimmed ribeye steaks or boneless beef top steak, cut ½ inch thick
- 3 teaspoons Cajun seasoning
- ¼ cup mayonnaise
- 1 tablespoon ketchup
- 1 teaspoon molasses
- 2 ciabatta rolls, split and toasted
- 1 tomato, sliced
  Sliced green onion (optional)

1. Preheat oven to 400°F. Spread sweet potatoes in a 15×10×1-inch baking pan. Sprinkle lightly with salt and pepper. Bake 18 to 20 minutes.

2. Meanwhile, cut steaks in half crosswise. Coat both sides of steaks with 1½ teaspoons seasoning. Heat a cast-iron or heavy skillet over medium-high heat. Cook steaks in hot skillet for 3 to 5 minutes on each side.
3. In a small bowl combine the mayonnaise, ketchup, molasses, and remaining seasoning.
4. Place one steak on each roll half. Top with some of the sauce, tomato slice, and, if desired, green onion. Serve remaining sauce with fries. Makes 4 servings.
EACH SERVING 583 cal, 29 g fat, 55 mg chol, 856 mg sodium, 59 g carb, 6 g fiber, 24 g pro.

Open-Face Beef and Tapenade Sandwiches

START TO FINISH 10 minutes

- ⅓ cup light mayonnaise or salad dressing
- 1 teaspoon Dijon or yellow mustard
- 4 slices crusty Italian country or sourdough bread
- ¼ cup olive tapenade
- 12 ounces thinly sliced deli roast beef
- 2 small tomatoes, thinly sliced
- 1 cup fresh baby spinach

1. In a small bowl combine mayonnaise and mustard. Lightly spread on one side of each bread slice. Spread with tapenade. Top with roast beef, tomato slices, and spinach. Makes 4 servings.
EACH SERVING 362 cal, 19 g fat, 46 mg chol, 1,681 mg sodium, 21 g carb, 2 g fiber, 21 g pro.

**OPEN-FACE
BEEF AND TAPENADE
SANDWICHES**

BEEF AND THREE-CHEESE TORTELLINI SALAD

Middle Eastern Beef Salad

PREP 30 minutes GRILL 10 minutes

- ¼ cup snipped fresh parsley
- ¼ cup snipped fresh mint
- 3 cloves garlic, minced
- 1 teaspoon olive oil
- 1 teaspoon honey
- 6 tablespoons plain low-fat yogurt
- 12 ounces beef tenderloin steaks, cut 1 inch thick
- ⅛ teaspoon salt
- ⅛ teaspoon black pepper
- 6 cups packaged fresh baby spinach
- 2 medium yellow or red tomatoes, cut into wedges
- 1 small cucumber, coarsely chopped
- 1 15-ounce can garbanzo beans (chickpeas), rinsed and drained

1. For mint-yogurt dressing, in a bowl combine parsley, mint, garlic, olive oil, and honey. Stir in yogurt until well combined. Set aside.
2. Trim fat from steaks. Season steaks with salt and pepper. For a charcoal grill, place steaks on a grill rack directly over medium coals. Grill, uncovered, until desired doneness, turning once halfway through. Allow 10 to 12 minutes for medium-rare (145°F) or 12 to 15 minutes for medium (160°F). (For a gas grill, preheat grill. Reduce heat to medium. Place steaks on grill rack over heat. Cover and grill as above.)
3. Meanwhile, on 4 dinner plates arrange spinach, tomatoes, cucumber, and garbanzo beans.
4. Thinly slice the grilled steak and place on top of salad. Serve with mint-yogurt dressing. Makes 4 servings.
EACH SERVING *282 cal, 9 g fat, 58 mg chol, 542 mg sodium, 25 g carb, 6 g fiber, 27 g pro.*

Beef and Three-Cheese Tortellini Salad

START TO FINISH 30 minutes

- 2 cups refrigerated or frozen cheese-filled tortellini
- 8 ounces cooked beef or cooked ham, cut into thin strips
- 1 cup Colby Jack or cheddar cheese cubes
- 1 cup broccoli florets
- 1 small yellow summer squash or zucchini, halved lengthwise and sliced
- ½ cup Parmesan Italian salad dressing
  Leaf lettuce
  Cherry tomatoes, halved (optional)

1. Cook tortellini according to package directions. Drain tortellini. Rinse with cold water; drain again.
2. In a large bowl combine tortellini, meat strips, cheese, broccoli, and squash. Drizzle salad dressing over beef mixture; toss gently to coat. Chill in the freezer for 10 minutes or until ready to serve (or chill in the refrigerator for 4 to 24 hours).
3. To serve, line 4 salad plates with leaf lettuce. Divide beef mixture among plates. If desired, garnish with cherry tomatoes. Makes 4 servings.
EACH SERVING *498 cal, 28 g fat, 97 mg chol, 822 mg sodium, 30 g carb, 3 g fiber, 31 g pro.*

MIDDLE EASTERN
BEEF SALAD

ALL-AMERICAN CHEESEBURGER SOUP

All-American Cheeseburger Soup

START TO FINISH **40 minutes**

- 1 pound ground beef
- 1 medium onion, chopped
- 1 stalk celery, chopped
- 2 cloves garlic, minced
- 2 tablespoons all-purpose flour
- 2 14.5-ounce cans lower-sodium beef broth
- 2 medium potatoes, scrubbed and coarsely chopped
- 1 14.5-ounce can diced tomatoes, drained
- 1 8-ounce package shredded cheddar and American cheese blend (2 cups)
- 1 6-ounce can tomato paste
- ¼ cup ketchup
- 2 tablespoons Dijon mustard
- 1 cup whole milk
   Toasted buns or rolls
   Cheeseburger toppings, such as pickles, onions, lettuce, mustard, and/or ketchup (optional)

1. In a 4-quart Dutch oven cook beef, onion, celery, and garlic over medium heat until meat is browned and vegetables are tender; drain off fat. Sprinkle flour on beef mixture; cook and stir 2 minutes. Stir in broth and potatoes. Bring to boiling, stirring occasionally. Reduce heat. Simmer, covered, 10 minutes or until potatoes are tender.

2. Stir in tomatoes, cheese, tomato paste, ketchup, and mustard. Cook and stir just until cheese is melted and smooth and soup comes to gentle boiling. Stir in milk; heat through. Serve with toasted buns and, if desired, cheeseburger toppings. Makes 6 servings.

EACH SERVING *477 cal, 27 g fat, 93 mg chol, 1,309 mg sodium, 28 g carb, 4 g fiber, 29 g pro.*

Basil, Beef, and Barley Soup

START TO FINISH **30 minutes**

- 1 pound boneless sirloin steak
- ¼ cup all-purpose flour
- 1 tablespoon dried basil, crushed
- ½ teaspoon salt
- 1 teaspoon black pepper
- 1 tablespoon vegetable oil
- 1 cup quick-cooking barley
- 1 14.5-ounce can diced tomatoes with basil, garlic, and oregano
- 1 cup packaged peeled fresh baby carrots, bias-sliced
- 1 cup lower-sodium beef broth
- 3 cups water
   Small fresh basil leaves (optional)

1. Cut steak into ½-inch pieces. In shallow dish combine flour, basil, salt, and black pepper; add meat and toss to coat.

2. In a 4- to 5-quart Dutch oven heat oil over medium-high heat. Cook steak in hot oil until browned on all sides. Stir in any remaining flour mixture. Stir in barley, tomatoes (undrained), carrots, broth, and the water. Bring to boiling; reduce heat. Cover and simmer 10 minutes.

3. Ladle soup into bowls and top with fresh basil. Makes 4 servings.

EACH SERVING *507 cal, 19 g fat, 53 mg chol, 1,014 mg sodium, 55 g carb, 7 g fiber, 31 g pro.*

TEXAS RED CHILI

Texas Red Chili

PREP 20 minutes COOK 57 minutes

- 3 dried guajillo or pasilla chiles (see tip, page 35)
- 2 dried ancho chiles
- 2 pounds 85% lean ground beef
- 6 slices thick-cut smoked bacon, cut into ½-inch pieces (8 ounces)
- 3 large Vidalia or other sweet onions, chopped
- 2 green sweet peppers, chopped
- 2 serrano peppers, finely chopped (see tip, page 35)
- 8 cloves garlic, minced
- 2 tablespoons chili powder
- 2 teaspoons ground cumin
- 1 28-ounce can diced tomatoes
- 1 cup water
- 1 tablespoon lime juice or cider vinegar
- ¼ teaspoon salt
  Cheddar cheese wedges and sliced green onions (optional)

1. In a large skillet over medium heat cook guajillo and ancho chiles 3 minutes, turning occasionally, until toasted. Cool; remove and discard stems and seeds. Transfer to a bowl; cover with boiling water. Let stand 20 minutes. Drain, reserving ⅓ cup soaking liquid. In a blender puree chiles and reserved liquid; set aside.
2. In a 5- to 6-quart Dutch oven over medium-high heat cook beef about 8 minutes, until beginning to brown. Drain off fat; transfer beef to a bowl.
3. In the same pan cook bacon 5 minutes, stirring occasionally, until browned. Stir in onions, sweet and serrano peppers, and garlic. Cook 7 minutes, stirring occasionally. Add pureed chiles; cook and stir 3 minutes. Add chili powder and cumin; cook and stir 1 minute. Add reserved beef, undrained tomatoes, and the water. Bring to boiling; reduce heat to medium-low. Simmer, covered, 30 minutes.
4. Remove from heat; stir in lime juice and salt. Top with cheese and onions. Makes 8 servings.

EACH SERVING 573 cal, 27 g fat, 77 mg chol, 961 mg sodium, 55 g carb, 13 g fiber, 36 g pro.

Game Day Chili

PREP 30 minutes
COOK 6 hours (low) or 3 hours (high)

- 1 recipe Chili Seasoning Puree
- 1½ pounds ground beef chuck
- 1 large chopped onion
- 2 stalks celery, sliced
- 1 28-ounce can diced tomatoes, undrained
- 1 14.5-ounce can beef broth
- 1½ cups pitted dried plums, chopped
- 1 6-ounce can tomato paste
- 2 tablespoons smoked paprika
- 2 teaspoons ground coriander
- 1 teaspoon crushed red pepper
- ¼ teaspoon ground cloves
- 1 ounce bittersweet chocolate, chopped

1. Prepare Chili Seasoning Puree. In a 6-quart Dutch oven cook beef, onion, and celery over medium-high heat, breaking up meat with a wooden spoon, until meat is browned and onion is tender. Drain off fat.
2. Transfer to a 5- or 6-quart slow cooker. Stir in Chili Seasoning Puree, tomatoes, broth, plums, 1½ cups *water*, tomato paste, paprika, coriander, crushed red pepper, and cloves. Cook, covered, on low-heat setting for 6 to 7 hours or on high-heat setting for 3 to 3½ hours. Stir in chocolate and serve. Makes 8 servings.
Chili Seasoning Puree In a bowl combine 2 dried ancho, mulato, or pasilla chile peppers (see tip, page 35) and enough boiling water to cover. Let stand 30 minutes; drain well. Remove stems and seeds from peppers. In a food processor or blender combine drained chile peppers, ¾ cup beef broth, 5 pitted dried plums, and 1 fresh jalapeño, seeded and chopped (see tip, page 35). Cover and process or blend until smooth.

EACH SERVING 343 cal, 14 g fat, 58 mg chol, 702 mg sodium, 38 g carb, 7 g fiber, 20 g pro.

GAME DAY CHILI

TWO-TOMATO STEW CHILI

Fiery Two-Pepper Chili

PREP 30 minutes
COOK 1 hour 11 minutes

   2 tablespoons olive oil
   2 pounds pork shoulder roast,
      trimmed and cut into 1-inch
      cubes
   2 cups chopped onion (2 large)
   6 cloves garlic, minced
   2 cups frozen corn
   2 tablespoons chili powder
   1 tablespoon ground ancho chile
      pepper
   ¼ teaspoon ground chipotle chile
      pepper
   2 15-ounce cans black beans,
      rinsed and drained
   3 10-ounce cans diced tomatoes
      with green chiles
   1½ cups water
   1 large yellow sweet pepper, cut
      into 1-inch pieces
      Salt

1. In a 4-quart Dutch oven heat oil over medium-high heat. Cook half the pork at a time about 4 minutes or until browned, turning occasionally. Remove with a slotted spoon; set aside.
2. Add onions and garlic to the Dutch oven. Cook, stirring occasionally, just until onion is tender. Stir in corn and cook 2 minutes more. Add the chili powder, ancho chile, and chipotle; cook 45 seconds. Stir in the pork, beans, tomatoes, and the water.
3. Bring to a boiling; reduce heat to medium-low; cover and simmer 40 minutes. Add yellow sweet pepper; cover and simmer 20 minutes longer or until pork is tender. Remove from heat. Season to taste with salt. Makes 8 servings.

EACH SERVING *337 cal, 8 g fat, 68 mg chol, 937 mg sodium, 35 g carb, 9 g fiber, 35 g pro.*

Two-Tomato Stew Chili

PREP 30 minutes COOK 1 hour

   1 8- to 8.5-ounce jar oil-packed
      dried tomatoes
   2 pounds beef chuck, cut into
      1-inch cubes
   3 cups chopped onions (3 large)
   6 cloves garlic, minced
   2 red sweet peppers, chopped
   2 green sweet peppers, chopped
   2 medium carrots, coarsely chopped
   ½ cup golden raisins
   4 teaspoons ground cumin
   ½ to 1 teaspoon crushed red pepper
   1 4.5-ounce can diced green chiles
   1 28-ounce can crushed tomatoes
   8 ounces smoked mozzarella,
      shredded
      Sliced dried tomatoes (optional)
      Toasted baguette slices (optional)

1. Drain tomatoes, reserving 2 tablespoons oil. Chop tomatoes; set aside. In a Dutch oven heat the reserved oil over medium-high. Brown half the beef at a time in the hot oil.
2. Return all meat to pan. Add onions, garlic, sweet peppers, and carrots; cook 2 minutes. Stir in chopped dried tomatoes, raisins, cumin, and crushed red pepper; cook 2 minutes. Stir in undrained green chiles; cook 1 minute. Add crushed tomatoes and 2 cups *water*; bring to boiling. Reduce heat to medium. Simmer, covered, for 1 to 1¼ hours, stirring occasionally, until meat is tender. Remove from heat. Add ¼ teaspoon each *salt* and *black pepper*. Top with mozzarella and, if desired, dried tomatoes. Serve with baguette slices. Makes 8 servings.

EACH SERVING *429 cal, 18 g fat, 82 mg chol, 676 mg sodium, 36 g carb, 7 g fiber, 34 g pro.*

FIERY TWO-PEPPER
CHILI

HOMINY AND CHORIZO CHILI

WINTER SQUASH AND SAGE SAUSAGE CHILI

Hominy and Chorizo Chili

PREP 45 minutes COOK 10 minutes

1½ pounds fresh or 1 pounds hard (cured) chorizo sausage links
¼ cup water
1 tablespoon olive oil
3 large onions, chopped
6 cloves garlic, minced
3 medium carrots, chopped
1 large green sweet pepper, chopped
1 teaspoon fresh thyme
1 tablespoon chili powder
½ teaspoon smoked paprika
3 15-ounce cans hominy, rinsed and drained
1 14.5-ounce can reduced-sodium chicken broth
2 tablespoons tomato paste
1 pint grape tomatoes, halved Snipped fresh oregano

1. In an extra-large skillet over medium-high heat bring sausage and the water to boiling. Cook, covered, 15 minutes, turning occasionally. Uncover; cook 8 to 10 minutes, turning to brown. Cool 5 minutes on cutting board. Diagonally cut into ½-inch slices.
2. In a large Dutch oven heat oil over medium-high. Cook onions, garlic, carrots, sweet pepper, and thyme 7 minutes, stirring occasionally, until almost tender. Stir in chili powder and paprika; cook 30 seconds. Add sausage;

cook 1 minute. Add hominy, broth, and tomato paste; bring to boiling. Reduce heat to medium; simmer, covered, 10 minutes, stirring occasionally. Stir in tomatoes; cook for 2 minutes. Sprinkle each serving with oregano. Makes 8 servings.
EACH SERVING *576 cal, 36 g fat, 75 mg chol, 1,455 mg sodium, 37 g carb, 7 g fiber, 25 g pro.*

Winter Squash and Sage Sausage Chili

START TO FINISH 20 minutes

1 pound bulk sage sausage or other sausage
1 15-ounce can cannellini beans, drained
1 12-ounce package frozen winter squash puree, thawed
1 cup chunky-style chipotle salsa or other salsa
1½ cups water
1 3.5-ounce package herb-flavored goat cheese, crumbled Fresh sage (optional)

1. In a large saucepan cook sausage over medium heat until browned and no pink remains, stirring to break up. Drain off fat. Stir in beans, squash, salsa, and water. Bring to boiling; reduce heat. Simmer, uncovered, for 10 minutes, stirring occasionally. Serve in bowls; sprinkle servings with goat cheese and fresh sage. Makes 4 servings.
EACH SERVING *385 cal, 14 g fat, 119 mg chol, 1,466 mg sodium, 34 g carb, 7 g fiber, 39 g pro.*

Cowboy Bowls

START TO FINISH 20 minutes

1 24-ounce package refrigerated mashed potatoes
1 17- to 18-ounce package refrigerated cooked shredded pork with barbecue sauce
1 15- to 16-ounce can chili beans in chili gravy
1 cup frozen whole kernel corn
½ cup chopped red sweet pepper
¼ cup finely chopped onion
½ cup shredded cheddar cheese

1. Heat mashed potatoes according to package directions.
2. Meanwhile, in a medium saucepan combine pork, undrained chili beans, corn, sweet pepper, and onion. Heat through.
3. Transfer mashed potatoes to shallow bowls. Top with pork mixture and sprinkle with cheese. Makes 4 servings.
EACH SERVING *600 cal, 21 g fat, 76 mg chol, 1,125 mg sodium, 74 g carb, 8 g fiber, 31 g pro.*

ZUCCHINI-WRAPPED
PORK

Zucchini-Wrapped Pork

PREP 35 minutes
ROAST 18 minutes at 450°F

  1 small zucchini
  1 12- to 16-ounce pork tenderloin
     Olive oil
     Salt and black pepper
 ⅓   cup purchased basil pesto
     Small fresh basil leaves
     (optional)
     Watercress or arugula (optional)

1. Preheat oven to 450°F. Line a
15×10×1-inch baking pan with foil; set
aside. With a sharp knife or vegetable
peeler, cut zucchini lengthwise into
8 thin slices. Cut pork tenderloin
crosswise into four equal portions. Press
meat with the palm of hand to flatten
slightly.
2. Wrap each tenderloin portion with
two zucchini slices (reserve remaining
zucchini for another use). Place in
prepared pan. Lightly brush with oil;
sprinkle with salt and pepper.
3. Roast, uncovered, 15 minutes
(12-ounce tenderloin) or 20 minutes
(16-ounce tenderloin) or until meat
registers 145°F. Let meat rest for at
least 3 minutes. Spoon some of the
pesto on each tenderloin just before
serving, if desired, sprinkle with basil
leaves. Serve with remaining pesto and
watercress. Makes 4 servings.
EACH SERVING *203 cal, 11 g fat, 62 mg chol,
382 mg sodium, 4 g carb, 1 g fiber, 21 g pro.*

Pecan-Crusted Sliders

START TO FINISH 25 minutes

 12 ounces pork tenderloin, sliced
     crosswise into 8 pieces
  1 egg
  2 tablespoons honey
  1 cup finely chopped pecans
  1 teaspoon salt
 ½   teaspoon black pepper
  1 small green apple
 1½ cups shredded broccoli (broccoli
     slaw) or coleslaw mix
 ¼   cup mayonnaise
  8 small buns or dinner rolls, split
     Dijon mustard (optional)

**PECAN-CRUSTED
SLIDERS**

1. With palm of hand, flatten pork slices
to ¼-inch thickness. In a shallow dish
whisk together egg and 1 tablespoon
of the honey. In another shallow
dish combine chopped nuts, salt, and
pepper. Dip pork in egg mixture, then
nut mixture, pressing to coat.
2. In an extra-large skillet heat oil over
medium-high heat. Cook pork in hot oil
2 minutes per side or until golden and
slightly pink in centers (145°F).
3. Meanwhile, for slaw, quarter apple;
remove core and seeds; thinly slice.
In a bowl combine apple, shredded
broccoli, mayonnaise, and remaining
honey. Season with salt and pepper. For
sliders, place pork on buns or rolls; top
with slaw. Pass mustard. Makes
4 servings.
EACH SERVING *694 cal, 44 g fat, 115 mg chol,
1,029 mg sodium, 49 g carb, 5 g fiber, 29 g pro.*

Sausage Jambalaya

PREP 15 minutes   COOK 4 hours
(low) or 2 hours (high)

 12 ounces cooked andouille sausage
     or cooked kielbasa
  1 pint miniature sweet peppers
     or 2 large yellow and/or orange
     sweet peppers
  1 15- to 16-ounce can red kidney
     beans, rinsed and drained
  1 14.5-ounce can fire-roasted diced
     tomatoes
  1 cup chopped celery (2 stalks)

1. Slice sausage into 1-inch chunks.
Halve, stem, and seed the miniature
peppers. If using large peppers, stem,
seed, and coarsely chop.
2. In a 3½- or 4-quart slow cooker
combine the sausage, sweet peppers,
drained beans, undrained tomatoes,
and celery. Cover and cook on low-heat
setting for 4 hours or on high-heat
setting for 2 hours. Stir before serving.
Makes 4 servings.
EACH SERVING *409 cal, 24 g fat, 56 mg chol,
1,295 mg sodium, 32 g carb, 8 g fiber, 18 g pro.*

PECAN-CRUSTED PORK WITH ORANGE-MAPLE GLAZE

1. Trim pork, then cut into ½-inch slices. Flatten slices with palm of hand; season with salt and pepper.
2. Place 3 tablespoons syrup in dish; place pecans in second dish. In an extra-large skillet heat oil over medium heat. Coat pork in syrup, then press in pecans. Place pork in skillet in single layer; top with remaining pecans and syrup from dish. Cook 3 minutes each side or until 145°F. Remove from skillet and let rest for at least 3 minutes.
3. Stir orange juice, remaining 1 tablespoon syrup, cumin, and cayenne into skillet. Cook, uncovered, 1 to 2 minutes until slightly thickened. Pour over pork. Serve with orange wedges. Makes 4 servings.

EACH SERVING *537 cal, 33 g fat, 111 mg chol, 381 mg sodium, 25 g carb, 4 g fiber, 38 g pro.*

Pork Chops, Apples, and Greens

START TO FINISH 30 minutes

- 4 5-ounce boneless pork chops
- 3 slices day-old bread
- 1 egg
- ½ teaspoon salt
- 2 tablespoons olive oil
- ¼ cup honey
- 2 tablespoons spicy brown mustard
- 2 tablespoons cider vinegar
- 2 cooking apples, cored and cut into wedges
- 6 cups packaged baby spinach

1. Place each chop between waxed paper or plastic wrap. With flat side of meat mallet, pound pork to ½-inch thickness. In a food processor process bread to crumbs; place in shallow dish. In a second shallow dish lightly beat egg with ¼ teaspoon of the salt. Dip pork in egg, then crumbs.
2. In an extra-large skillet cook chops in hot oil 3 minutes per side or until 145°F and golden. Let chops rest for at least 3 minutes. Transfer to platter. Stir honey, mustard, and vinegar into skillet drippings. Add apples; cook about 3 minutes, until crisp-tender. Toss in spinach. Sprinkle with remaining salt. Makes 4 servings.

EACH SERVING *446 cal, 21 g fat, 150 mg chol, 700 mg sodium, 26 g carb, 5 g fiber, 35 g pro.*

Caramelized Pork with Melon

START TO FINISH 25 minutes

- 1 small cantaloupe
- ¼ cup orange juice
- 3 tablespoons hoisin sauce
- 4 center-cut pork chops, ½ inch thick
- 1 tablespoon vegetable oil
- 3 green onions, thinly sliced
   Shredded napa cabbage (optional)

1. Remove rind and seeds from the cantaloupe; chop. Place 2 cups chopped melon in a food processor or blender; reserve remaining melon. Add orange juice and process until smooth. For sauce, transfer ½ cup pureed melon to a small bowl; add hoisin sauce. Strain remaining puree; reserve juice and discard solids.
2. Sprinkle pork lightly with *salt* and *black pepper;* brush generously with the sauce. Heat oil in an extra-large skillet. Cook chops for 3 minutes on each side or until 145°F and browned. Let chops rest for at least 3 minutes.
3. Meanwhile combine remaining chopped melon, strained juice, and green onions. Remove chops from skillet; add remaining sauce mixture to skillet. Cook and stir until heated through. Spoon onto serving plates. Top each with a chop. Add melon mixture to skillet, if desired, to warm slightly; serve over chops. If desired, serve with shredded napa cabbage. Makes 4 servings.

EACH SERVING *327 cal, 10 g fat, 117 mg chol, 452 mg sodium, 19 g carb, 2 g fiber, 39 g pro.*

Pecan-Crusted Pork with Orange-Maple Glaze

START TO FINISH 30 minutes

- 1 pork tenderloin (1½ pounds)
- ½ teaspoon salt
- ¼ teaspoon black pepper
- 4 tablespoons pure maple syrup
- 1 cup pecan pieces, finely chopped
- 2 tablespoons vegetable oil
- 2 oranges (1 juiced; 1 cut into wedges)
- ¼ teaspoon ground cumin
- ¼ teaspoon cayenne pepper

Pork Loin with Butternut Squash

PREP 20 minutes COOK 4 hours (low) or 2 hours (high)

- 1 small butternut squash
- ½ teaspoon each salt, pepper, pumpkin pie spice, and onion or garlic powder
- 1 to 1½ pounds boneless pork loin roast
- 1 tablespoon olive oil
- 1 18.8-ounce can caramelized French onion soup
- ½ cup chunky-style applesauce

1. Halve and peel squash, discard seeds, then cut squash in large chunks. Place squash in a 3- or 3½-quart slow cooker.
2. In a small bowl combine salt, pepper, spice, and onion or garlic powder; rub seasoning on all sides of pork. Heat oil in a large skillet; brown pork on all sides in the hot oil. Place pork on the squash in slow cooker. Pour soup and applesauce over all. Cover and cook on low-heat setting for 4 hours or high-heat setting for 2 hours.
3. Slice pork on cutting board. To serve, drizzle sauce over pork and squash. Makes 4 servings.
EACH SERVING 322 cal, 14 g fat, 76 mg chol, 732 mg sodium, 22 g carb, 3 g fiber, 26 g pro.

Herb-and-Garlic-Crusted Pork Roast

PREP 25 minutes
MARINATE overnight
ROAST 1 hour at 425°F/350°F
STAND 15 minutes

- ½ cup kosher salt
- ¼ cup brown sugar
- 8 cups cold water
- 3 tablespoons peanut oil or vegetable oil
- 1 3- to 3½-pound center-cut boneless pork loin
- 4 slices Black Forest bacon or other bacon, cut into 1-inch pieces (uncooked)
- 1 tablespoon apricot preserves
- 2 teaspoons finely chopped garlic
- 1 tablespoon fresh rosemary, chopped
- 1½ cups fresh bread crumbs
- 3 tablespoons fresh parsley, chopped
- 3 tablespoons melted butter
- ½ teaspoon kosher salt
- ½ teaspoon black pepper

1. For brine, in a large bowl dissolve salt and sugar in the cold water. Transfer pork to brine; cover and refrigerate overnight or up to 2 days, turning occasionally if roast isn't fully submerged.
2. Remove loin from brine and blot dry with paper towels. Heat oil in a nonstick skillet. Brown roast on all sides, about 10 minutes. Set aside to cool slightly.
3. In a food processor puree bacon to a smooth paste. Transfer half the bacon to a mixing bowl.* Stir in apricot preserves, garlic, and 2 teaspoons of the chopped rosemary.
4. Place cooled pork loin on waxed paper. Spread with a thin coat of pureed bacon. In a separate bowl mix bread crumbs, remaining rosemary, parsley, melted butter, salt and pepper. Toss well to mix. Press crumb mixture on roast, except ends, applying pressure for crumbs to adhere.
5. Position oven rack in lowest position; preheat oven to 425°F. Transfer roast to a wire rack in a foil-lined baking dish or roasting pan. Roast 15 minutes. Reduce temperature to 350°F. Roast 45 minutes more or until an instant-read thermometer registers 145°F. (If crust begins to brown too deeply, tent with foil.) Remove from oven and allow roast to rest for 15 minutes, tented with foil, in a warm place. Makes 6 servings, plus leftovers.
*Tip This amount of bacon is required to process well. Serve remaining pureed bacon spread on baguette slices and broiled until golden as an appetizer.
EACH SERVING 412 cal, 23 g fat, 118 mg chol, 621 mg sodium, 13 g carb, 1 g fiber, 36 g pro.

HERB-AND-GARLIC-CRUSTED PORK ROAST

PORK TENDERLOIN WITH CUCUMBER-MANGO SALAD

Spiced Pork and Apples

PREP 25 minutes   MARINATE 4 hours
BAKE 15 minutes at 425°F

- 4 boneless pork chops, cut about ½ inch thick
- ¼ cup peanut oil or vegetable oil
- ¼ cup honey or packed brown sugar
- ¼ cup reduced-sodium soy sauce
- 2 tablespoons rice wine or sherry
- 1 teaspoon toasted sesame oil
- 1 teaspoon five-spice powder
- 1 2-inch piece fresh ginger, peeled and thinly sliced
- 2 large baking apples (such as Cortland, Pippin, Rome Beauty, or Winesap), cored and cut into wedges
- ¼ teaspoon ground cinnamon or five-spice powder
- 4 green onions, diagonally sliced into 2-inch pieces
- 1 tablespoon honey

1. Place pork chops in a resealable plastic bag set in a shallow dish; set aside. For marinade, in a small bowl combine peanut oil, honey, soy sauce, rice wine, sesame oil, five-spice powder, and ginger. Pour marinade over pork chops. Seal bag; turn to coat chops. Marinate in the refrigerator for 4 to 12 hours, turning occasionally.
2. Preheat oven to 425°F. Drain chops, reserving ¼ cup marinade. Arrange chops in an ungreased 3-quart rectangular baking dish. Arrange apples around chops. Drizzle apples with the reserved ¼ cup marinade. Sprinkle apples with cinnamon.
3. Bake, uncovered, for 10 minutes. Add green onions. Bake, uncovered, for 5 minutes more or until chops are cooked through (145°F) and apples are tender. Let chops rest for at least 3 minutes. Arrange chops and apples on a serving platter. Drizzle apples with honey. Makes 4 servings.
EACH SERVING *539 cal, 28 g fat, 98 mg chol, 473 mg sodium, 42 g carb, 3 g fiber, 31 g pro.*

Pork Tenderloin with Cucumber-Mango Salad

PREP 30 minutes
ROAST 15 minutes at 425°F

- 2 tablespoons packed brown sugar
- 2 teaspoons five-spice powder
- ½ teaspoon salt
- 1½ pounds pork tenderloin
- 4 green onions
- 1 mango, peeled, seeded, and chopped
- 1 small English cucumber, sliced and/or chopped
- 1 fresh jalapeño, seeded and sliced (see tip, page 35) (optional)

1. Preheat oven to 425°F. For rub, in a small bowl combine brown sugar, five-spice powder; set aside 1 teaspoon rub. Rub remaining rub into pork tenderloin. Place tenderloin in foil-lined baking pan.
2. Roast, uncovered, for 15 minutes or until a meat thermometer registers 145°F. Cover with foil and let rest at least 3 minutes.
3. Meanwhile, for the salad, slice the green portion of green onions in thin strips; chop the white portion. In a medium bowl combine onions, mango, cucumber, jalapeño (if using), and reserved rub. Slice pork and serve with mango salad. Makes 4 servings.
EACH SERVING *258 cal, 3 g fat, 110 mg chol, 370 mg sodium, 19 g carb, 2 g fiber, 37 g pro.*

SPICED PORK
AND APPLES

PECAN-
PARMESAN PORK
WITH PORT
SAUCE

Pecan-Parmesan Pork with Port Sauce

PREP 25 minutes ROAST 20 minutes at 425°F STAND 15 minutes

- 2 1-pound pork tenderloins
- 1 cup broken pecans
- ⅔ cup finely shredded Parmesan cheese
- 2 tablespoons yellow mustard
- 2 teaspoons Worcestershire sauce or soy sauce
- 2 cups port or dry Marsala
- 1 cup snipped dried Calimyrna or Mission figs
- 2 tablespoons packed brown sugar

1. Preheat oven to 425°F. Trim fat from tenderloins; set tenderloins aside. In a blender or food processor combine pecans, cheese, mustard, and Worcestershire sauce. Cover and blend or process until pecans are finely chopped. Press mixture onto all sides of the tenderloins to coat with a thin layer.
2. Place tenderloins, side by side, on a rack in a 3-quart baking dish. Roast, uncovered, for 20 minutes or until tenderloin is 145°F. Cover with foil; let stand for at least 3 minutes.
3. Meanwhile, for sauce, in a medium saucepan stir together port, figs, and brown sugar. Bring to boiling; reduce heat. Simmer, uncovered, for 10 minutes or until sauce is reduced to 1 cup. Cool slightly.
4. Transfer half the sauce to a blender or processor. Cover and blend or process until nearly smooth. Pour sauce through a sieve over a bowl, pressing solids to release juices. Discard solids. Repeat with remaining sauce. Return all the sauce to saucepan. Cook and stir over low heat just until heated through. To serve, slice meat. Serve with warm sauce. Makes 4 servings.

EACH SERVING 428 cal, 15 g fat, 78 mg chol, 253 mg sodium, 31 g carb, 4 g fiber, 29 g pro.

CARNITAS

Carnitas

PREP 10 minutes COOK 10 hours (low) or 4½ hours (high)

- 1 2-pound boneless pork shoulder roast, cut into 2-inch pieces
- ¼ teaspoon salt
- ¼ teaspoon black pepper
- 1 tablespoon whole black peppercorns
- 2 teaspoons cumin seeds
- 4 cloves garlic, minced
- 1 teaspoon dried oregano, crushed
- 3 bay leaves
- 2 14.5-ounce cans reduced-sodium chicken broth
- 2 teaspoons finely shredded lime peel
- 2 tablespoons lime juice
- 12 6-inch crisp corn tortillas
- 2 green onions, thinly sliced
- ⅓ cup light sour cream (optional)
- ⅓ cup purchased salsa (optional)

1. Sprinkle pork with salt and pepper. Place in a 3½- or 4-quart slow cooker.
2. To make a bouquet garni, cut a 6-inch square from a double thickness of 100%-cotton cheesecloth. Place peppercorns, cumin seeds, garlic, oregano, and bay leaves in center of cheesecloth square. Bring up corners of cheesecloth and tie with clean 100%-cotton kitchen string. Add to slow cooker. Add broth.
3. Cover and cook on low-heat setting for 10 to 12 hours or on high-heat setting for 4½ to 5 hours.
4. Using a slotted spoon, remove meat from slow cooker. Discard bouquet garni and cooking liquid. Using two forks, coarsely shred meat; discard any fat. Sprinkle meat with lime peel and lime juice; toss to mix. Serve on tortillas with green onions and, if desired, sour cream and salsa. Makes 6 servings.

EACH SERVING 318 cal, 10 g fat, 90 mg chol, 377 mg sodium, 24 g carb, 4 g fiber, 32 g pro.

Pork Chop Casserole

PREP 25 minutes
BAKE 25 minutes at 350°F

    8   boneless pork loin chops, cut
        about ¾ inch thick
    ⅓   cup all-purpose flour
    ¼   teaspoon salt
    ¼   teaspoon black pepper
    2   tablespoons vegetable oil
    1   10.75-ounce can condensed
        cream of mushroom soup
    ⅔   cup chicken broth
    ½   cup sour cream
    ½   teaspoon ground ginger
    ½   teaspoon dried rosemary,
        crushed
    1½ cups french-fried onions
        Hot cooked noodles or thick
        slices of toasted bread

1. Preheat oven to 350°F. Trim fat from chops. In a shallow dish combine flour, salt, and pepper. Dip chops in flour mixture, turning to coat.
2. In a large skillet heat oil over medium-high heat. Cook chops, half at a time, in hot oil until brown on both sides. Remove from heat.
3. For sauce, in a medium bowl combine soup, broth, sour cream, ginger, and rosemary. Stir in half the french-fried onions. Pour sauce into an ungreased 3-quart baking dish, spreading evenly. Top with chops.
4. Bake, covered, for 20 minutes. Sprinkle with the remaining french-fried onions. Bake, uncovered, for 5 minutes or until chops are tender and juices run clear (145°F). Serve on hot cooked noodles toasted bread. Makes 8 servings.

EACH SERVING *411 cal, 19 g fat, 95 mg chol, 536 mg sodium, 31 g carb, 1 g fiber, 28 g pro.*

MEXI-PORK WRAPS

Mexi-Pork Wraps

START TO FINISH **35 minutes**

- 1 tablespoon olive oil
- 8 ounces lean boneless pork, cut into thin bite-size strips
- 1 clove garlic, minced
- ½ cup frozen whole kernel corn, thawed
- ½ cup chopped bottled roasted red sweet peppers
- ¼ cup sliced green onions
- 3 tablespoons lime juice
- ½ teaspoon ground cumin
- ⅛ teaspoon cayenne pepper
- ½ cup canned refried black beans or regular refried beans
- 4 8-inch whole grain tortillas
- ½ cup shredded romaine lettuce
- ½ cup chopped tomatoes
  Light sour cream (optional)

1. In a large skillet heat oil over medium-high heat. Add pork and garlic to skillet; cook for 4 minutes or until pork is cooked through and juices run clear, stirring occasionally. Set aside.
2. In a medium bowl stir together corn, roasted red peppers, green onions, 2 tablespoons of the lime juice, the cumin, and cayenne pepper; set aside. In a small bowl stir together refried black beans and the remaining 1 tablespoon lime juice.
3. To assemble, spread 2 tablespoons of the black bean mixture in a 2-inch-wide strip on the center of each tortilla. Top with pork strips, corn mixture, romaine, and tomatoes. Fold lower edge of each tortilla up and over filling. Roll tortillas around filling. If desired,

BARBECUED PORK SANDWICHES

serve wraps with sour cream. Makes 4 servings.

EACH SERVING *280 cal, 9 g fat, 39 mg chol, 419 mg sodium, 26 g carb, 12 g fiber, 23 g pro.*

Barbecued Pork Sandwiches

START TO FINISH **30 minutes**

  Nonstick cooking spray
- ½ cup chopped onion (1 medium)
- 2 cloves garlic, minced
- ⅔ cup water
- ½ 6-ounce can tomato paste
- 2 tablespoons red wine vinegar
- 1 tablespoon packed brown sugar
- 1½ teaspoons chili powder
- 1 teaspoon dried oregano, crushed
- 1 teaspoon Worcestershire sauce
- 12 ounces pork tenderloin
- ¼ teaspoon salt
- 1 medium green sweet pepper, cut into thin strips
- 6 whole wheat hamburger buns, split and toasted

1. For sauce, lightly coat a medium unheated saucepan with nonstick cooking spray. Preheat saucepan over medium heat. Add onion and garlic; cook and stir about 5 minutes or until onion is tender. Stir in the water, tomato paste, vinegar, brown sugar, chili powder, oregano, and Worcestershire sauce. Bring to boiling; reduce heat. Simmer, uncovered, about 10 minutes or until desired consistency, stirring occasionally.
2. Meanwhile, trim fat from meat. Cut meat into bite-size strips. Lightly coat a large unheated skillet with nonstick cooking spray. Preheat skillet over medium-high heat. Add meat; sprinkle with salt. Cook and stir for 2 minutes or until meat is cooked. Stir in the sauce and sweet pepper; heat through. Serve the barbecued pork in toasted buns. Makes 6 servings.

EACH SERVING *208 cal, 2 g fat, 37 mg chol, 365 mg sodium, 29 g carb, 3 g fiber, 17 g pro.*

CORN BREAD-TOPPED SAUSAGE BAKE

TORTELLINI EMILIA

Corn Bread-Topped Sausage Bake

PREP 25 minutes
BAKE 20 minutes at 425°F

- 1 8.5-ounce packages corn muffin mix
- ½ cup carrot, chopped (1 medium)
- ¼ cup chopped onion
- ¼ cup chopped green sweet pepper
- ¼ cup chopped celery
- 2 tablespoons vegetable oil
- 1 11.5-ounce can condensed bean with bacon soup
- ¾ cup milk
- 2 teaspoons yellow mustard
- 1 pound cooked smoked Polish sausage, sliced
  Shredded cheddar cheese (optional)

1. Preheat oven to 425°F. For corn bread, prepare muffin mix according to package directions (do not bake).
2. In a large saucepan cook carrot, onion, sweet pepper, and celery in hot oil over medium heat until tender. Stir in soup, milk, and mustard; stir in sausage. Cook and stir until bubbly. Transfer to an ungreased roaster or 2-quart baking dish. Pour corn bread batter over hot sausage mixture, spreading evenly.
3. Bake, uncovered, for 20 minutes or until a toothpick inserted in corn bread comes out clean. If desired, sprinkle each serving with cheese. Makes 6 servings.

EACH SERVING 562 cal, 34 g fat, 94 mg chol, 1,566 mg sodium, 43 g carb, 6 g fiber, 20 g pro.

Tortellini Emilia

PREP 25 minutes
BAKE 20 minutes at 400°F

- 2 8-ounce packages dried cheese-filled tortellini
- 3 tablespoons finely chopped red onion
- 2 tablespoons finely chopped shallot
- 1 tablespoon butter
- 2 cups half-and-half or light cream
- ½ cup milk
- 2 egg yolks
- ¼ cup grated Parmesan cheese
- 1 tablespoon snipped fresh sage
- ¼ teaspoon black pepper
- ½ cup shredded Gruyère cheese or Swiss cheese
- ½ cup broken walnuts
- 2 ounces thinly sliced prosciutto or cooked ham, finely chopped

1. Preheat oven to 400°F. Cook tortellini according to package directions; drain.
2. For sauce, in a medium saucepan cook onion and shallot in hot butter over medium heat until tender. Stir in half-and-half and milk. Bring just to boiling. Remove from heat. Stir about 1 cup of the hot sauce into egg yolks. Stir yolk mixture into sauce in saucepan. Cook and stir on medium-low heat about 10 minutes or until slightly thickened and just starting to bubble. Stir in Parmesan cheese, sage, and pepper.
3. Spread half the tortellini in a 2-quart baking dish. Sprinkle with Gruyère cheese. Add half the sauce. Top with remaining tortellini, walnuts, prosciutto, and remaining sauce.

4. Bake, uncovered, about 20 minutes or until heated through and top is lightly browned. Makes 8 servings.

EACH SERVING 455 cal, 25 g fat, 96 mg chol, 824 mg sodium, 38 g carb, 1 g fiber, 21 g pro.

Sausage-Stuffed Manicotti

PREP 20 minutes
BAKE 30 minutes at 350°F

- 12 dried manicotti pasta
- 1 pound bulk Italian sausage
- 1 15-ounce carton ricotta cheese
- 1 cup finely shredded Parmesan cheese
- 2 teaspoons dried basil, crushed
- 3 cups marinara pasta sauce
- 1½ cups shredded smoked mozzarella cheese
  Snipped fresh parsley (optional)

1. Preheat oven to 350°F. Cook pasta according to package directions; drain.
2. In a large skillet cook sausage over medium heat until browned. Drain off fat. In a medium bowl combine ricotta cheese, Parmesan cheese, and basil. Stir in cooked sausage. Using a small spoon, fill pasta with sausage mixture. Arrange filled pasta in an ungreased 3-quart baking dish. Pour marinara sauce over pasta. Sprinkle with mozzarella cheese.
3. Bake, covered, for 20 minutes. Uncover and bake about 10 minutes or until manicotti is heated through and cheese is melted. If desired, sprinkle with fresh snipped parsley. Makes 6 servings.

EACH SERVING 756 cal, 47 g fat, 128 mg chol, 1,541 mg sodium, 45 g carb, 4 g fiber, 36 g pro.

SAUSAGE AND POTATO LASAGNA

Sausage and Potato Lasagna

PREP 30 minutes
BAKE 35 minutes at 350°F
STAND 10 minutes

- 1 20-ounce package refrigerated sliced potatoes
- ½ cup water
- 1 pound bulk Italian sausage or bulk pork sausage
- 2 cups sliced mushrooms
- ½ cup chopped onion
- 2 cloves garlic, minced
- 1 cup milk
- 1 tablespoon all-purpose flour
- ½ teaspoon salt
- ¼ teaspoon black pepper
- ¼ teaspoon ground nutmeg
- 1 15-ounce carton ricotta cheese
- 1 10-ounce package frozen chopped spinach, thawed and well drained
- ½ cup grated Parmesan cheese
- 1 egg, slightly beaten
- 2 cups shredded mozzarella cheese

1. Preheat oven to 350°F. Grease a 3-quart rectangular baking dish; set aside. In a medium microwave-safe bowl combine potatoes and the water. Microwave, covered, on high about 5 minutes or until potatoes are almost tender, stirring once; drain and set aside.
2. In a very large skillet combine sausage, mushrooms, onion, and garlic. Cook over medium heat until sausage is browned. Drain off fat. In a medium bowl combine milk, flour, salt, pepper, and nutmeg. Stir milk mixture into sausage mixture in skillet. Cook and stir until thickened and bubbly; set aside.
3. In an extra-large bowl stir together ricotta cheese, spinach, Parmesan cheese, and egg. Layer half the sliced potatoes into the prepared dish. Spread half the ricotta cheese mixture and half the meat mixture on top. Sprinkle with half the mozzarella cheese. Repeat with remaining potatoes, ricotta cheese mixture, and meat mixture.

4. Bake, covered, for 25 minutes. Uncover; sprinkle with remaining mozzarella cheese. Bake for 10 minutes more or until potatoes are tender and lasagna is bubbly around edges. Let stand for 10 minutes before serving. Makes 12 servings.
EACH SERVING *462 cal, 27 g fat, 116 mg chol, 888 mg sodium, 22 g carb, 2 g fiber, 28 g pro.*

Cheesy Baked Penne and Sausage

PREP 25 minutes
BAKE 25 minutes at 350°F

- 8 ounces dried penne pasta
- 8 ounces bulk mild Italian sausage
- ⅓ cup sliced green onions
- 2 tablespoons all-purpose flour
- 2 tablespoons whole-grain mustard
- 1¼ cups milk
- ¼ teaspoon pepper
- ½ 8-ounce carton mascarpone cheese
- 1 cup shredded fontina cheese, shredded
- 1 cup shredded provolone cheese

1. Preheat oven to 350°F. Cook pasta according to package directions; drain. Meanwhile, in an extra-large skillet cook sausage until browned; drain off fat well. Stir in green onions; cook 1 minute. Add flour and mustard; gradually stir in milk and pepper. Cook and stir until slightly thickened and bubbly. Reduce heat; stir in mascarpone cheese until blended. Add remaining cheeses and pasta.
2. Transfer pasta mixture to a 2-quart baking dish. Bake, uncovered, for 25 minutes or until heated through. Makes 6 servings.
EACH SERVING *461 cal, 24 g fat, 74 mg chol, 687 mg sodium, 36 g carb, 1 g fiber, 26 g pro.*

CHEESY BAKED PENNE AND SAUSAGE

SPICY SHRIMP PASTA WITH DRIED TOMATOES, RECIPE PAGE 163

fish & shellfish

THE CATCH OF THE DAY Take a trip to the salty sea or paddle through clear inland waters. The sweet, rich taste of fish and shellfish makes even the simplest meal seem special.

FISH TOSTADAS
WITH CHILI-LIME
CREAM

Fish Tostadas with Chili-Lime Cream

START TO FINISH **20 minutes**

  1 pound fresh tilapia or cod fillets
  ½ teaspoon chili powder
  ¼ teaspoon salt
  1 lime, halved
  ½ cup sour cream
  ½ teaspoon garlic powder
  8 6-inch tostada shells
  2 cups shredded cabbage mix
  1 avocado, halved, seeded, peeled, and sliced (optional)
  1 cup cherry tomatoes, quartered (optional)
     Bottled hot pepper sauce (optional)

1. Preheat broiler. Sprinkle fish with ¼ teaspoon of the chili powder and the salt. For chili-lime cream, in a bowl squeeze 2 teaspoons juice from half the lime. Stir in sour cream, garlic powder, and remaining chili powder; set aside. Cut remaining lime half in wedges.
2. Place fish on unheated greased broiler rack; tuck under thin edges. Place shells on baking sheet on lowest rack. Broil fish 4 inches from heat for 4 to 6 minutes per ½-inch thickness until fish flakes with fork. Break in chunks. Serve with tostadas, cabbage, chili-lime cream, lime wedges, and, if desired, avocado, tomatoes, and pepper sauce. Makes 4 servings.

EACH SERVING *278 cal, 14 g fat, 67 mg chol, 303 mg sodium, 17 g carb, 2 g fiber, 25 g pro.*

Steamed Cod with Gingery Mushrooms

START TO FINISH **30 minutes**

  1 pound fresh or frozen skinless Alaska or gray cod, or tilapia fillets
  ½ teaspoon ground ginger
  ¼ teaspoon salt
  ¼ teaspoon black pepper
  1 tablespoon finely chopped fresh ginger
  2 teaspoons canola oil
  8 ounces fresh shiitake mushrooms, stemmed and halved

STEAMED COD WITH GINGERY MUSHROOMS

1 large red sweet pepper, seeded and cut into rings
½ cup sliced green onions
¼ cup dry white wine or reduced-sodium chicken broth
⅔ cup reduced-sodium chicken broth
Thin strips green onions (optional)
Thin slices fresh ginger (optional)

1. Thaw fish, if frozen. In a bowl combine the ½ teaspoon ground ginger, salt, and black pepper. Sprinkle on fish; set aside.
2. In skillet cook the 1 tablespoon fresh ginger in hot oil over medium-high heat for 15 seconds. Add mushrooms, sweet pepper, and the ½ cup onions. Cook 5 minutes or until mushrooms are tender, stirring occasionally. Remove skillet from heat; add wine. Return to heat. Cook and stir until wine is almost evaporated. Add broth; bring to boiling.
3. Place fish on vegetables in skillet. Reduce heat; maintain gentle boiling. Cook, covered, 4 to 6 minutes for each ½-inch thickness of fish or until fish flakes easily when tested with a fork. If desired, serve fish and vegetables topped with onion strips and fresh ginger. Spoon cooking liquid over all. Makes 4 servings.

EACH SERVING *155 cal, 3 g fat, 48 mg chol, 308 mg sodium, 6 g carb, 2 g fiber, 23 g pro.*

FISH AND GREEN BEANS WITH WASABI MAYONNAISE

Fish and Green Beans with Wasabi Mayonnaise

PREP 10 minutes
BAKE 20 minutes at 450°F

Nonstick cooking spray
1 lime
1 to 3 teaspoons wasabi paste
⅓ cup mayonnaise
1 to 1½ pounds firm white fish fillets, ½ inch thick, rinsed and dried
1 cup panko (Japanese-style bread crumbs)
1 tablespoon melted butter
12 ounces tender young green beans, cooked

1. Preheat oven to 450°F. Coat baking pan with cooking spray. Shred the peel and juice half the lime; cut remaining into wedges. Stir together juice, peel, wasabi paste, and mayonnaise; transfer 1 tablespoon to a bowl. Cover and refrigerate remaining.
2. Sprinkle fish with *salt*. Place fish in a baking pan. Coat with the 1 tablespoon wasabi mayonnaise, then ¾ cup panko. Drizzle with melted butter. Bake for 20 minutes or until fish flakes easily with a fork.
3. Remove fish from pan. Toss beans with panko that remains in pan. Sprinkle with ¼ cup panko. Serve with wasabi mayonnaise and lime wedges. Makes 4 servings.

EACH SERVING *349 cal, 19 g fat, 56 mg chol, 384 mg sodium, 18 g carb, 4 g fiber, 26 g pro.*

**CRISPY FISH
AND PEPPERS**

Crispy Fish and Peppers

START TO FINISH 20 minutes

1 pound fresh or frozen (thawed) small fish fillets (such as grouper, catfish, or tilapia)
¾ cup buttermilk
1 egg
1 teaspoon Cajun seasoning
1 cup all-purpose flour
3 to 4 tablespoons vegetable oil
1 cup sliced and/or chopped miniature sweet peppers
1 lemon, cut up

1. Rinse fish and pat dry with paper towels.
2. In a shallow dish whisk together buttermilk, egg, and Cajun seasoning. Place flour in another shallow dish. Dip fish in buttermilk, then flour. Repeat twice.
3. Heat 3 tablespoons of the oil in a large heavy skillet over medium-high heat. Carefully add fish to hot oil (working in batches if necessary). Cook for 3 minutes on each side or until golden. Add more oil if needed. Drain on paper towels.
4. Drain oil from skillet; wipe clean with paper towels. Add peppers to skillet and cook 2 minutes or until crisp-tender. Serve fish with peppers and lemon. Makes 4 servings.

EACH SERVING 251 cal, 13 g fat, 97 mg chol, 188 mg sodium, 8 g carb, 2 g fiber, 26 g pro.

Coconut-Poached Mahi Mahi

START TO FINISH 20 minutes

1 small lime
1 15-ounce can light coconut milk
1 Thai green chile, thinly sliced (see tip, page 35)
1 tablespoon sugar
1 pound skinless, boneless mahi mahi or other firm whitefish fillets
1 teaspoon salt
1 small head bok choy, torn (about 3 cups)
  Crystallized ginger, green chiles (optional)

1. Finely shred peel from lime, then juice the lime. Set aside peel. In a large saucepan over medium heat combine lime juice, coconut milk, green chile, and sugar.
2. Cut fish into 8 portions; rinse and pat dry with paper towels. Rub salt onto fish portions, then place in coconut milk mixture. Cook fish, covered, for 5 minutes. Uncover; gently stir in bok choy. Cook for 3 minutes more or until fish flakes easily when tested with a fork. Ladle fish with cooking liquid into bowls. Top with lime peel and, if desired, ginger and green chiles. Makes 4 servings.

EACH SERVING 189 cal, 7 g fat, 83 mg chol, 744 mg sodium, 10 g carb, 1 g fiber, 22 g pro.

Mediterranean-Style Snapper

START TO FINISH 15 minutes

8 small cloves garlic
½ 6.5-ounce jar oil-packed dried tomato halves with herbs (⅓ cup)
½ cup pitted mixed green olives
4 5- to 6-ounce red snapper fillets or other firm-flesh white fish
¼ cup crumbled feta cheese
  Fresh oregano leaves (optional)
  Pepperoncini (optional)

1. Peel garlic cloves. With side of wide knife, smash garlic. For cooking oil, drain 1 tablespoon oil from dried tomatoes; heat the oil in an extra-large skillet. Add tomatoes, olives, and garlic to hot oil. Cook 2 minutes, until garlic is golden. Use slotted spoon to remove tomato-olive mixture. Reserve oil in skillet to cook fish; set aside.
2. Rinse fish and pat dry. Season with *salt* and *pepper*. Cook fish, skin sides down, in hot oil 4 minutes for each ½-inch thickness of fish or until skin is golden and crisp and fish flakes easily when tested with a fork, turning once halfway through cooking. Remove skin, if desired.
3. To serve, top fish with tomato-olive mixture, cheese, and, if desired, fresh oregano and pepperoncini. Makes 4 servings.

EACH SERVING 245 cal, 9 g fat, 61 mg chol, 808 mg sodium, 8 g carb, 1 g fiber, 32 g pro.

MEDITERRANEAN-STYLE SNAPPER

LEMONY COD WITH ASPARAGUS

SMOKED SALMON AND APPLE SUPPER SALAD

Lemony Cod with Asparagus

START TO FINISH 25 minutes

- 1 pound fresh or frozen skinless cod or flounder fillets
- 4 slices crusty bread, cut into 4 pieces
- 2 tablespoons butter, melted
- ¼ teaspoon garlic salt
- 12 ounces asparagus spears, trimmed
- 1 tablespoon lemon juice
- ½ teaspoon dried thyme, crushed
- ⅛ teaspoon black pepper
  Lemon wedges, halved crosswise

1. Thaw fish, if frozen. Preheat broiler. Place bread on the unheated rack of a broiler pan. Brush with 1 tablespoon of the melted butter and sprinkle with the garlic salt. Broil 4 inches from heat for 1 minute or until golden brown, turning once. Remove from pan; keep warm.
2. Rinse fish; pat dry with paper towels. Arrange fish and asparagus in a single layer on the same broiler pan rack.
3. In a bowl stir together the remaining 1 tablespoon butter and the lemon juice. Drizzle butter mixture over fish and brush over asparagus. Sprinkle fish and asparagus with thyme and pepper.
4. Broil 4 inches from heat for 4 to 6 minutes or just until fish begins to flake easily when tested with a fork and asparagus is crisp-tender, turning asparagus once. Serve fish and asparagus with bread and lemon wedges. Makes 4 servings.
EACH SERVING 293 cal, 8 g fat, 64 mg chol, 454 mg sodium, 29 g carb, 3 g fiber, 27 g pro.

Smoked Salmon and Apple Supper Salad

START TO FINISH 27 minutes

- 4 ounces thinly sliced lox-style smoked salmon or smoked salmon, flaked, with skin and bones removed
- 3 medium carrots, cut lengthwise into ½-inch-wide sticks
- 3 stalks celery, cut lengthwise into ½-inch-wide sticks
- 2 medium fennel bulbs, cored and thinly sliced
- 1 medium green apple, cored and thinly sliced
- ¼ cup olive oil
- 1 medium lemon (finely shredded peel and juice)
- 1 teaspoon sugar
- ½ teaspoon salt
- 1 tablespoon capers, drained
  Lemon slices and/or fennel fronds (optional)

1. In an extra-large bowl combine salmon, carrots, celery, fennel, and apple.
2. In a screw-top jar combine oil, finely shredded peel and juice from lemon, sugar, and salt. Cover; shake well to combine. Drizzle over salad. Let stand 10 minutes; toss halfway through.
3. Toss in capers. If desired, serve with lemon slices. Makes 4 servings.
EACH SERVING 246 cal, 15 g fat, 7 mg chol, 1,039 mg sodium, 24 g carb, 8 g fiber, 8 g pro.

Cajun Snapper with Red Beans and Rice

START TO FINISH 25 minutes

- 2 frankfurters, chopped
- 1 8.8-ounce package fully cooked rice
- 1 tablespoon salt-free Cajun seasoning
- 1 15- to 16-ounce can red beans, rinsed and drained
  Bottled hot pepper sauce (optional)
- 1 pound red snapper fillet, cut in 4 pieces
- 2 tablespoons butter
- 2 tablespoons all-purpose flour
  Fresh snipped parsley (optional)

1. In a saucepan cook frankfurters over medium heat for 2 to 3 minutes. Stir in rice, ½ cup *water*, and 1 teaspoon of the Cajun seasoning. Stir in beans and hot pepper sauce if using. Cover; cook over medium-low heat for 15 minutes.
2. Rinse fish; pat dry. In an extra-large skillet melt butter over medium heat. In a shallow dish combine flour and remaining Cajun seasoning. Press top side of fish into flour mixture, then place fish, skin side down, in hot butter. Cook 3 minutes or until skin is crisp. Carefully turn using a spatula; cook fish 3 minutes more or until fish flakes easily with a fork.
3. Serve fish over rice and beans. If desired, sprinkle with fresh snipped parsley. Makes 4 servings.
EACH SERVING 438 cal, 16 g fat, 69 mg chol, 544 mg sodium, 41 g carb, 6 g fiber, 36 g pro.

CAJUN SNAPPER
WITH RED BEANS
AND RICE

HERBED SALMON

Herbed Salmon

PREP 15 minutes
BAKE 3 minutes at 350°F

- 1 pound skinless salmon fillet, cut into 4 portions
- 1 lemon
- 1 tablespoon snipped fresh dill
- 1 tablespoon snipped fresh tarragon
- 1 tablespoon snipped fresh parsley or bias-sliced chives
- ½ teaspoon salt
- ½ teaspoon black pepper
- 2 tablespoons butter, softened
  Lemon peel and fresh herbs (optional)

1. Preheat oven to 350°F. Rinse fish; pat dry. Shred 1 teaspoon of peel from lemon; set aside. Juice half the lemon. In a small bowl combine lemon peel, snipped herbs, salt, pepper, and butter; stir to combine. Spread evenly on the salmon.
2. Heat a very large nonstick oven-going skillet over medium heat. Add salmon, herb side down. Cook 3 minutes or until golden brown. Turn salmon; pour lemon juice over. Place pan in oven and bake 3 to 7 minutes or until salmon flakes easily with a fork.
3. Transfer to serving plates; drizzle with pan juices. If desired, top with additional shredded lemon peel and snipped fresh herbs. Makes 4 servings.
EACH SERVING *294 cal, 21 g fat, 78 mg chol, 400 mg sodium, 3 g carb, 1 g fiber, 24 g pro.*

Catfish-and-Slaw Tacos

START TO FINISH 25 minutes

- 1 pound fresh or frozen catfish fillets
- 1 lime
- ¼ cup mayonnaise or salad dressing
- ½ teaspoon bottled hot pepper sauce
- ½ a small head cabbage, shredded (about 2½ cups)
- 1 tablespoon Cajun seasoning
- ¼ cup cornmeal
- ¼ cup all-purpose flour
- ¼ cup vegetable oil (more as needed)
- 16 4-inch corn tortillas
  Lime wedges
  Bottled hot pepper sauce (optional)

1. Thaw fish, if frozen; set aside. For slaw, squeeze about 3 tablespoons juice from lime. In a medium bowl combine juice, mayonnaise, and the ½ teaspoon

CATFISH-AND-SLAW TACOS

hot pepper sauce. Add cabbage; toss to combine. Set aside.
2. Rinse fish; pat dry with paper towels. Cut fish into 1-inch strips. Toss strips with Cajun seasoning. In a large bowl combine cornmeal and flour. Add catfish strips. Toss to coat with cornmeal mixture.
3. In a large skillet cook catfish strips, half at a time, in hot oil over medium heat about 2 minutes on each side or until golden brown and fish flakes when tested with a fork. Remove from skillet.
4. Wrap tortillas in paper towels. Heat in microwave on high for 1 minute. Stack two tortillas for each taco. Top with 2 or 3 pieces of fish and some of the slaw. Reserve any remaining dressing to serve with tacos. Serve with limes, reserved dressing, and, if desired, additional hot pepper sauce. Serve immediately. Makes 8 tacos.
EACH TACO *310 cal, 18 g fat, 29 mg chol, 150 mg sodium, 26 g carb, 2 g fiber, 12 g pro.*

Salmon with Roasted Vegetables

PREP 25 minutes   BAKE 4 minutes per ½-inch thickness at 450°F

- 4 4- to 5-ounce fresh or frozen skinless salmon fillets, about 1 inch thick
  Nonstick cooking spray
- 1 tablespoon snipped fresh dill
- ½ teaspoon salt
- ¼ teaspoon black pepper
- 2 medium zucchini and/or yellow summer squash, cut crosswise into ¼-inch slices (2½ cups)
- 1 cup grape or cherry tomatoes, halved
- 4 green onions, cut into 1-inch pieces
- 1 tablespoon Dijon mustard

1. Preheat oven to 450°F. Thaw fish, if frozen. Rinse fish and pat dry with paper towels. Set aside. Line a 15×10×1-inch baking pan with foil; lightly coat foil with cooking spray.
2. In a small bowl combine dill, salt, and pepper; set aside. In a large bowl combine zucchini, tomatoes, and onions. Generously coat vegetables with cooking spray; toss to coat evenly. Sprinkle with half of the dill mixture; toss to coat evenly.
3. Spoon vegetables on one side of prepared baking pan. Place fish opposite. Stir mustard into remaining dill mixture. Spread evenly on fish. Measure thickness of fillets in the thickest part.
4. Bake, uncovered, for 4 to 6 minutes per ½-inch thickness of fish or until fish begins to flake when tested with a fork and zucchini is crisp-tender. Makes 4 servings.
EACH SERVING *239 cal, 12 g fat, 66 mg chol, 463 mg sodium, 6 g carb, 2 g fiber, 24 g pro.*

SALMON-DILL PENNE AND CHEESE

SALMON-PASTA TOSS

Salmon-Dill Penne and Cheese

PREP 25 minutes
BAKE 30 minutes at 350°F

6	ounces dried multigrain penne pasta
⅔	cups whole milk
8	ounces Havarti cheese with dill, shredded
1½	teaspoons all-purpose flour
1	teaspoon finely shredded lemon peel
⅛	teaspoon salt
4	ounces smoked salmon, flaked, with skin and bones removed
½	cup crushed crisp rye crackers

1. Preheat oven to 350°F. Cook pasta according to package directions for minimum cooking time. Drain and return to pan. Stir in milk. In a medium bowl toss cheese with flour, lemon peel, and salt; stir into pasta mixture. Stir in salmon. Transfer to a 2-quart rectangular baking dish.
2. Cover and bake for 25 minutes; uncover. Gently stir and sprinkle with crushed crackers. Bake, uncovered, 5 minutes more or until heated through. Makes 4 servings.
EACH SERVING *791 cal, 51 g fat, 160 mg chol, 1,181 mg sodium, 43 g carb, 4 g fiber, 43 g pro.*

Salmon-Pasta Toss

START TO FINISH 25 minutes

1	0.5-ounce envelope pesto mix
3	tablespoons olive oil
1	pound salmon fillets
12	ounces dried fettuccine
1	16-ounce jar dried-tomato Alfredo sauce
1	14.5-ounce can diced tomatoes with basil, oregano, and garlic, undrained
1	7-ounce jar roasted red sweet peppers, drained and coarsely chopped
½	cup finely shredded Parmesan cheese
⅓	cup milk

1. Combine pesto mix and olive oil. Remove 1 tablespoon of the pesto and brush on salmon fillets. Broil salmon, 4 inches from heat for 4 to 6 minutes per ½-inch thickness turning once halfway through cooking, or until salmon flakes easily. Set aside.
2. Meanwhile, in a large pot cook fettuccine according to package directions. Drain well; return to pot. Stir in remaining pesto, Alfredo sauce, undrained tomatoes, sweet peppers, ¼ cup of the Parmesan cheese, and the milk. Heat through.
3. Break salmon into large chunks; gently fold into pasta mixture. Heat through. Transfer to a serving bowl. Sprinkle with the remaining Parmesan cheese. Makes 4 servings.
EACH SERVING *561 cal, 24 g fat, 59 mg chol, 1,166 mg sodium, 56 g carb, 3 g fiber, 29 g pro.*

Salmon- and Asparagus-Sauced Pasta

START TO FINISH 25 minutes

1	pound asparagus spears
2⅔	cups dried cavatappi or penne pasta
1	small red or yellow sweet pepper, cut into bite-size strips
½	cup chopped onion
1	tablespoon butter or margarine
1	10-ounce container refrigerated Alfredo pasta sauce
¼	cup milk
⅛	teaspoon black pepper
3	ounces lox-style smoked salmon, coarsely chopped
2	teaspoons snipped fresh tarragon

1. Snap off and discard woody bases from asparagus. If desired, scrape off scales. Bias-slice asparagus into 2-inch pieces.
2. In a large saucepan cook pasta according to package directions, except add asparagus the last 3 minutes of cooking. Drain; keep warm.
3. Meanwhile, for sauce, in a medium saucepan cook and stir sweet pepper and onion in hot butter over medium heat until tender. Stir in Alfredo sauce, milk, and black pepper; heat through. Gently stir in salmon and tarragon; heat through. Add to pasta mixture and gently stir to combine. Makes 4 servings.
EACH SERVING *446 cal, 18 g fat, 54 mg chol, 910 mg sodium, 53 g carb, 4 g fiber, 18 g pro.*

SALMON-AND
ASPARAGUS-SAUCED
PASTA

**CITRUS SALSA
SALMON**

SALMON AND RAVIOLI

TUNA AND FRUIT SALSA

Citrus Salsa Salmon

START TO FINISH 20 minutes

- 4 4- to 5-ounce skinless salmon fillets (¾ to 1 inch thick)
  Salt and black pepper
- ⅓ cup red jalapeño jelly
- 3 medium oranges, peeled, seeded, and coarsely chopped
- 1 medium grapefruit, peeled and sectioned
- 1 cup grape or cherry tomatoes, halved

1. Preheat broiler. Lightly sprinkle salmon with salt and pepper. In a small saucepan over low heat melt the jelly. Brush 2 tablespoons of the melted jelly on the salmon; reserve remaining jelly. Place salmon on an unheated rack of broiler pan. Broil 4 inches from heat for 8 minutes or until salmon flakes when tested with a fork.
2. Meanwhile, for fresh citrus salsa, in a medium bowl combine chopped oranges, grapefruit sections, halved tomatoes, and remaining jelly. Season with salt and pepper. Serve salmon with citrus salsa. Makes 4 servings.

EACH SERVING *362 cal, 13 g fat, 67 mg chol, 223 mg sodium, 40 g carb, 4 g fiber, 24 g pro.*

Salmon and Ravioli

START TO FINISH 25 minutes

- 1 9-ounce package refrigerated four-cheese ravioli
- 1 lemon, halved
- 2 6-ounce skinless, salmon fillets
  Salt and black pepper
- 2 tablespoons olive oil
- 1 6-ounce package baby spinach
- 3 cloves garlic, thinly sliced
- 2 tablespoons butter
  Shredded Parmesan cheese

1. Cook ravioli according to package directions; drain and set aside.
2. Meanwhile, halve lemon. Squeeze juice from one half of the lemon; cut remaining half into small wedges. Set lemon juice and wedges aside. Rinse salmon; pat dry. Sprinkle with salt and pepper.
3. In a large skillet heat olive oil over medium heat; add salmon; cook for 6 to 8 minutes, just until salmon flakes, turning once. Remove salmon; add spinach to skillet. Cook 1 minute or just until spinach begins to wilt. Remove spinach from skillet. Add lemon juice, garlic, and butter to hot skillet. Cook and stir over medium heat until butter is melted. Cook and stir 1 minute more.
4. Slice salmon and divide among four plates. Add ravioli and spinach; pour pan juices over. Serve with lemon wedges and pass Parmesan. Makes 4 servings.

EACH SERVING *525 cal, 31 fat, 102 mg chol, 689 mg sodium, 31 g carb, 3 g fiber, 29 g pro.*

Tuna and Fruit Salsa

START TO FINISH 25 minutes

- 4 5- to 6-ounce fresh tuna steaks, 1 inch thick
- 2 fresh peaches, halved and pitted
- 2 tablespoons olive oil
  Salt and cracked black pepper
- 2 tablespoons apricot preserves
- 1 tablespoon vinegar
- ½ cup fresh raspberries
- 3 green onions, thinly sliced

1. Lightly brush tuna steaks and peach halves with olive oil; sprinkle with salt and pepper. In a skillet cook tuna and peaches over medium-high heat for 5 minutes. Remove peaches; set aside to cool. Turn tuna and cook 6 minutes more or until it flakes easily; remove to a platter and cover to keep warm.
2. Coarsely chop peaches. In a medium microwave-safe bowl heat apricot preserves on high for 15 seconds. Stir in vinegar; fold in raspberries and peaches. Serve with tuna steaks. Sprinkle with green onions. Makes 4 servings.

EACH SERVING *333 cal, 14 g fat, 54 mg chol, 133 mg sodium, 17 g carb, 3 g fiber, 34 g pro.*

TUNA AND HUMMUS WRAPS

SALSA-SAUCED TUNA
TORTILLA ROLLS

Tuna and Hummus Wraps

START TO FINISH 20 minutes

- 1 6-ounce can very low-sodium chunk white tuna (water pack), drained
- 1 small cucumber, peeled, seeded, and finely chopped
- 1 small tomato, seeded and chopped
- 2 tablespoons olive oil
- 1 tablespoon snipped fresh dill or 1 teaspoon dried dill, crushed
- ¼ teaspoon black pepper
- 4 8-inch whole wheat tortillas
- ⅓ cup refrigerated cucumber-dill hummus
- 4 cups torn packaged lettuce (such as hearts of romaine, European blend, or Mediterranean blend)

1. In a medium bowl stir together tuna, cucumber, tomato, oil, dill, and pepper. **2.** Spread hummus on one side of each tortilla. Toss tuna mixture with lettuce. Divide evenly among tortillas. Fold or roll up filled tortillas. Makes 4 servings.
EACH SERVING 280 cal, 11 g fat, 19 mg chol, 482 mg sodium, 32 g carb, 4 g fiber, 16 g pro.

Salsa-Sauced Tuna Tortilla Rolls

PREP 30 minutes
BAKE 40 minutes at 350°F

- Nonstick cooking spray
- 2 12-ounce cans solid white tuna (water pack), drained and flaked
- 4 cups finely chopped Granny Smith apples
- ½ cup chopped green onions
- 1½ cups red or green seedless grapes, halved
- 1 cup mayonnaise or salad dressing
- ½ teaspoon seasoned salt
- ½ teaspoon black pepper
- 24 7-inch flour tortillas
- 2 16-ounce jars pineapple salsa
- 1 cup sliced almonds, toasted (see tip, page 31)
- 2 tablespoons snipped fresh cilantro

1. Preheat oven to 350°F. Coat a 3-quart baking dish with cooking spray. **2.** In a large bowl combine tuna, apples, green onions, grapes, mayonnaise, seasoned salt, and pepper; mix well. Spoon tuna mixture along one edge of each tortilla. Roll up, starting from edge with filling. Arrange rolls, seam sides down, in baking dish. **3.** Spoon salsa evenly over tortillas. Cover with foil. Bake for 35 minutes. Sprinkle with almonds. Bake, uncovered, about 5 minutes more or until heated through. Sprinkle with cilantro. Makes 12 servings.
EACH SERVING 500 cal, 27 g fat, 30 mg chol, 679 mg sodium, 45 g carb, 4 g fiber, 20 g pro.

TUNA FOCACCIA

Tuna Focaccia

START TO FINISH 15 minutes

- 1 3-ounce package cream cheese, softened
- 2 tablespoons sweet red chili dipping sauce
- 2 small focaccia or four 6-inch pita bread rounds, halved and split
- 1 12-ounce can solid white albacore tuna (drained)
- 1 12-ounce bag frozen edamame-blend vegetables (edamame, corn, and peppers), thawed Asian sweet chili sauce

1. In a small bowl combine cream cheese and the 2 tablespoons sweet red chili dipping sauce; spread on focaccia halves or inside pita bread halves. **2.** Flake tuna; combine in a medium bowl with the vegetables; spoon filling on or into bread. Pass Asian sweet chili sauce. Makes 4 servings.
EACH SERVING 480 cal, 12 g fat, 58 mg chol, 1,050 mg sodium, 59 g carb, 5 g fiber, 34 g pro.

TUNA SALAD WITH WONTON CRISPS

Tuna Salad with Wonton Crisps

START TO FINISH 30 minutes

  5   tablespoons olive oil
  8   wonton wrappers, cut into strips
 12   ounces fresh or frozen tuna
       steaks, thawed
  ¼   cup cider vinegar
  1   tablespoon sugar
  1   teaspoon finely shredded lime
       peel (optional)
  ½   medium head napa cabbage,
       shredded (6 cups)
  ½   medium seedless cucumber,
       sliced and/or cut into strips

1. In an extra-large skillet heat 3 tablespoons of the olive oil over medium-high heat. Cook wonton strips in hot oil until browned, stirring occasionally. Transfer with slotted spoon to paper towels; set aside.
2. Lightly season tuna with *salt* and *pepper*. Cook tuna in the same hot skillet for 3 minutes per side or until some pink remains in centers. Transfer tuna to cutting board; slice tuna for salads.
3. For dressing, whisk together remaining olive oil, vinegar, sugar, and lime peel. Serve cabbage, cucumber, and sliced tuna in shallow bowls. Drizzle salads with dressing and sprinkle with wonton crisps. Makes 4 servings.
EACH SERVING *358 cal, 22 g fat, 34 mg chol, 282 mg sodium, 18 g carb, 2 g fiber, 23 g pro.*

Creamy Lemon-Dill Tuna Salad

START TO FINISH 20 minutes

  ¾   cup mayonnaise or salad
       dressing
  1   tablespoon Dijon mustard
  1   tablespoon lemon juice
  1   tablespoon snipped fresh dill or
       ¼ teaspoon dried dill
  1   tablespoon honey
  ¼   teaspoon salt
  ⅛   teaspoon black pepper
  1   15- to 19-ounce can cannellini
       beans (white kidney beans),
       rinsed and drained
  1   12-ounce can solid white tuna
       (water pack), drained and
       broken into chunks

CREAMY LEMON-DILL TUNA SALAD

½ cup halved red onion slices
½ cup bottled roasted yellow or red sweet peppers, drained and chopped
1 stalk celery, sliced
2 to 3 tablespoons capers, drained
½ 5-ounce package arugula or baby spinach
2 large tomatoes, sliced

1. In a medium bowl mix together mayonnaise, mustard, lemon juice, dill, honey, salt, and pepper.
2. In a large bowl combine beans, tuna, and half the dressing. Stir in onions, peppers, celery, and capers. Serve over greens and tomatoes. Pass remaining dressing. Makes 4 servings.

EACH SERVING *343 cal, 23 g fat, 35 mg chol, 686 mg sodium, 18 g carb, 5 g fiber, 20 g pro.*

Tarragon Tuna Melts

START TO FINISH **30 minutes**

⅓ cup mayonnaise or salad dressing
2 tablespoons snipped fresh parsley
2 tablespoons snipped fresh chives
1 tablespoon snipped fresh tarragon
1 teaspoon finely shredded lemon peel
2 teaspoons lemon juice
2 teaspoons Dijon mustard
¼ teaspoon black pepper
1 12-ounce can solid white tuna (water pack), drained and flaked

8 ½-inch slices sourdough bread
8 thin tomato slices (optional)
1 cup shredded sharp white cheddar cheese
2 tablespoons butter, softened

1. In a large bowl combine mayonnaise, parsley, chives, tarragon, lemon peel, lemon juice, mustard, and pepper; stir until well combined. Stir in tuna, breaking up any large pieces with a fork.
2. Place 4 bread slices on work surface; evenly divide tuna filling on bread. Top each with tomato, if desired, and cheese. Spread one side of remaining bread slices with half the butter. Place

TARRAGON TUNA MELTS

bread, buttered sides up, on cheese. Place sandwiches, buttered sides down, on a large nonstick griddle over medium heat. (Or cook sandwiches, half at a time, in a large nonstick skillet.) Carefully butter top bread slices.
3. Cook sandwiches for 6 minutes or until cheese is melted and bread is golden, carefully turning once halfway through cooking. Serve warm. Makes 4 servings.

EACH SERVING *550 cal, 34 g fat, 95 mg chol, 988 mg sodium, 27 g carb, 2 g fiber, 32 g pro.*

SPICY SHRIMP
PASTA WITH DRIED
TOMATOES

SHRIMP
BRUSCHETTA
SALAD

STIR-FRY SHRIMP
WITH CHEESY GRITS

Spicy Shrimp Pasta with Dried Tomatoes

START TO FINISH 20 minutes

- 8 ounces dried angel hair pasta
- 3 cups fresh broccoli florets
- 1 6.5-ounce jar sun-dried tomato strips with Italian herbs packed in oil
  Olive oil
- 2 shallots, finely chopped
- 1 pound frozen shrimp, peeled and deveined, tails intact, thawed and drained
- ¼ teaspoon crushed red pepper
  Salt and black pepper
- ¼ cup small fresh basil leaves

1. In a 4-quart Dutch oven cook pasta according to package directions. Drain; return to pan. Cover to keep warm.
2. Meanwhile, drain tomatoes, reserving oil. If necessary, add olive oil to equal ¼ cup. In an extra-large skillet heat oil over medium-high heat. Add shallots; cook and stir 2 minutes or until tender. Add shrimp and crushed red pepper; cook and stir for 2 minutes. Add sun-dried tomatoes; cook and stir for 1 minute or until shrimp are opaque.
3. Toss shrimp with cooked pasta. Season with salt and black pepper. Drizzle with additional olive oil. Transfer to 4 serving bowls and sprinkle with snipped fresh basil. Makes 4 servings.
EACH SERVING *526 cal, 19 g fat, 172 mg chol, 394 mg sodium, 55 g carb, 5 g fiber, 34 g pro.*

Shrimp Bruschetta Salad

START TO FINISH 20 minutes

- 1 pound large peeled fresh or frozen (thawed) cooked shrimp
- 1 pint yellow and/or red cherry tomatoes, quartered
- ¼ cup snipped fresh parsley
- ¼ cup Asian sweet chili sauce
- 1 small baguette or French bread loaf
- 3 tablespoons mayonnaise
  Bottled hot pepper sauce (optional)

1. Preheat broiler. Remove tails from shrimp if present. In a medium bowl combine shrimp, tomatoes, parsley, and chili sauce. Set aside.
2. Halve bread loaf lengthwise and crosswise. Brush cut surfaces with mayonnaise. Place on a baking sheet. Broil bread 4 to 5 inches from heat for 2 minutes or until golden brown.
3. Top toasted bread with shrimp salad. If desired, pass hot pepper sauce. Makes 4 servings.
EACH SERVING *404 cal, 11 g fat, 225 mg chol, 885 mg sodium, 44 g carb, 3 g fiber, 31 g pro.*

Stir-Fry Shrimp with Cheesy Grits

START TO FINISH 25 minutes

- 2 red and/or yellow sweet peppers
- ½ cup quick-cooking hominy grits
- ½ cup shredded Mexican cheese blend (2 ounces)
  Salt and black pepper
- 1½ pounds medium shrimp, peeled and deveined, tails intact
- ½ teaspoon chili powder
- ¼ cup olive oil
- 1 cup cilantro sprigs
- 1 tablespoon cider vinegar
  Lemon wedges (optional)
  Cilantro sprigs (optional)

1. Halve, seed, and coarsely chop peppers. In a medium saucepan heat 1¾ cups *water* to boiling. Stir in grits and peppers. Return to boiling. Reduce heat. Simmer, covered, 5 minutes or until most of the water is absorbed and grits are tender. Stir in cheese. Sprinkle with salt and black pepper. Cover and keep warm.
2. In a bowl toss shrimp with chili powder. Heat 1 tablespoon of the oil in a large skillet over medium-high heat. Add shrimp. Cook and stir for 3 minutes or until shrimp are opaque.
3. In a food processor process remaining oil, cilantro, vinegar, and 2 tablespoons *water*. Drizzle on shrimp and grits. If desired, serve with lemon wedges and cilantro. Makes 4 servings.
EACH SERVING *385 cal, 21 g fat, 185 mg chol, 423 mg sodium, 421 g carb, 3 g fiber, 29 g pro.*

SHRIMP RELLENO CASSEROLE

Shrimp Relleno Casserole

PREP 30 minutes
BAKE 35 minutes at 350°F

16 ounces fresh or frozen cooked
    shrimp, peeled and deveined
 3 tablespoons butter
 4 large poblano chiles, seeded and
    chopped (see tip, page 35)
 1 cup finely chopped onion
 4 cloves garlic, minced
 1 8-ounce package cream cheese,
    cut up
 3 medium roma tomatoes,
    chopped
 2 cups shredded Monterey Jack
    cheese
 2 cups shredded cheddar cheese
 1 cup all-purpose flour
 1 teaspoon baking powder
 1 teaspoon baking soda
 ½ teaspoon salt
 1 egg, lightly beaten
 1 cup milk
 2 tablespoons vegetable oil

1. Thaw shrimp, if frozen. Preheat oven
to 350°F. Grease a 3-quart baking dish;
set aside.
2. In a large skillet melt butter over
medium heat. Add poblano chiles,
onion, and garlic; cook about 5 minutes
or until onion is tender. Add cream
cheese, stirring until smooth. Stir in
shrimp and tomatoes. Remove from
heat. Stir in 1 cup of the Monterey Jack
cheese and 1 cup of the cheddar cheese.
Transfer mixture to the prepared
baking dish.
3. In a medium bowl stir together flour,
baking powder, baking soda, and salt.
In a small bowl combine egg, milk, and
oil. Add to flour mixture; stir just until
batter is smooth. Pour over shrimp
mixture, spreading evenly. Sprinkle
with the remaining Monterey Jack
cheese and remaining cheddar cheese.

4. Bake, uncovered, for 35 minutes
or until top is set and golden. Makes
10 servings.
EACH SERVING 449 cal, 30 g fat, 190 mg chol,
742 mg sodium, 18 g carb, 1 g fiber, 26 g pro.

Seafood Lasagna

PREP 40 minutes BAKE 45 minutes
at 350°F STAND 10 minutes

12 ounces fresh or frozen cooked
    shrimp, peeled, deveined, and
    halved lengthwise
 8 dried lasagna noodles
 2 tablespoons butter or margarine
 1 cup chopped onion
 1 3-ounce package cream cheese,
    softened and cut up
 1 12-ounce carton cream-style
    cottage cheese
 1 egg, lightly beaten
 2 teaspoons dried basil, crushed
 ¼ teaspoon salt
 ⅛ teaspoon black pepper
 2 10.75-ounce cans condensed
    cream of mushroom soup
 ⅓ cup milk
 1 6.5-ounce can crabmeat,
    drained, flaked, and cartilage
    removed
 ¼ cup finely shredded Parmesan
    cheese

1. Thaw shrimp, if frozen. Rinse
shrimp; pat dry with paper towels.
Cook lasagna noodles according to
package directions; drain and set aside.
2. Preheat oven to 350°F. Arrange four
noodles in the greased 3-quart baking
dish. Set aside.
3. In a medium skillet melt butter over
medium heat. Add onion; cook until
tender. Remove from heat. Add cream
cheese and stir until melted. Stir in
cottage cheese, egg, basil, salt, and
pepper. Spread half the cheese mixture
over the noodles.
4. In a large bowl combine soup and
milk; stir in shrimp and crabmeat.
Spread half the shrimp mixture over
cheese layer. Repeat layers. Sprinkle
with Parmesan cheese.
5. Bake, uncovered, about 45 minutes
or until hot and bubbly. Let stand for
10 minutes before serving. Makes
12 servings.
EACH SERVING 243 cal, 11 g fat, 112 mg chol,
720 mg sodium, 18 g carb, 1 g fiber, 17 g pro.

SEAFOOD LASAGNA

ICEBERG WEDGES WITH
SHRIMP AND BLUE
CHEESE DRESSING

Iceberg Wedges with Shrimp and Blue Cheese Dressing

START TO FINISH 35 minutes

1½ pounds fresh or frozen large shrimp in shells
3 tablespoons lemon juice
¼ teaspoon black pepper
½ cup light mayonnaise or salad dressing
¼ teaspoon bottled hot pepper sauce
2 tablespoons crumbled blue cheese
3 tablespoons fat-free milk
  Nonstick cooking spray
1 large head iceberg lettuce, cut into 12 wedges
1 large tomato, chopped
⅓ cup thinly sliced, quartered red onion
2 slices turkey bacon, cooked and crumbled

1. Thaw shrimp, if frozen. Peel and devein shrimp, leaving tails intact if desired. Rinse shrimp; pat dry with paper towels. In a medium bowl combine shrimp, 2 tablespoons of the lemon juice, and ⅛ teaspoon of the black pepper. Toss to coat. Set aside.
2. For dressing, in a small bowl combine the remaining 1 tablespoon lemon juice, the remaining ⅛ teaspoon black pepper, the mayonnaise, and hot pepper sauce. Stir in blue cheese. Stir in enough of the milk to make desired consistency.
3. Coat an unheated grill pan with cooking spray. Preheat grill pan over medium-high heat. Thread shrimp onto six 10- to 12-inch-long skewers.* Place kabobs on grill pan. Cook for 3 to 5 minutes or until shrimp are opaque, turning once halfway through cooking. (If necessary, cook kabobs half at a time.)
4. Place two of the lettuce wedges on each of 6 serving plates. Top with shrimp, tomato, red onion, and bacon. Serve with dressing. Makes 6 servings.
*Tip If using wooden skewers, soak them in water for 30 minutes before using to prevent them from burning.
EACH SERVING *190 cal, 10 g fat, 129 mg chol, 360 mg sodium, 8 g carb, 1 g fiber, 18 g pro.*

GREEK LEEKS AND SHRIMP STIR-FRY

Greek Leeks and Shrimp Stir-Fry

START TO FINISH 30 minutes

1¼ pounds fresh or frozen medium shrimp, peeled and deveined
⅔ cups water
⅓ cup lemon juice
1 tablespoon cornstarch
¼ teaspoon bouquet garni seasoning or dried oregano, crushed
1 cup quick-cooking couscous
½ teaspoon dried oregano, crushed
¼ teaspoon salt
1½ cups boiling water
1 tablespoons olive oil
1⅓ cups thinly sliced leeks
½ cup crumbled feta cheese

1. Thaw shrimp, if frozen. Rinse shrimp and pat dry with paper towels; set aside.
2. In a small bowl combine the ⅔ cup water, lemon juice, cornstarch, and bouquet garni seasoning; set aside.
3. In a small bowl combine couscous, oregano, and salt. Pour boiling water over couscous. Cover and let stand for 5 minutes.
4. Meanwhile, heat oil in a wok or an extra-large skillet over medium-high heat. Cook and stir leeks in hot oil for 2 minutes or until tender. Remove leeks from wok; set aside. Stir lemon juice mixture. Add to wok and bring to boiling. Add shrimp and cook 2 minutes or until opaque. Stir in cooked leeks and half the feta cheese.
5. To serve, fluff couscous with a fork; transfer to a serving bowl. Spoon shrimp mixture over couscous and sprinkle with remaining feta. Makes 4 servings.
EACH SERVING *424 cal, 9 g fat, 228 mg chol, 527 mg sodium, 45 g carb, 3 g fiber, 37 g pro.*

2. In an extra-large skillet heat the remaining 2 tablespoons olive oil over medium-high heat. Stir in sweet peppers, onions, and garlic; stir-fry for 4 minutes or until crisp-tender. Add shrimp and cayenne pepper. Cook for 2 to 3 minutes or until shrimp are opaque, stirring occasionally.
3. If desired, stir in basil. Serve shrimp over pasta. Makes 4 servings.

EACH SERVING *477 cal, 18 g fat, 229 mg chol, 256 mg sodium, 45 g carb, 4 g fiber, 33 g pro.*

Pasta with White Clam Sauce

START TO FINISH 30 minutes

- 10 ounces dried linguine or fettuccine
- 2 6.5-ounce cans chopped or minced clams
- 2 cups half-and-half, light cream, or whole milk
- ½ cup chopped onion
- 2 cloves garlic, minced
- 2 tablespoons butter or margarine
- ¼ cup all-purpose flour
- ¼ teaspoon salt
- ⅛ teaspoon black pepper
- 2 teaspoons snipped fresh oregano
- ¼ cup snipped fresh parsley
- ¼ cup dry white wine, nonalcoholic dry white wine, or chicken broth
- ¼ cup finely shredded or grated Parmesan cheese

1. In a large saucepan cook pasta according to package directions. Drain; keep warm. Meanwhile, drain canned clams, reserving the juice from 1 can (should have about ½ cup). Add enough half-and-half to reserved clam juice to equal 2½ cups liquid. Set clams and clam juice mixture aside.
2. In a medium saucepan cook onion and garlic in hot butter over medium heat until tender but not brown. Stir in flour, salt, and pepper. Add clam juice mixture all at once. Cook and stir until thickened and bubbly. Cook and stir for 1 minute more. Stir in drained clams, oregano, parsley, and wine or broth. Heat through. Serve over hot pasta. Sprinkle with Parmesan cheese. Makes 4 servings.

EACH SERVING *680 cal, 24 g fat, 125 mg chol, 430 mg sodium, 72 g carb, 3 g fiber, 40 g pro.*

Mediterranean Scallops and Pasta

START TO FINISH 30 minutes

- 1 pound fresh or frozen sea scallops
- 2 tablespoons olive oil
- 2 tablespoons lemon juice
- 2 teaspoons dried Mediterranean seasoning, crushed
- 8 ounces dried fettuccine
- 1 6-ounce jar quartered marinated artichoke hearts, drained
- ¼ cup oil-pack dried tomatoes, well drained and sliced
- ¼ cup purchased basil pesto

1. Thaw scallops, if frozen. Rinse scallops; pat dry with paper towels. Halve any large scallops. In a medium bowl combine oil, lemon juice, and Mediterranean seasoning; add scallops and toss to coat. Cover and chill for 15 minutes.
2. Meanwhile, in a 4-quart Dutch oven or saucepan cook pasta according to package directions. Drain well; return to hot Dutch oven. Add artichokes, tomatoes, and pesto to cooked pasta. Toss to combine. Keep warm.
3. In a large skillet bring scallop mixture to boiling over medium-high heat. Boil gently, uncovered, for 3 minutes or until scallops are opaque, turning scallops occasionally. Add scallops to pasta. Toss to combine. Heat through. Serve immediately. Makes 4 servings.

EACH SERVING *537 cal, 22 g fat, 40 mg chol, 592 mg sodium, 54 g carb, 2 g fiber, 29 g pro.*

Garlicky Peppers and Shrimp

START TO FINISH 20 minutes

- 1 9-ounce package refrigerated spinach or plain fettuccine
- 4 tablespoons olive oil
- 3 small red, green, yellow, and/or orange sweet peppers, seeded and cut into thin strips
- 2 medium onions, cut into thin wedges
- 4 cloves garlic, thinly sliced
- 1 pound peeled and deveined medium shrimp
- ⅛ teaspoon cayenne pepper
- 1 cup small fresh basil leaves (optional)

1. Cook pasta according to package directions; drain and return to pan. Toss with 2 tablespoons of the olive oil. Keep warm.

CRAB-FENNEL SALAD

BAYSIDE ENCHILADAS

Shrimp Pasta Diavolo

START TO FINISH 20 minutes

1 9-ounce package refrigerated linguine
12 ounces medium fresh shrimp, peeled and deveined
1 medium onion, cut into thin wedges
3 cloves garlic, minced
¼ teaspoon crushed red pepper
2 tablespoons olive oil
1 14.5-ounce can diced tomatoes, undrained
½ cup torn fresh basil
2 cups fresh baby spinach
½ cup finely shredded Parmesan cheese

1. Cook linguine according to package directions. Drain pasta and transfer to an extra-large bowl; set aside. Rinse shrimp; pat dry with paper towels.
2. Meanwhile, in a large skillet cook onion, garlic, and crushed red pepper in hot oil until tender. Stir in tomatoes. Bring to boiling; reduce heat. Simmer, uncovered, for 3 minutes. Add shrimp to skillet; cover and simmer for 3 minutes or until shrimp are opaque. Add shrimp mixture to pasta. Stir in basil and spinach. Top each serving with Parmesan cheese. Makes 4 servings.

EACH SERVING 412 cal, 13 g fat, 204 mg chol, 528 mg sodium, 44 g carb, 4 g fiber, 30 g pro.

Crab-Fennel Salad

START TO FINISH 20 minutes

⅔ cup plain low-fat yogurt
¼ cup mayonnaise or salad dressing
¼ cup milk
1 teaspoon curry powder
4 cups coarsely chopped fresh fruit, such as cantaloupe, strawberries, honeydew melon, and/or pineapple
2 6- to 8-ounce packages chunk-style imitation crabmeat or lobster
1½ cups sliced fennel
8 cups torn mixed salad greens

1. For dressing, in a small bowl stir together yogurt, mayonnaise, milk, and curry powder. If desired, thin dressing with additional milk.
2. In a large bowl combine fresh fruit, crabmeat, and fennel; set aside. Divide salad greens among salad plates. Top with crabmeat and fruit; drizzle with dressing. Makes 6 servings.

EACH SERVING 176 cal, 5 g fat, 16 mg chol, 601 mg sodium, 24 g carb, 3 g fiber, 10 g pro.

Bayside Enchiladas

PREP 30 minutes BAKE 30 minutes at 350°F STAND 10 minutes

8 ounces fresh or frozen medium shrimp
8 ounces fresh or frozen bay scallops
1 8-ounce carton sour cream
½ cup purchased salsa
2 cups shredded Monterey Jack cheese
6 7- to 8-inch flour tortillas
¼ cup cottage cheese
¼ cup milk
2 tablespoons grated Parmesan cheese
¼ cup sliced green onions
¼ cup sliced pitted ripe olives

1. Thaw shrimp and scallops, if frozen. Peel and devein shrimp. Rinse shrimp and scallops; pat dry with paper towels. Set aside. Lightly grease one 3-quart baking dish; set aside. Preheat oven to 350°F.
2. In a large bowl combine sour cream and salsa. Stir in shrimp, scallops, and 1 cup Monterey Jack cheese. Spoon about 1 cup of the shrimp mixture onto each tortilla near an edge; roll up. Place filled tortillas, seam sides down, in prepared dish; set aside.
3. For sauce, in a blender or food processor combine cottage cheese, milk, and Parmesan cheese. Cover and blend or process until nearly smooth (sauce will be thin). Pour sauce over tortillas in dish. Sprinkle with green onions and olives.
4. Bake, uncovered, for 25 minutes. Sprinkle with the remaining 1 cup Monterey Jack cheese. Bake about 5 minutes more or until cheese is melted. Cover; let stand for 10 minutes before serving. Makes 6 servings.

EACH SERVING 404 cal, 24 g fat, 109 mg chol, 604 mg sodium, 20 g carb, 1 g fiber, 27 g pro.

**LOBSTER MANICOTTI
WITH CHIVE
CREAM SAUCE**

Lobster Manicotti with Chive Cream Sauce

PREP 45 minutes
BAKE 30 minutes at 350°F

12 dried manicotti
1 tablespoon butter or margarine
1 tablespoon all-purpose flour
1¼ cups milk
1 8-ounce tub cream cheese with chives and onion
¼ cup grated Romano or Parmesan cheese
12 ounces chopped cooked lobster or chunk-style imitation lobster
1 10-ounce package frozen chopped broccoli, thawed and well drained
½ 7-ounce jar roasted red sweet peppers, drained and chopped
¼ teaspoon black pepper
Paprika

1. Cook manicotti shells according to package directions; drain and set aside.
2. Meanwhile, for cheese sauce, in a medium saucepan melt butter over medium heat. Add flour and stir until combined. Add 1 cup of the milk all at once. Cook and stir over medium heat until sauce is thickened and bubbly. Reduce heat to low. Gradually add cream cheese, stirring until smooth. Stir in Romano cheese.
3. Preheat oven to 350°F. For filling, in a medium bowl combine ¾ cup of the cheese sauce, the lobster, broccoli, roasted peppers, and black pepper. Using a small spoon, carefully fill each manicotti shell with about ⅓ cup of the filling. Arrange filled shells in an ungreased 3-quart baking dish or 6 individual casseroles. Stir the remaining ¼ cup milk into the remaining sauce. Pour sauce over the shells. Sprinkle with paprika.
4. Cover dish (or dishes) with foil. Bake 30 minutes or until heated through. Makes 6 servings.

EACH SERVING *386 cal, 17 g fat, 90 mg chol, 471 mg sodium, 34 g carb, 2 g fiber, 21 g pro.*

DIVINE CRAB CAKES

Divine Crab Cakes

PREP 15 minutes
COOK 6 minutes per batch

2 beaten eggs
⅔ cup soft bread crumbs
⅓ cup mayonnaise or salad dressing
1 teaspoons dry mustard
1 teaspoon lemon juice
1 teaspoons Worcestershire sauce
1 teaspoons salt
⅛ teaspoon black pepper
Dash bottled hot pepper sauce (optional)
1 pound cooked crabmeat, finely flaked
⅓ cup fine dry bread crumbs
2 tablespoons cooking oil

1. In a large bowl combine the eggs, soft bread crumbs, mayonnaise, mustard, lemon juice, Worcestershire sauce, salt, black pepper, and, if desired, hot pepper sauce. Stir in crabmeat; mix well. Shape mixture into eight ½-inch-thick patties.
2. Coat patties with the dry bread crumbs. In a large skillet heat oil over medium heat. Cook crab cakes, 4 at a time, in hot oil about 3 minutes on each side or until golden brown. Keep warm while cooking remaining crab cakes. Add additional oil to skillet if necessary. Makes 4 servings.

EACH SERVING *399 cal, 27 g fat, 226 mg chol, 975 mg sodium, 10 g carb, 0 g fiber, 28 g pro.*

GARDEN VEGGIE LINGUINE WITH
CILANTRO PESTO, RECIPE PAGE 178

vegetarian

FRESH AND FLAVORFUL These main-dish recipes take advantage of the abundance from gardens, farmer's markets, and produce stands. Every bite shouts "delicious"!

SMOKY MUSHROOM STROGANOFF

PEACH AND TOMATO PASTA

Smoky Mushroom Stroganoff

START TO FINISH **18 minutes**

- 1   8.8-ounce package dried pappardelle (wide egg noodles)
- 1½ pounds packaged sliced mushrooms, such as button, cremini, and/or shiitake
- 2   cloves garlic, minced
- 1   tablespoon olive oil
- 1   8-ounce carton light sour cream
- 2   tablespoons all-purpose flour
- 1½ teaspoons smoked paprika
- ¼   teaspoon black pepper
- 1   cup vegetable broth
       Snipped fresh parsley (optional)

1. Cook noodles according to package directions. Drain; keep warm.
2. In an extra-large skillet cook mushrooms and garlic in hot oil over medium-high heat for 5 minutes or until tender, stirring occasionally. (Reduce heat if mushrooms brown quickly.) Remove with slotted spoon; cover to keep warm.
3. For sauce, in a bowl combine sour cream, flour, paprika, and pepper. Stir in broth until smooth. Add to skillet. Cook and stir until thickened and bubbly; cook and stir 1 minute more. Serve mushrooms and sauce over noodles. If desired, sprinkle with parsley. Makes 4 servings.
EACH SERVING *407 cal, 13 g fat, 72 mg chol, 443 mg sodium, 59 g carb, 4 g fiber, 17 g pro.*

Peach and Tomato Pasta

START TO FINISH **30 minutes**

- 12 ounces spaghetti or linguine
- 3   cloves garlic, thinly sliced
- 1   tablespoon canola oil
- 1   pint grape tomatoes
- 2   pounds peaches (about 6), pitted and sliced and/or coarsely chopped
- ½   cup pitted Kalamata olives, halved
- ⅓   cup chopped basil leaves
- ¼   teaspoon salt
- ¼   to ½ teaspoon crushed red pepper
- ⅛   teaspoon black pepper
       Toasted slivered almonds (see tip, page 31) (optional)

1. Prepare spaghetti according to package directions. Reserve ¼ cup of the spaghetti cooking liquid. Drain spaghetti and return to pot; keep warm.
2. In an extra-large skillet cook garlic in hot oil over medium heat for 1 minute. Add tomatoes. Cook, uncovered, for 2 minutes. Add peaches. Cook 4 minutes or just until peaches are soft, stirring occasionally. Stir in olives, basil, salt, and both peppers; heat through.
3. Add peach mixture to spaghetti along with reserved spaghetti cooking liquid. Toss to combine. Season to taste with *salt* and *black pepper*. Serve warm or at room temperature. If desired, sprinkle with almonds just before serving. Makes 6 servings.
EACH SERVING *321 cal, 5 g fat, 0 mg chol, 227 mg sodium, 61 g carbo, 5 g fiber, 9 g pro.*

Spinach Tortellini with Beans and Feta

START TO FINISH **20 minutes**

- 1   9-ounce package refrigerated cheese-filled spinach tortellini
- 1   15-ounce can cannellini (white kidney) beans, rinsed and drained
- ¾   cup crumbled garlic-and-herb-flavored feta cheese (3 ounces)
- 2   tablespoons olive oil
- 1   large tomato, chopped
       Black pepper
- 4   cups baby spinach

1. Cook tortellini according to package directions. Drain and return to saucepan.
2. Add drained beans, feta cheese, and olive oil to tortellini in saucepan. Heat and gently stir over medium heat until beans are hot and cheese begins to melt. Add chopped tomato; heat 1 minute more. Sprinkle with pepper.
3. Divide spinach among 4 dinner plates or shallow bowls. Top with tortellini mixture. Makes 4 servings.
EACH SERVING *448 cal, 18 g fat, 61 mg chol, 858 mg sodium, 55 g carb, 9 g fiber, 24 g pro.*

LINGUINE IN FRESH TOMATO SAUCE WITH GARLIC-BASIL TOAST

1. For sauce, drain dried tomatoes, reserving 1 tablespoon oil. Halve large tomatoes. In an extra-large skillet cook garlic in oil from tomatoes over medium heat about 1 minute or until tender. Add cherry and oil-packed tomatoes. Cook and stir about 8 minutes or until fresh tomato skins blister. Season with salt and pepper.
2. Meanwhile, cook spaghetti, with 1 tablespoon salt added to water, according to package directions. Reserve 1 cup pasta cooking water. Drain pasta.
3. Toss spaghetti with tomato mixture in skillet, adding enough cooking water to thin sauce. Serve immediately with fresh mozzarella balls and parsley. Makes 8 servings.

EACH SERVING *264 cal, 6 g fat, 10 mg chol, 229 mg sodium, 47 g carb, 7 g fiber, 8 g pro.*

Garden Veggie Linguine with Cilantro Pesto

START TO FINISH **30 minutes**

- 8   ounces dried linguine or fettuccine
- 8   ounces baby zucchini, halved lengthwise, or 1 small zucchini, sliced
- 8   ounce package peeled fresh baby-cut carrots, halved
- 2   seedless oranges
- ½   cup olive oil
- 1   cup fresh cilantro leaves
- 1   teaspoon dry mustard
- 1   teaspoon minced garlic
- ½   teaspoon crushed red pepper
      Cilantro and/or finely shredded orange peel (optional)

1. Cook pasta according to package directions, adding zucchini and carrots the last 5 minutes. Drain; reserve ¼ cup pasta water. Return pasta to pan.
2. For pesto, peel and quarter 1 orange. In a food processor combine orange, olive oil, cilantro, pasta water, 1 teaspoon *salt*, mustard, garlic, and red pepper. Cover and process until smooth. Peel and chop remaining orange. Toss all together; if desired, top with cilantro and orange peel. Makes 4 servings.

EACH SERVING *518 cal, 28 g fat, 0 mg chol, 644 mg sodium, 58 g carb, 6 g fiber, 10 g pro.*

Linguine in Fresh Tomato Sauce with Garlic-Basil Toast

START TO FINISH **20 minutes**

- 10   ounces dried linguine
- 3   tablespoons olive oil
- 6   cloves garlic, minced, or 1 tablespoon bottled minced garlic
- 2   English muffins, split
- ⅔   cup fresh basil, chopped
- 1   pint small tomatoes, halved
- ½   cup chicken broth or pasta water
- 1   teaspoon sugar
- ½   cup halved, pitted Kalamata olives (optional)
       Grated Parmesan cheese (optional)
       Fresh basil (optional)

1. Heat broiler. Cook pasta according to package directions. Drain; set aside.
2. Meanwhile, in bowl combine 1 tablespoon of the oil and about one-third of the minced garlic; brush on cut sides of muffins. Place muffins on baking sheet. Broil 3 to 4 inches from heat for 2 minutes or until golden. Sprinkle 1 tablespoon of the chopped basil; set aside.

3. In a large saucepan heat remaining oil over medium-high. Add remaining garlic, basil, and the tomatoes. Cook for 2 minutes; add broth and sugar. Cook for 3 minutes, until tomatoes soften. Season with *salt* and *pepper*. Stir in pasta and, if desired, olives; heat through. If using, sprinkle with cheese and basil. Makes 4 servings.

EACH SERVING *450 cal, 12 g fat, 1 mg chol, 403 mg sodium, 72 g carb, 3 g fiber, 12 g pro.*

Spaghetti with Two-Tomato Toss

START TO FINISH **35 minutes**

- ½   7- to 8-ounce jar oil-packed dried tomatoes
- 4   cloves garlic, minced
- 2   pints red and/or yellow cherry or grape tomatoes
- ½   teaspoon salt
- 1   teaspoon cracked black pepper
- 1   14- to 16-ounce package dried corn, multigrain, whole wheat, or regular spaghetti
- 4   ounce bite-size fresh mozzarella cheese balls (bocconcini), halved
- ½   cup chopped fresh parsley

GARDEN VEGGIE
LINGUINE WITH
CILANTRO PESTO

Broccoli Spaghetti

START TO FINISH 25 minutes

- 6 ounces dried spaghetti
- 3 cups broccoli florets
- 1 15- to 19-ounce can cannellini beans (white kidney), rinsed and drained
- 1 10-ounce container refrigerated light Alfredo sauce
- 3 cloves garlic, minced
- ½ cup croutons, coarsely crushed
- ¼ teaspoon crushed red pepper
  Olive oil

1. Cook pasta according to package directions, adding broccoli the last 3 minutes of cooking; drain, reserving ½ cup of the pasta water. Return pasta mixture to pan; keep warm.
2. Meanwhile, in a blender or food processor combine beans, Alfredo sauce, garlic, and the reserved pasta water; cover and blend or process until nearly smooth. Transfer to a small saucepan; heat through over medium heat, stirring frequently.
3. Spoon sauce onto serving plates. Top with pasta mixture, crushed croutons, crushed red pepper, and a drizzle of olive oil. Makes 4 servings.
EACH SERVING 402 cal, 12 g fat, 18 mg chol, 659 mg sodium, 60 g carb, 8 g fiber, 19 g pro.

Two-Potato Frittata

PREP 28 minutes ROAST 15 minutes at 450°F BAKE 7 minutes at 400°F

- 2 small sweet potatoes, scrubbed, thinly sliced or chopped
- 1 medium Yukon gold potato, chopped
- 1 small red onion, cut in thin wedges or chopped
- 2 tablespoons olive oil
- 8 eggs
- ½ 5.2-ounce package semisoft cheese with garlic and roasted pepper
  Fresh oregano (optional)

1. Preheat oven to 450°F. In a round 3-quart baking dish combine potatoes and red onion. Toss with olive oil and sprinkle with *salt*. Roast, uncovered, 15 minutes.
2. Meanwhile, in a medium bowl whisk eggs, cheese, and a pinch of *salt* until

combined. Reduce oven to 400°F. Pour egg mixture over roasted vegetables; return to oven. Bake 7 minutes or until eggs are set.
3. Invert frittata onto a large cutting board; cut into wedges. Turn wedges top sides up and place on plates. If desired, sprinkle with oregano. Makes 4 servings.
EACH SERVING 344 cal, 25 g fat, 424 mg chol, 566 mg sodium, 17 g carb, 2 g fiber, 15 g pro.

Grilled Vegetables with Couscous

START TO FINISH 30 minutes

- 2 limes
- ⅓ cup olive oil
- ½ teaspoon ground cumin
- ½ teaspoon salt
- ½ teaspoon black pepper
- 2 small zucchini and/or yellow summer squash
- 1 small head cauliflower, trimmed
- 1 small red onion
- 1½ cups water
- 1 cup couscous
  Snipped fresh parsley (optional)

GRILLED VEGETABLES WITH COUSCOUS

1. From 1 lime, shred 1 teaspoon peel; set aside. Juice limes for ¼ cup juice. In a small bowl whisk together lime juice, olive oil, cumin, salt, and pepper.
2. Cut zucchini lengthwise into ½-inch slices. Cut cauliflower crosswise into 4 equal slices. Cut red onion crosswise into ½-inch slices. Brush vegetable slices with some of the olive oil mixture.
3. For a charcoal grill, grill vegetable slices on the rack of an uncovered grill directly over medium coals until crisp-tender, turning vegetables once. Allow 5 to 6 minutes for zucchini slices and 10 to 12 minutes for cauliflower and onion slices. (For a gas grill, preheat grill. Reduce heat to medium. Place vegetables on grill rack over heat. Cover and grill as directed.) Remove vegetables from grill as they get done.
4. Meanwhile, in a medium saucepan bring water to boiling. Stir in couscous and 1 teaspoon lime peel. Remove from heat; cover and let stand 5 minutes. Fluff couscous with a fork. To serve, drizzle vegetables and couscous with remaining oil mixture. If desired, top with parsley. Makes 4 servings.
EACH SERVING 386 cal, 19 g fat, 0 mg chol, 336 mg sodium, 49 g carb, 7 g fiber, 9 g pro.

MUSHROOM AND POBLANO ENCHILADAS

AUTUMN COUSCOUS BOWL

WINTER GARDEN POLENTA

Mushroom and Poblano Enchiladas

START TO FINISH 30 minutes

6 ounces firm tofu
1 small poblano chile (see tip, page 35)
  Vegetable oil
1 8-ounce package sliced cremini mushrooms
1 teaspoon ground cumin
¼ cup sour cream
1 cup shredded cheddar and Monterey Jack cheese (4 ounces)
8 corn tortillas
  Chopped tomato and green onion (optional)

1. Drain tofu; cut into cubes. Stem and seed poblano chile; cut into strips.
2. In a skillet heat 1 tablespoon oil over medium heat. Add tofu, peppers, mushrooms, cumin, and ½ teaspoon salt. Cook 8 to 10 minutes or until mushrooms and pepper are tender, turning occasionally. Stir in sour cream and ½ cup of the cheese.
3. Preheat broiler. Lightly oil a 13×9×2-inch baking pan; set aside. Wrap tortillas in dampened microwave-safe paper towels and heat on high for 30 seconds or until warm and softened. Spoon mushroom filling into tortillas; fold over and place in prepared pan. Sprinkle with remaining cheese. Broil 4 to 5 inches from heat for 1 to 2 minutes until cheese is melted. If desired, top with tomato and green onion. Makes 4 servings.

EACH SERVING *335 cal, 18 g fat, 36 mg chol, 521 mg sodium, 29 g carb, 4 g fiber, 15 g pro.*

Autumn Couscous Bowl

START TO FINISH 35 minutes

1 2-pound butternut squash, peeled and chopped into ½-inch cubes (about 4 cups)
2 cups small cauliflower florets
½ teaspoon salt
½ teaspoon black pepper
1 10-ounce package couscous
3 tablespoons butter
¼ cup sweet Asian chili sauce
¼ cup shelled pistachio nuts
  Fresh thyme (optional)

1. Preheat broiler. Place squash and 2 tablespoons water in a large microwave-safe bowl; cover with vented plastic wrap. Cook on high 5 minutes or until crisp-tender, stirring once.
2. Transfer squash and cauliflower to 15×10×1-inch baking pan; sprinkle with salt and black pepper. Lightly coat with *cooking spray*. Broil 4 to 5 inches from heat for 10 minutes, until tender and beginning to brown, stirring once.
3. Meanwhile, prepare couscous according to package directions; set aside. In a small microwave-safe bowl combine butter and chili sauce. Heat on high just until melted. Divide couscous among 4 bowls. Top with vegetables, pistachios, chili-butter, and, if desired, thyme. Makes 4 servings.

EACH SERVING *521 cal, 13 g fat, 23 mg chol, 633 mg sodium, 90 g carb, 9 g fiber, 14 g pro.*

Winter Garden Polenta

PREP 15 minutes COOK 3 hours (low) or 1½ hours (high)

½ cup oil-packed dried tomatoes
5 cups boiling water
1½ cups coarse polenta or cornmeal
½ cup finely shredded Parmesan cheese
1 teaspoon salt
1 teaspoon dried basil, crushed
¼ teaspoon crushed red pepper
1 8-ounce package sliced fresh mushrooms
4 cups fresh baby spinach
  Crumbled Parmesan cheese (optional)

1. Drain tomatoes, reserving 1 tablespoon oil. Snip tomatoes. In a 3½- or 4-quart slow cooker combine tomatoes, boiling water, polenta, the ½ cup Parmesan, salt, the basil, and crushed red pepper; stir to combine. Cover and cook on low-heat setting for 3 hours or high-heat setting for 1½ hours or until polenta is tender.
2. About 15 minutes before serving, in a large skillet heat reserved oil from tomatoes. Add mushrooms. Cook and stir for 5 minutes or until tender. Add spinach. Cook and stir just until wilted. Season to taste with salt. Stir polenta, then spoon into bowls. Top with spinach and mushroom mixture and, if desired, crumbled Parmesan. Makes 4 servings.

EACH SERVING *293 cal, 10 g fat, 7 mg chol, 859 mg sodium, 43 g carb, 6 g fiber, 11 g pro.*

BLACK BEAN CAKES WITH SALSA

5 large eggs
2 teaspoons chopped fresh thyme or ½ teaspoon dried thyme, crushed
½ teaspoon salt
¼ teaspoon black pepper
1 tablespoon canola oil
1 recipe Spring Greens
  Mixed peppercorns, crushed (optional)

1. Preheat oven to 425°F. Lightly coat two small baking sheets with nonstick cooking spray; set aside.
2. Drain zucchini in a colander; press to squeeze out excess liquid. In a large bowl combine zucchini, potatoes, carrot, flour, 1 egg, thyme, salt, and pepper.
3. In an extra-large large nonstick skillet heat half the oil over medium heat. To make a pancake, spoon about a 1-cup portion of potato mixture into skillet; evenly press and round edges with back of spatula to form a pancake. Cook, two pancakes at a time, 4 minutes each side or until golden brown, turning once. Transfer to prepared baking sheet. Repeat with remaining oil and potato mixture.
4. With the back of a wooden spoon or a ¼-cup measure, gently press each pancake, slightly off-center, to make a 3-inch-diameter depression, deep enough to hold an egg. Pour 1 egg in each nest. Place pancakes with eggs in oven, being careful not to tilt baking sheet. Bake, uncovered, 10 minutes or until eggs are cooked through. Transfer pancakes to serving plates. Serve with Spring Greens. If desired, sprinkle with crushed peppercorns. Makes 4 servings.
Spring Greens In a large bowl combine 3 cups watercress and 1 small carrot, peeled and cut into long strips with a vegetable peeler. For dressing, in a bowl combine 2 teaspoons white wine vinegar, 1 teaspoon Dijon mustard, ¼ teaspoon salt, and a dash of black pepper. Slowly whisk in 3 tablespoons olive oil. Toss with watercress and carrot strips.
EACH SERVING *362 cal, 20 g fat, 264 mg chol, 599 mg sodium, 34 g carb, 4 g fiber, 13 g pro.*

Black Bean Cakes with Salsa

START TO FINISH 25 minutes

1½ cups prepared salsa
1 jalapeño (see tip, page 35)
2 15-ounce cans black beans, rinsed and drained
1 8.5-ounce package corn muffin mix
1 tablespoon chili powder
2 tablespoons olive oil
½ cup sour cream
½ teaspoon chili powder

1. In a colander drain ½ cup of the salsa. Seed and finely chop half the jalapeño; thinly slice remaining half. In a large bowl mash beans with vegetable masher or fork. Stir in muffin mix, drained salsa, 2½ teaspoons chili powder, and chopped jalapeño.
2. In an extra-large skillet heat 1 tablespoon oil over medium-high heat. Add four ½-cup mounds of bean mixture to skillet. Flatten mounds with spatula to 3½-inch round cakes. Cook 3 minutes each side until browned. Remove from skillet. Repeat with remaining oil and bean mixture.
3. In a bowl combine sour cream and the ½ teaspoon chili powder. Top cakes with remaining salsa, sliced jalapeño, and seasoned sour cream. Makes 4 servings.
EACH SERVING *519 cal, 19 g fat, 11 mg chol, 1,553 mg sodium, 79 g carb, 12 g fiber, 20 g pro.*

Potato, Zucchini, and Carrot Pancakes

PREP 30 minutes COOK 8 minutes per batch ROAST 10 minutes at 425°F

Nonstick cooking spray
1 medium zucchini, shredded (about 1¼ cups)
1½ pounds baking potatoes, peeled and shredded (about 4 cups)
1 large carrot, shredded (about 1 cup)
¼ cup all-purpose flour

POTATO, ZUCCHINI,
AND CARROT
PANCAKES

TOFU STACK-UP

FALAFEL PATTY MELT

Farmer's Market Grilled Cheese

START TO FINISH 30 minutes

¼ cup mayonnaise
2 cups baby spinach
1 teaspoon minced garlic
¼ teaspoon salt
¼ teaspoon black pepper
8 ½-inch slices sourdough bread
2 tablespoons olive oil
½ 3.4- to 4-ounce package garlic-and-herb goat cheese, softened
1 small zucchini, thinly sliced lengthwise
1 tomato, sliced

1. In a blender or food processor combine the mayonnaise, 1 cup of the spinach, garlic, salt, and pepper. Blend or process until smooth. Set aside.
2. Brush one side of each slice of bread with the olive oil; place, oiled sides down, on waxed paper. Spread goat cheese on half the slices; layer zucchini, tomato, and remaining spinach on top. Spread some of the spinach mayonnaise on remaining slices; place on vegetables, spread sides down.
3. Cook sandwiches in a very large skillet over medium-high heat for 6 to 8 minutes or until bread is golden brown, turning once. Pass any remaining spinach mayonnaise. Makes 4 servings.

EACH SERVING *369 cal, 22 g fat, 15 mg chol, 636 mg sodium, 32 g carb, 3 g fiber, 10 g pro.*

Falafel Patty Melt

PREP 20 minutes
BAKE 5 minutes at 400°F

½ cup frozen peas
1 16-ounce can garbanzo beans (chickpeas), rinsed and drained
1 medium carrot, shredded
2 tablespoons all-purpose flour
2 tablespoons olive oil
¼ teaspoon salt
½ teaspoon black pepper
4 flatbreads or pita bread rounds
8 slices dilled Havarti cheese (4 to 6 ounces)
Romaine leaves and sliced tomato (optional)

1. Preheat oven to 400°F. Place peas in a 1-quart microwave-safe dish. Cover and cook on high 2 minutes. In a food processor bowl or with an immersion blender puree garbanzo beans, carrot, flour, 1 tablespoon of the oil, salt, and pepper. Stir in peas. Form mixture into 8 patties.
2. Heat remaining oil in a large nonstick skillet over medium-high heat. Add patties. Cook 2 minutes per side or until browned and heated through.
3. Meanwhile, place flatbreads on baking sheet. Place 2 slices of cheese on each. Bake 5 minutes or until cheese is melted. Place two patties on each flatbread; fold over. Cut into halves and, if desired, serve with romaine and tomato. Makes 4 servings.

EACH SERVING *508 cal, 17 g fat, 21 mg chol, 1,006 mg sodium, 66 g carb, 8 g fiber, 18 g pro.*

Tofu Stack-Up

START TO FINISH 30 minutes

2 ears fresh sweet corn
2 12- to 16-ounce packages firm or extra-firm tofu, drained
⅓ cup yellow cornmeal
2 teaspoons chili powder
½ teaspoon salt
3 to 4 tablespoons olive oil
1 medium red sweet pepper, seeded and sliced
2 medium green tomatoes, sliced
Lime wedges
Fresh cilantro leaves (optional)

1. In a large saucepan cook corn, covered, in boiling salted water for 7 minutes. Drain.
2. Meanwhile, slice each block of tofu horizontally into 4 slices. In a shallow dish combine cornmeal, chili powder, and salt; dip tofu into mixture to coat.
3. In an extra-large skillet heat 1 tablespoon oil over medium-high heat. Cook tofu in batches for 2 to 3 minutes per side or until crisp and golden brown, adding more oil as needed. Remove tofu from skillet; add remaining oil, sweet pepper, and green tomatoes. Cook about 3 minutes or until tomatoes are heated through and lightly browned and peppers are crisp-tender.
4. Cut corn from cob. Place one slice tofu on each of four serving plates. Top with half the corn, peppers and tomatoes, remaining tofu slices, corn, peppers and tomatoes. Serve with lime wedges and, if desired, cilantro leaves. Makes 4 servings.

EACH SERVING *306 cal, 16 g fat, 0 mg chol, 382 mg sodium, 28 g carb, 4 g fiber, 15 g pro.*

TOMATO EGG SALAD

FOCACCIA-CAMEMBERT PIZZAS

Tomato Egg Salad

START TO FINISH 25 minutes

6	eggs
6	roma tomatoes
⅓	seedless cucumber, chopped (about ¾ cup)
¼	cup chopped red onion
⅓	cup mayonnaise
1	tablespoon Dijon mustard
1	bunch watercress, trimmed
½	teaspoon salt
½	teaspoon black pepper

1. In a medium saucepan cover eggs with water. Bring to boiling over high heat. Remove from heat; cover and let stand 12 minutes. Drain, rinse, peel, and chop cooked eggs.
2. Meanwhile, halve tomatoes lengthwise and remove seeds. In a bowl combine cucumber, onion, mayonnaise, mustard, salt, and pepper. Fold in chopped eggs.
3. Divide watercress among 4 plates. Top each with 3 tomato halves; spoon on egg salad. Makes 4 servings.
EACH SERVING 276 cal, 22 g fat, 324 mg chol, 610 mg sodium, 8 g carb, 2 g fiber, 12 g pro.

Focaccia-Camembert Pizzas

PREP 20 minutes   BROIL 3 minutes

4	6-inch Italian flatbreads (focaccia)
2	large tomatoes, sliced Salt and black pepper
1	8-ounce round Camembert cheese, chilled
⅓	cup chopped walnuts
2	tablespoons snipped fresh chives

1. Preheat broiler. Place flatbreads on the unheated rack of a broiler pan. Top with tomato slices; sprinkle with salt and pepper. Cut cheese into thin slices. Place cheese slices on tomato slices.
2. Broil 4 to 5 inches from heat about 2 minutes or until cheese begins to melt. Sprinkle with walnuts; broil 1 minute more. Sprinkle with fresh chives. Makes 4 servings.
EACH SERVING 449 cal, 24 g fat, 41 mg chol, 1,027 mg sodium, 41 g carb, 6 g fiber, 21 g pro.

Chickpea Salad with Grilled Pita

START TO FINISH 15 minutes

2	15-ounce cans no-salt-added garbanzo beans (chickpeas) or regular garbanzo beans (chickpeas), rinsed and drained
6	Campari or roma tomatoes, sliced
4	ounces crumbled feta cheese with tomato and basil
¼	cup lightly packed small fresh mint leaves
⅓	cup white wine vinegar
¼	cup olive oil
1	tablespoon sugar
½	teaspoon black pepper
1	to 2 pita bread rounds

1. For salad, in a large bowl combine beans, tomatoes, feta, and mint. For dressing, in a screw-top jar combine vinegar, oil, sugar, and pepper; shake to combine. Pour over salad; set aside.
2. Grill pita bread on an indoor or outdoor grill over medium heat until warm and toasted. Transfer to a cutting board and cut into wedges. Serve salad with pita wedges. Makes 4 servings.
EACH SERVING 454 cal, 22 g fat, 21 mg chol, 878 mg sodium, 49 g carb, 10 g fiber, 17 g pro.

CHICKPEA SALAD WITH GRILLED PITA

SWEET POTATO SOUP WITH CURRIED CHEESE CRISPS

Sweet Potato Soup with Curried Cheese Crisps

PREP 15 minutes COOK 10 minutes
BAKE 4 minutes at 425°F

- 2 pounds sweet potatoes
- 3 green onions, coarsely chopped
- 1 14.5-ounce can vegetable or chicken broth
- 1 cup whipping cream
- 1 teaspoon curry powder
- ¼ teaspoon salt
- ¼ teaspoon black pepper
  Nonstick cooking spray
- ½ cup white cheddar cheese, shredded (2 ounces)
  Paprika (optional)

1. Preheat oven to 425°F. Pierce potatoes in several places with a knife. Cook potatoes on paper towels in the microwave on high for 10 minutes or until tender, turning once. Halve potatoes lengthwise. Hold with oven mitt; scoop flesh into food processor. Add onions and half the broth. Process until smooth.
2. Transfer potatoes, cream, and remaining broth to a large saucepan. Heat over medium-high heat, stirring occasionally, until heated through. Stir in ¾ teaspoon of the curry powder, the salt, and pepper.
3. Meanwhile, for crisps, lightly coat a baking sheet with cooking spray. In a small bowl toss cheese and remaining curry powder. Evenly divide into 8 mounds, 2 inches apart, on baking sheet; flatten slightly. Bake 4 minutes, until melted and beginning to brown. Cool slightly; remove with metal spatula. If desired, sprinkle with paprika. Serve with soup. Makes 4 servings.

EACH SERVING 416 cal, 27 g fat, 97 mg chol, 737 mg sodium, 37 g carb, 5 g fiber, 8 g pro.

Beer and Cheese Soup

START TO FINISH 25 minutes

- 1 bunch green onions
- 3 tablespoons olive oil
- ¾ cup bottled roasted red sweet peppers, drained
- ¾ cup pale lager or nonalcoholic beer

BEER AND CHEESE SOUP

- 2 cups refrigerated shredded hash brown potatoes
- 2 cups milk
- 8 ounces American cheese, shredded
- ¼ teaspoon paprika plus additional for sprinkling

1. Slice green onions; set aside green parts. In a Dutch oven cook white portions of green onions over medium heat in 1 tablespoon hot oil until tender.
2. In a blender combine red peppers, cooked onion, beer, and 1 cup of the potatoes; process until smooth. Transfer to Dutch oven. Bring to boiling. Reduce heat. Simmer, uncovered, 5 minutes.
3. Add milk and cheese to Dutch oven. Cook and stir over medium heat until cheese is melted and soup is hot (do not boil).
4. In a skillet cook remaining potatoes in remaining hot oil over medium-high heat 8 minutes or until golden, stirring occasionally. Drain on paper towels; sprinkle with ¼ teaspoon paprika. Top soup with potatoes, onion tops, and paprika. Makes 4 servings.

EACH SERVING 467 cal, 30 g fat, 63 mg chol, 1,096 mg sodium, 28 g carb, 2 g fiber, 19 g pro.

**PORK CHOP AND SQUASH,
RECIPE PAGE 208**

grilling

FLAME-KISSED FOOD Why heat up the kitchen when it's so easy to grill in the backyard? Discover the smoky, delicious flavors when meat, poultry, fish, and shellfish meet your grill.

OPEN-FACE PESTO-CHICKEN BURGERS

Rosemary-Brie Chicken Burgers

PREP 25 minutes STAND 10 minutes
GRILL 14 minutes

- ½ cup dried cranberries, finely chopped
- ½ cup finely chopped walnuts, toasted
- ½ cup fine dry bread crumbs
- 2 teaspoons snipped fresh rosemary
- ½ teaspoon salt
- ½ teaspoon black pepper
- 2 pounds uncooked ground chicken or turkey
- 4 ounces Brie cheese, thinly sliced
  Mayonnaise (optional)
  Fresh spinach or arugula (optional)
- 6 kaiser or ciabatta rolls, split

1. Place cranberries in a small bowl; add enough boiling water to cover. Let stand for 10 minutes; drain well.
2. In a large bowl combine cranberries, walnuts, bread crumbs, rosemary, salt, and pepper. Add ground chicken; mix well. Shape mixture into six ¾-inch-thick patties.
3. For a charcoal grill, grill patties on the greased rack of an uncovered grill directly over medium coals for 14 to 18 minutes or until no longer pink (165°F), turning once halfway through grilling and topping patties with cheese during the last 2 to 3 minutes of grilling. (For a gas grill, preheat grill. Reduce heat to medium. Place patties on greased grill rack over heat. Cover and grill as above.)
4. Spread bottoms of rolls with mayonnaise and top with spinach (if using). Top with patties, then roll tops. Makes 6 servings.
EACH SERVING 578 cal, 27 g fat, 149 mg chol, 780 mg sodium, 46 g carb, 3 g fiber, 39 g pro.

Open-Face Pesto-Chicken Burgers

PREP 25 minutes GRILL 11 minutes

- 1 pound uncooked ground chicken or ground turkey
- 4 tablespoons basil pesto
- ¼ cup finely shredded Parmesan cheese
- 3 cloves garlic, minced
- ¼ teaspoon kosher salt or salt
- 2 3-inch slices ciabatta or four ¾-inch slices rustic Italian bread
- 2 tablespoons olive oil
- 4 slices fresh mozzarella cheese
- 2 cups fresh basil leaves, arugula, or spring garden mix
- 8 small tomato slices
  Coarsely ground black pepper

1. In a bowl combine the chicken, half the pesto, the Parmesan cheese, garlic, and salt. Shape into four ½-inch-thick oval patties.

2. Horizontally halve ciabatta. Brush cut sides of ciabatta or both sides of Italian bread with olive oil; set aside.
3. For a charcoal grill, place patties on a greased rack directly over medium coals. Grill, uncovered, 10 to 13 minutes or until chicken is no longer pink (165°F), turning once halfway through grilling. Top each patty with mozzarella cheese. Cover grill. Grill 1 to 2 minutes more or until cheese is melted. Add bread to grill rack; grill 1 to 2 minutes each side or until toasted. (For a gas grill, preheat grill. Reduce heat to medium. Place patties on grill rack over heat. Cover; grill as above.)
4. Arrange basil or greens on toasted bread. Top with chicken patties, tomato slices, and remaining pesto. Sprinkle with coarsely ground black pepper. Makes 4 servings.
EACH SERVING 348 cal, 13 g fat, 194 mg chol, 504 mg sodium, 33 g carb, 2 g fiber, 25 g pro.

ROSEMARY-BRIE CHICKEN BURGERS

PEACH-GLAZED CHICKEN

Peach-Glazed Chicken

PREP 15 minutes GRILL 50 minutes

2½ to 3 pounds meaty chicken
  pieces (breast halves, thighs,
  drumsticks, hindquarters)
  Salt and coarsely ground black
  pepper
½ cup peach preserves
1 tablespoon white wine vinegar
1 tablespoon prepared horseradish
1 teaspoon freshly grated ginger
½ teaspoon salt
½ teaspoon coarsely ground black
  pepper

1. Skin chicken if desired. Sprinkle
chicken with salt and pepper. For a
charcoal grill, arrange preheated coals
around a drip pan. Test for medium
heat above the pan. Place chicken on
grill rack above the drip pan. Cover and
grill for 40 minutes. (For a gas grill,
preheat grill. Reduce heat to medium.
Adjust for indirect cooking. Place
chicken on grill rack over burner that is
turned off. Grill as above.)
2. Meanwhile, for glaze, place peach
preserves in a small microwave-safe
bowl; snip any large pieces. Stir in
vinegar, horseradish, ginger, salt, and
pepper. Heat, uncovered, on high for
30 to 60 seconds or until preserves are
melted, stirring once.
3. Brush glaze over chicken pieces.
Cover and grill for 10 to 20 minutes
more or until chicken is no longer
pink (170°F for breast halves; 180°F
for thighs and drumsticks), brushing
occasionally with glaze. Spoon any
remaining glaze over chicken. Makes
4 servings.
EACH SERVING *356 cal, 9 g fat, 115 mg chol,
565 mg sodium, 28 g carb, 1 g fiber, 37 g pro.*

Chicken-Berry Salad

PREP 30 minutes MARINATE 1 hour
GRILL 12 minutes

½ cup fresh orange juice
¼ cup fresh lime juice
¼ cup fresh lemon juice
1 tablespoon extra virgin olive oil
1 teaspoon chopped fresh basil
¾ teaspoon salt
½ teaspoon black pepper
4 medium skinless, boneless
  chicken breast halves (1¼ to
  1½ pounds total)
3 cups fresh blackberries
¼ cup red wine vinegar
3 tablespoons sugar
1 teaspoon Dijon mustard
¼ teaspoon dried oregano, crushed
½ cup extra virgin olive oil
1 8-ounce package Mediterranean
  mixed salad greens
2 medium pears, cored and thinly
  sliced
¾ cup crumbled feta cheese
  (3 ounces)

1. In small bowl stir together orange,
lime, and lemon juices; 1 tablespoon
oil; basil; ½ teaspoon of the salt; and
¼ teaspoon pepper. Place chicken in
resealable plastic bag set in large bowl.
Pour juice mixture over chicken; seal
bag. Marinate 1 to 4 hours, turning bag
occasionally.
2. For dressing, in blender combine
1 cup of the blackberries, vinegar,
sugar, mustard, oregano, ¼ teaspoon
salt, and ¼ teaspoon pepper. Cover
and blend until smooth. With blender
running, slowly add ½ cup oil in thin
steady stream until well combined.
Transfer to serving container. Cover
and refrigerate until serving time.
3. Drain chicken; discard marinade.
For charcoal grill, place chicken on
the rack of an uncovered grill directly
over medium coals. Grill for 12 to
15 minutes or until done (170°F),
turning once halfway through grilling.
(For gas grill, preheat grill. Reduce heat
to medium. Add chicken to grill rack.
Cover and grill as above.)
4. Slice chicken. Divide greens among
4 serving plates. Top with chicken,
pears, and remaining 2 cups berries.
Top each with some of the dressing and
feta cheese. Pass remaining dressing.
Makes 4 servings.
EACH SERVING *603 cal, 35 g fat, 101 mg chol,
427 mg sodium, 36 g carb, 9 g fiber, 38 g pro.*

CHICKEN-BERRY
SALAD

SIZZLING STEAK AND PEACHES

Tangy Peach Sauce In a food processor combine 2 cups peeled and sliced peaches (2 medium), ¼ cup peach nectar, 2 tablespoons condensed beef broth, 2 tablespoons balsamic vinegar, 1 tablespoon packed brown sugar, 1 tablespoon finely chopped onion, and ¼ teaspoon ground cinnamon. Cover and process until nearly smooth. Transfer mixture to a small saucepan. Bring to boiling; reduce heat. Simmer, uncovered, about 10 minutes or until mixture reaches desired consistency, stirring occasionally. Makes about 1 cup.

EACH SERVING *690 cal, 16 g fat, 88 mg chol, 840 mg sodium, 87 g carb, 7 g fiber, 47 g pro.*

Pepper-Punched T-Bones

PREP 15 minutes GRILL 7 minutes

- ½ cup steak sauce
- 2 tablespoons snipped fresh thyme
- 2 tablespoons whole green peppercorns in brine, chopped
- 2 teaspoons cracked black pepper
- ½ teaspoon cayenne pepper
- 4 beef T-bone steaks, cut ¾ inch thick

1. In a small bowl combine steak sauce, thyme, green peppercorns, black pepper, and cayenne pepper. Trim fat from steaks. Spread half of the pepper mixture on one side of each steak.
2. For a charcoal grill, place steaks, pepper sides down, on the rack of an uncovered grill directly over medium coals. Spread the remaining pepper mixture on tops of steaks. Grill for 7 to 10 minutes for medium-rare (145°F) or 10 to 13 minutes for medium (160°F), turning once halfway through grilling. (For a gas grill, preheat grill. Reduce heat to medium. Place steaks on grill rack over heat. Spread the remaining pepper mixture on tops of steaks. Cover and grill as above.) Makes 4 servings.

EACH SERVING *583 cal, 38 g fat, 146 mg chol, 567 mg sodium, 5 g carb, 1 g fiber, 52 g pro.*

Sizzling Steak and Peaches

PREP 30 minutes GRILL 10 minutes

- 1 recipe Tangy Peach Sauce
- 4 slices thick-sliced bacon, cut crosswise into thirds
- 4 6-ounce boneless beef shoulder top blade (flat-iron), ribeye, or top loin steaks, cut 1 inch thick
   Salt
   Freshly ground black pepper
- 2 peaches, halved lengthwise
- 4 slices Texas toast, toasted

1. Prepare Tangy Peach Sauce. Remove ½ cup of the sauce for basting. Set aside remaining sauce until ready to serve.
2. In a large skillet cook bacon on medium heat until crisp. Remove bacon and drain on paper towels. Trim fat from steaks. Sprinkle steaks with salt and pepper.
3. For a charcoal grill, place steaks on the rack of an uncovered grill directly over medium coals. Grill for 10 to 12 minutes for medium-rare (145°F) or 12 to 15 minutes for medium (160°F), turning once halfway through grilling and brushing with the reserved ½ cup sauce during the last 5 minutes of grilling. (For a gas grill, preheat grill. Reduce heat to medium. Place steaks on grill rack over heat. Cover and grill as above.)
4. While steaks are grilling, add peach halves to grill. Grill about 3 minutes or until peaches are heated through and light brown, turning once halfway through grilling. Cut each peach half into 4 wedges.
5. To serve, place toast slices on dinner plates. Top with bacon, steaks, and grilled peach wedges. Pass the remaining sauce. Makes 4 servings.

PEPPER-PUNCHED
T-BONES

**HONEY-LIME LAMB AND
MELON KABOBS**

Honey-Lime Lamb and Melon Kabobs

PREP 25 min. MARINATE 30 minutes
GRILL 12 minutes

1¼ to 1½ pounds boneless lamb
    sirloin steak, cut into 1-inch
    cubes
  3 teaspoons shredded lime peel
  ⅓ cup lime juice
  ⅓ cup honey
  1 tablespoon snipped fresh
    tarragon or ½ teaspoon dried
    tarragon, crushed
  1 clove garlic, minced
  ½ teaspoon salt
  ½ teaspoon black pepper
12 1-inch cubes cantaloupe
12 1-inch cubes honeydew
  1 6-ounce carton plain yogurt
  6 soft flatbreads, warmed
    Fresh arugula (optional)

1. Place lamb in resealable plastic bag
set in dish. For marinade, in bowl whisk
together 2 teaspoons of the peel, lime
juice, honey, 2 teaspoons of the fresh
tarragon (1 teaspoon dried), garlic, salt,
and pepper. Reserve ¼ cup marinade.
Pour remaining over lamb. Seal bag;
turn to coat. Refrigerate 30 minutes to
2 hours, turning once. Remove lamb;
discard marinade.
2. On twelve 6-inch skewers thread
lamb and melon pieces, leaving ¼ inch
between. For charcoal grill, place on
rack directly over medium coals. Grill,
uncovered, 12 to 14 minutes or until
meat is slightly pink in center, turning
and brushing often with reserved
marinade.
3. Stir remaining lime peel and tarragon
into yogurt. Serve kabobs with yogurt,
flatbreads, and, if desired, arugula.
Makes 6 servings.
EACH SERVING *409 cal., 6 g fat, 62 mg chol,
616 mg sodium, 62 g carb, 3 g fiber, 27 g pro.*

SMOKY
BARBECUED
BISON BURGERS

Smoky Barbecued Bison Burgers

PREP 25 minutes GRILL 14 minutes

  ¼ cup mayonnaise
  2 tablespoons barbecue sauce
  1 tablespoon chopped dill pickle
  2 teaspoons prepared horseradish
  1 cup shredded smoked Gouda
    cheese (4 ounces)
  1 tablespoon country Dijon
    mustard
  4 cloves garlic, minced
  2 teaspoons smoked paprika
  ½ teaspoon black pepper
  ¼ teaspoon salt
1½ pounds ground bison (buffalo)
  4 whole grain hamburger buns,
    split and toasted
    Tomato slices
    Red onion slices

1. For sauce, in a bowl combine
mayonnaise, 1 tablespoon of the barbecue
sauce, the pickle, and horseradish. Cover
and chill until ready to serve.
2. In a large bowl combine the remaining
1 tablespoon barbecue sauce, cheese,
mustard, garlic, paprika, pepper, and
salt. Add ground bison; mix well, but do
not overmix. Shape mixture into four
¾-inch-thick patties.
3. For a charcoal grill, grill patties on
the greased rack of an uncovered grill
directly over medium coals for 14 to
16 minutes or until done (160°F),
turning once halfway through grilling.
(For a gas grill, preheat grill. Reduce
heat to medium. Place patties on greased
grill rack over heat. Cover and grill as
above.)
4. Spread bottoms of buns with sauce.
Add burgers, tomato, and red onion.
Replace tops of buns. Makes 4 servings.
EACH SERVING *550 cal, 30 g fat, 111 mg chol,
1,187 mg sodium, 30 g carb, 3 g fiber, 40 g pro.*

MEDITERRANEAN
BURGERS

MEATBALL AND
VEGETABLE KABOBS

Mediterranean Burgers

PREP 15 minutes   GRILL 14 minutes

- 1 pound lean ground lamb or beef
- 2 teaspoons freshly ground black pepper
- 4 kaiser rolls, split and toasted
- 4 lettuce leaves
- 4 tomato slices
- ½ cup thinly sliced cucumber
- ½ cup crumbled feta cheese (2 ounces)
- 1 tablespoon snipped fresh mint

1. Shape ground meat into four ¾-inch-thick patties. Sprinkle pepper evenly over patties; press in with your fingers.
2. For a charcoal grill, grill patties on the rack of an uncovered grill directly over medium coals for 14 to 18 minutes or until done (160°F), turning once halfway through grilling. (For a gas grill, preheat grill. Reduce heat to medium. Place patties on grill rack over heat. Cover and grill as above.)
3. Line bottoms of rolls with lettuce. Top with burgers, tomato, cucumber, cheese, and mint; replace tops of rolls. Makes 4 servings.

EACH SERVING *435 cal, 21 g fat, 88 mg chol, 535 mg sodium, 33 g carb, 1 g fiber, 28 g pro.*

Meatball and Vegetable Kabobs

PREP 20 minutes   GRILL 8 minutes

- ½ of a 6-ounce can tomato paste with Italian seasonings (⅓ cup)
- ½ teaspoon Italian seasoning, crushed
- 16 1-inch cooked refrigerated or frozen Italian-style meatballs, thawed
- 2 small zucchini
- 8 large cherry tomatoes
  Nonstick cooking spray

1. In a medium bowl combine tomato paste, ¼ cup water, and Italian seasoning to make a thick sauce. Add meatballs; stir to coat; set aside.
2. With vegetable peeler, cut 4 evenly spaced strips from zucchini. Cut zucchini into 1-inch cubes. On 8 metal or bamboo skewers (see tip, page 167) alternately thread meatballs and zucchini, leaving ¼ inch between pieces; thread a tomato at end of each. Lightly coat kabobs with cooking spray.
3. For a charcoal grill, grill kabobs on the rack of an uncovered grill directly over medium coals for 8 to 10 minutes or until meatballs are heated through and vegetables are crisp-tender. Brush remaining tomato paste mixture on meatballs during last 2 minutes of cooking. (For a gas grill, preheat grill. Reduce heat to medium. Place kabobs on grill rack over heat. Cover and grill as above.) Makes 4 servings.

EACH SERVING *222 cal, 15 g fat, 43 mg chol, 623 mg sodium, 12 g carb, 3 g fiber, 10 g pro.*

Apple-Bacon Burger

PREP 20 minutes   GRILL 8 minutes

- 6 slices bacon
- 2 small green apples
- ½ pound ground beef
- ½ pound bulk Italian sausage
- 2 tablespoons mayonnaise
- 1 tablespoon Dijon mustard
- 1 teaspoon honey
- 4 kaiser rolls, split and toasted

1. In a very large skillet cook bacon over medium-high heat until crisp. Drain on paper towels.
2. Core and finely chop one of the apples; combine in a large mixing bowl with beef and sausage. Shape into four ½-inch-thick patties.
3. For a charcoal grill, grill patties on the rack of an uncovered grill directly over medium coals for 8 to 10 minutes or until done (160°F), turning once halfway through grilling. (For a gas grill, preheat grill. Reduce heat to medium. Place patties on grill rack over heat. Cover and grill as above.)
3. Meanwhile, in a small bowl combine mayonnaise, mustard, and honey. Core and slice remaining apple.
4. To assemble the burgers, layer apple slices and grilled burgers on toasted bun bottoms. Top each with 1½ slices of bacon. Generously spread mayonnaise mixture on the cut sides of bun tops place on burgers. Makes 4 servings.

EACH SERVING *659 cal, 42 g fat, 99 mg chol, 1,164 mg sodium, 40 g carb, 3 g fiber, 28 g pro.*

APPLE-BACON
BURGER

ROASTED GARLIC-
MOZZARELLA
BURGERS

Roasted Garlic-
Mozzarella Burgers

PREP 20 minutes
ROAST 30 minutes at 400°F
STAND 30 minutes GRILL 20 minutes

2 bulbs garlic
1 tablespoon olive oil
¾ cup freshly grated Parmesan
   cheese (3 ounces)
⅓ cup finely chopped onion
   (1 small)
⅓ cup snipped oil-packed dried
   tomatoes, drained
½ cup snipped fresh basil
½ teaspoon freshly ground black
   pepper
¼ teaspoon salt
1½ pounds lean ground beef
8 ounces bulk Italian sausage
6 ounces fresh mozzarella cheese
6 ciabatta rolls, split, or
   hamburger buns
   Olive oil
   Fresh baby spinach leaves
1 recipe Olive Mayonnaise
   Ripe olives (optional)

1. Preheat oven to 400°F. Peel off the outer papery layer of the garlic bulbs. Cut off the top third of the garlic bulbs, exposing the tops of the cloves. Place a sheet of foil on a flat surface; place bulbs in the middle of the foil. Drizzle bulbs with the 1 tablespoon olive oil; fold foil up and over to form a packet. Roast garlic for 30 minutes or until soft and cloves are pulling away from papery covering. Cool about 30 minutes or until cool enough to handle. Squeeze the garlic cloves from the bulbs into a small bowl; mash with a fork to form a paste.

2. In a large bowl combine the garlic paste, Parmesan cheese, onion, tomatoes, basil, pepper, and salt. Add ground beef and Italian sausage. Mix well. Shape meat mixture into twelve ½-inch-thick patties.

3. Cut the mozzarella into six ¼-inch slices. Top 6 patties with a mozzarella slice. Top each with the remaining 6 patties. Pinch edges of top and bottom patties together to form one large burger patty, sealing all sides.

4. For a charcoal grill, arrange medium-hot coals around a drip pan. Test for medium heat above the pan. Place patties on grill rack over drip pan. Cover and grill about 20 minutes or until done (160°F), turning once halfway through grilling. (For a gas grill, preheat grill. Reduce heat to medium. Adjust for indirect grilling. Place patties on grill rack over burner that is off. Cover and grill as directed.)

5. Brush cut sides of rolls with additional olive oil. During the last 1 to 2 minutes of grilling, place buns, oil sides down, on grill directly over heat to lightly toast. Remove burgers and buns. Let burgers stand for 2 minutes before eating (the cheese inside is hot).

6. Serve burgers in rolls topped with spinach leaves and Olive Mayonnaise. If desired, garnish with an additional spinach leaf and a ripe olive. Makes 6 servings.

Olive Mayonnaise In a small bowl combine ½ cup mayonnaise, 1 to 2 tablespoons purchased Kalamata olive tapenade, and 1 tablespoon snipped fresh basil. Cover and chill for at least 1 hour before serving.

EACH SERVING *876 cal, 67 g fat, 145 mg chol, 1,101 mg sodium, 27 g carb, 2 g fiber, 39 g pro.*

Grilled Poblano Chile Burgers

PREP **25 minutes**
ROAST **20 minutes at 425°F**
STAND **15 minutes** GRILL **14 minutes**

- 2 fresh medium poblano or Anaheim chile peppers
- 1 egg, lightly beaten
- ¾ cup soft bread crumbs (1 slice)
- ½ cup shredded carrot (1 medium)
- 2 tablespoons water
- 1 teaspoon dried oregano, crushed
- 2 cloves garlic, minced
- ½ teaspoon salt
- ¼ teaspoon black pepper
- 1 pound lean ground beef
- 4 kaiser rolls, split and toasted
- 4 slices red and/or yellow tomato
  Frozen avocado dip (guacamole), thawed (optional)

GRILLED POBLANO CHILE BURGERS

1. Preheat oven to 425°F. To roast chile peppers, cut peppers in half lengthwise; remove stems, seeds, and membranes (see tip, page 35). Place pepper halves, cut sides down, on a foil-lined baking sheet. Roast for 20 to 25 minutes or until peppers are charred and very tender. Bring the foil up around the peppers and fold edges together to enclose. Let stand about 15 minutes or until cool enough to handle. Use a sharp knife to loosen edges of the skins; gently pull off the skins in strips and discard. Chop roasted peppers.

2. In a large bowl combine egg, bread crumbs, carrot, the water, oregano, garlic, salt, black pepper, and roasted peppers. Add beef; mix well. Shape meat mixture into four ¾-inch-thick patties.

3. For a charcoal grill, grill patties on the rack of an uncovered grill directly over medium coals for 14 to 18 minutes or until done (160°F), turning once halfway through grilling. (For a gas grill, preheat grill. Reduce heat to medium. Place patties on grill rack over heat. Cover and grill as above.) Serve burgers on rolls with tomato and, if desired, avocado dip. Makes 4 servings.

EACH SERVING *478 cal, 21 g fat, 130 mg chol, 751 mg sodium, 41 g carb, 2 g fiber, 31 g pro.*

BACON-WRAPPED
PORK AND BEANS

Bacon-Wrapped Pork and Beans

PREP 15 minutes GRILL 18 minutes

1 1½- to 1¾-pound center-cut pork loin fillet
8 slices center-cut bacon
16 green onions
1 pint cherry or grape tomatoes, halved
1 16-ounce can pinto beans, rinsed and drained
⅓ cup ketchup
1 teaspoon yellow mustard

1. Cut pork loin crosswise into 8 slices. Sprinkle lightly with *salt* and *pepper*. Wrap 1 slice of bacon around each pork slice; secure with small skewers or wooden picks.
2. For charcoal grill, arrange medium-hot coals around drip pan. Test for medium heat above pan. Place pork on grill rack over pan. Cover and grill 15 to 20 minutes or until pork is slightly pink in center and juices run clear (145°F), turning once halfway through grilling. Allow meat to rest for at least 3 minutes. (For a gas grill, preheat grill. Reduce heat to medium. Adjust for indirect cooking. Place slices on grill rack over the burner that is turned off. Grill as directed.)
2. Meanwhile, chop 4 of the green onions. Place remaining onions on grill rack over coals. Grill 3 minutes, turning occasionally, or until just tender.
3. In a saucepan combine the chopped onions, tomatoes, beans, ketchup, 2 tablespoon *water*, and mustard. Bring to boiling; reduce heat. Cover and simmer until pork is done. Serve with pork and green onions. Makes 4 servings.

EACH SERVING *452 cal, 11 g fat, 107 mg chol, 1,147 mg sodium, 33 g carb, 8 g fiber, 55 g pro.*

Stuffed Pork Rib Chops

PREP 20 minutes GRILL 35 minutes

1 cup crumbled semisoft goat cheese (chèvre) or feta cheese (4 ounces)
½ cup dried cherries or cranberries
1 tablespoon snipped fresh oregano or 1 teaspoon dried oregano, crushed
1 tablespoon snipped fresh rosemary or 1 teaspoon dried rosemary, crushed
2 cloves garlic, minced
¼ to ½ teaspoon crushed red pepper
½ teaspoon salt
¼ teaspoon black pepper
4 bone-in pork rib chops or boneless pork top loin chops, cut 1½ inches thick
½ cup bottled raspberry chipotle barbecue sauce or other barbecue sauce
   Snipped rosemary (optional)

1. For stuffing, in a medium bowl stir together goat cheese, cherries, oregano, rosemary, garlic, crushed red pepper, ¼ teaspoon of the salt, and ⅛ teaspoon of the black pepper.
2. Trim fat from chops. Make a pocket in each chop by cutting horizontally from the fat side almost to the bone (or the opposite side). Spoon one-fourth of the stuffing into each pocket. Secure the openings with wooden toothpicks. Sprinkle chops with ¼ teaspoon salt and ⅛ teaspoon black pepper.
3. For a charcoal grill, arrange medium-hot coals around a drip pan. Test for medium heat above the pan. Place chops on the grill rack over pan. Cover and grill for 20 to 25 minutes or until chops are slightly pink in center (145°F), turning once and brushing frequently with barbecue sauce during the last 10 minutes of grilling. Allow chops to rest for at least 3 minutes. (For a gas grill, preheat grill. Reduce heat to medium. Adjust for indirect cooking. Place chops on grill rack over the burner that is turned off. Grill as directed.) Remove toothpicks before serving. If desired, sprinkle with rosemary. Makes 4 servings.

EACH SERVING *359 cal, 14 g fat, 70 mg chol, 556 mg sodium, 32 g carb, 2 g fiber, 26 g pro.*

STUFFED PORK RIB CHOPS

PORK CHOP AND SQUASH

Peach-Glazed Chops

PREP 20 minutes
MARINATE 30 minutes
GRILL 12 minutes

- 2 medium peaches, coarsely chopped
- 1 medium lime, juiced (2 tablespoons)
- ½ cup reduced-sodium soy sauce
- 1 tablespoon Sriracha sauce
- 2 cloves garlic
- 4 center-cut pork chops, about 1 inch thick
- 4 peaches, halved and pitted
- 1 red sweet pepper, quartered
- 1 tablespoon honey
- ½ bunch fresh parsley or basil, coarsely chopped

1. In a blender combine the chopped peaches, lime juice, soy sauce, and Sriracha sauce. Blend until nearly smooth. Transfer to a resealable plastic bag set in a shallow dish. Smash garlic with the side of a wide knife or the bottom of a skillet. Add garlic and pork to bag; seal and turn to coat. Let stand up to 30 minutes at room temperature or refrigerate 2 to 4 hours, turning occasionally.
2. Remove pork from marinade, reserving marinade. For a charcoal grill, grill chops on rack of uncovered grill directly over medium coals for 12 to 15 minutes or until chops are slightly pink in centers and juices run clear (145°F), turning once halfway through grilling and adding the peach halves and pepper quarters for the last 7 minutes of grilling. Allow chops to rest for at least 3 minutes. (For a gas grill, preheat grill. Reduce heat to medium. Place meat on grill rack over heat. Cover and grill as above.)
3. Meanwhile, pour marinade into a small saucepan. Add honey and bring to a simmer. Simmer 2 to 3 minutes or until slightly reduced and thickened (discard garlic cloves). Remove pork, peaches, and peppers from grill and brush with reduced marinade. Chop peaches and peppers as desired for serving. Pass remaining marinade. Sprinkle with parsley. Makes 4 servings.
EACH SERVING 476 cal, 16 g fat, 117 mg chol, 1,227 mg sodium, 43 g carb, 4 g fiber, 41 g pro.

Pork Chop and Squash

PREP 20 minutes GRILL 6 minutes

- 4 pork loin chops, cut ¾ inch thick
- 4 small zucchini and/or yellow summer squash, halved lengthwise
- 1 tablespoon olive oil
  Salt and black pepper
- 1 orange, peeled and chopped
- ½ cup bottled chipotle salsa

1. Lightly brush chops and squash with olive oil and sprinkle with salt and pepper.
2. For a charcoal grill, grill chops and squash, cut sides down, directly over medium coals for 6 to 8 minutes turning once halfway through grilling, until squash are tender chops are slightly pink in center and juices run clear (145°F). Allow chops to rest for at least 3 minutes. (For a gas grill, preheat grill. Reduce heat to medium. Place meat on grill rack over heat. Cover and grill as above.)
3. Meanwhile, stir together orange and salsa. Slice squash into bite-size pieces. Spoon salsa mixture on chops. Makes 4 servings.
EACH SERVING 268 cal, 14 g fat, 78 mg chol, 340 mg sodium, 10 g carb, 3 g fiber, 26 g pro.

**PEACH-GLAZED
CHOPS**

GRILLED SEA BASS
WITH TOMATOES

Grilled Sea Bass with Tomatoes

PREP 15 minutes
MARINATE 15 minutes
GRILL 4 minutes per ½-inch thickness

- 4 6-ounce fresh or frozen sea bass or halibut fillets
- 4 cloves garlic, minced
- 1 tablespoon grated fresh ginger
- 2 teaspoons toasted sesame oil
- ¾ teaspoon salt
- ½ teaspoon ground cardamom
- 1 tablespoon olive oil
- 1 medium red onion, sliced ¼ inch thick
- 2 fresh jalapeños, seeded and finely chopped (see tip, page 35)
- 3 small yellow or red tomatoes, halved and cut into wedges
- 1 tablespoon snipped fresh oregano
- ¾ teaspoon snipped fresh thyme
- ¼ teaspoon black pepper

1. Thaw fish, if frozen. Rinse fish; pat dry with paper towels. Set aside.
2. For paste, stir together 2 cloves minced garlic, ginger, sesame oil, ½ teaspoon of the salt, and the cardamom. Rub both sides of fish evenly with paste. Cover and chill for 15 minutes.
3. Measure thickness of fish. Grill fish on the greased rack of an uncovered grill directly over medium coals until fish flakes easily with a fork, turning once halfway through grilling. Allow 4 to 6 minutes per ½-inch thickness. (For a gas grill, preheat grill. Reduce heat to medium. Place fish on greased grill rack. Cover and grill as above.)
4. Meanwhile, in a heavy large skillet heat olive oil over medium-high heat. Add onion; cook until tender, stirring frequently. Add the remaining 2 cloves minced garlic and the jalapeños; continue cooking until onions are golden. Add tomatoes, oregano, thyme, black pepper, and the remaining ¼ teaspoon salt. Stir gently until heated through.
5. To serve, place tomato-onion mixture on a serving platter; top with the fish. Makes 4 servings.

EACH SERVING 252 cal, 9 g fat, 69 mg chol, 580 mg sodium, 8 g carb, 2 g fiber, 33 g pro.

LEMON AND HERB GRILLED TROUT SANDWICH

Lemon and Herb Grilled Trout Sandwich

PREP 15 minutes GRILL 6 minutes per ½-inch thickness

- 1 large lemon
- ½ cup mayonnaise
- ¼ cup snipped fresh basil or 2 tablespoon snipped fresh dill
- ¼ teaspoon salt
- ¼ teaspoon black pepper
- 1 pound ruby or rainbow trout fillets
- 4 ciabatta buns, halved
  Fresh basil (optional)

1. Finely shred peel and squeeze juice from half the lemon; thinly slice the remaining half and set aside. In a small bowl combine mayonnaise, lemon peel and juice, basil, salt, and pepper.
2. Rinse fish; pat dry. Measure thickness of fish. Remove 2 tablespoon of the mayonnaise mixture and brush on fish. Grill fish, skin sides up, on the greased rack of an uncovered grill directly over medium-high heat for 1 minute. Carefully turn skin sides down and grill 5 to 7 minutes per ½-inch thickness or until fish flakes easily with a fork. After turning fish add lemon slices and buns, cut sides down, to the grill. (For a gas grill, preheat grill. Reduce heat to medium. Place fish on greased grill rack. Cover and grill as above.)
3. Remove fish, buns, and lemon slices from grill. Remove skin from fish. Cut fish into bun-size pieces. Spread some of the mayonnaise mixture on bun bottoms. Add fish, lemon slices, and additional basil. Pass remaining mayonnaise mixture. Makes 4 servings.

EACH SERVING 518 cal, 30 g fat, 77 mg chol, 667 mg sodium, 32 g carb, 3 g fiber, 29 g pro.

BARBECUED SALMON
WITH CORN RELISH

Lemon-Grilled Salmon with Corn Salad

PREP 20 minutes GRILL 8 minutes per ½-inch thickness

- 1½ cups cooked and cooled fresh or frozen yellow corn kernels
- ⅓ cup chopped red sweet pepper
- ¼ cup snipped fresh chives or thinly sliced green onions
- 3 tablespoons thinly sliced fresh basil
- 2 tablespoons pure maple syrup
- 2 tablespoons lemon juice
- ¼ teaspoon salt
- 1½ cups fresh blueberries
- 2 teaspoons finely shredded lemon peel
- 1 teaspoon ground cumin
- ½ teaspoon salt
- ¼ teaspoon black pepper
- 4 4- to 5-ounces fresh skinless salmon fillets
  Nonstick cooking spray
  Lemon slices and/or fresh basil sprigs (optional)

1. For corn salad, in bowl combine corn, sweet pepper, chives, basil, maple syrup, lemon juice, and the ¼ teaspoon salt. Add blueberries; toss gently to combine.
2. In small bowl combine lemon peel, cumin, the ½ teaspoon salt, and the black pepper. Sprinkle mixture on salmon fillets. Lightly coat both sides of salmon fillets with cooking spray. Measure thickness of fish.
3. For charcoal grill, grill salmon fillets on the rack of an uncovered grill directly over medium coals for 8 to 12 minutes or until fish flakes easily when tested with a fork, carefully turning once halfway through grilling. (For gas grill, preheat grill. Reduce heat to medium. Place salmon fillets on grill rack over heat. Cover and grill as above.)
4. Serve grilled salmon with corn salad. If desired, garnish with lemon slices and/or fresh basil sprigs. Makes 4 servings.

EACH SERVING *342 cal, 13 g fat, 67 mg chol, 507 mg sodium, 32 g carbo, 4 g fiber, 25 g pro.*

Barbecued Salmon with Corn Relish

PREP 20 minutes GRILL 4 minutes per ½-inch thickness

- 1 fresh jalapeño (see tip, page 35)
- 1 red sweet pepper, chopped
- 2 fresh ears of corn, husked
- 4 5- to 6-ounces skinless salmon fillets, ½ to 1 inch thick
- ½ cup bottled barbecue sauce
- 2 teaspoons olive oil
- ¼ teaspoon salt
- ¼ teaspoon black pepper
  Fresh oregano (optional)

1. Thinly slice half the jalapeño; seed and finely chop remaining half. In a bowl combine chopped jalapeño and sweet pepper; set aside.
2. Place corn on grill rack directly over medium heat; grill, turning occasionally, 10 to 15 minutes or until crisp-tender. Transfer corn to cutting board; cool slightly.
3. Meanwhile, rinse salmon and pat dry; measure thickness of fish. Sprinkle with salt and black pepper. For charcoal grill, grill salmon fillets on the rack of an uncovered grill directly over medium coals for 4 to 6 minutes per ½-inch thickness or until fish flakes easily when tested with fork, turning once halfway through grilling. Cover salmon to keep warm. (For gas grill, preheat grill. Reduce heat to medium. Place salmon fillets on grill rack over heat. Cover and grill as above.) Cut corn from cob. Add to chopped peppers with 1 tablespoon of the barbecue sauce, olive oil, salt, and black pepper.
4. Serve salmon with corn and relish. Top with remaining barbecue sauce and, if desired, fresh oregano. Makes 4 servings.

EACH SERVING *395 cal, 22 g fat, 78 mg chol, 470 mg sodium, 18 g carb, 2 g fiber, 31 g pro.*

**LEMON-GRILLED
SALMON WITH
CORN SALAD**

SESAME SALMON
WITH ASIAN
SLAW

Sesame Salmon with Asian Slaw

PREP 20 minutes
MARINATE 30 minutes
GRILL 6 minutes

- 1½ pounds fresh or frozen skinless salmon fillets
- ⅔ cup reduced-sodium soy sauce
- ⅓ cup sesame oil (not toasted)
- ⅓ cup sherry vinegar
- 3 tablespoons grated fresh ginger
- 4 cloves garlic, minced
- ¼ teaspoon cayenne pepper
  Asian Slaw
  Sesame seeds, toasted

1. Thaw fish, if frozen. Rinse fish; pat dry with paper towels. Cut fish into 1-inch pieces. Place fish in a resealable plastic bag set in a shallow dish.
2. For marinade, combine soy sauce, sesame oil, vinegar, ginger, garlic, and cayenne. Pour over fish. Seal bag; turn to coat fish. Marinate in refrigerator 30 minutes, turning once.
3. Drain fish, discarding marinade. Thread fish onto twelve 4-inch wooden skewers (see tip, page 167), leaving ¼ inch between pieces.
4. For a charcoal grill, grill fish kabobs on the greased rack of an uncovered grill directly over medium coals for 6 to 8 minutes or until fish flakes easily when tested with a fork, turning once halfway through grilling. (For a gas grill, cook fish kabobs over medium heat as above.)
5. Arrange fish kabobs on top of Asian Slaw. Sprinkle with sesame seeds. Makes 6 servings.

Asian Slaw In a small screw-top jar combine 2 tablespoons vegetable oil, 1 tablespoon lime juice, 1 tablespoon rice vinegar, 1 teaspoon packed brown sugar, 1 teaspoon grated fresh ginger, 1 teaspoon soy sauce, ¼ teaspoon salt, and ¼ teaspoon crushed red pepper. Cover and shake well. In a large bowl combine 4 cups shredded cabbage, 1 cup shredded bok choy, 1 cup shredded carrots (2 medium), ½ cup thinly sliced radishes, ½ cup cucumber strips, ½ cup chopped sweet green or orange pepper (1 small), ¼ cup cilantro, and ¼ cup toasted sliced almonds. Shake dressing. Pour over cabbage mixture; toss gently to coat. Makes 6 cups.

EACH SERVING *519 cal, 38 g fat, 67 mg chol, 1,460 mg sodium, 17 g carb, 5 g fiber, 29 g pro.*

Port-Glazed Grilled Salmon with Basil-Peach Relish

PREP 30 minutes GRILL 8 minutes per ½-inch thickness

- 1 cup port
- 4 6-ounce fresh or frozen skinless salmon fillets, about 1 inch thick
- 2 tablespoons honey
- 2 tablespoons lemon juice
- 2 tablespoons olive oil
- 3 large ripe peaches, peeled, pitted, and chopped
- ⅓ cup snipped fresh basil
  Small fresh basil leaves (optional)

1. For glaze, in a small saucepan bring port to boiling; reduce heat. Boil gently, uncovered, for 15 to 20 minutes or until reduced to ¼ cup. Set aside.
2. Meanwhile, thaw fish, if frozen. Rinse fish; pat dry with paper towels.
3. For relish, in a medium bowl combine honey, lemon juice, and oil. Add peaches and the snipped basil; toss gently to combine.
4. Measure fish. For a charcoal grill, grill fish on the greased rack of an uncovered grill directly over medium coals for 8 to 12 minutes per ½-inch thickness or until fish flakes easily when tested with a fork, turning once halfway through grilling and brushing frequently with glaze during the last 5 minutes of grilling. (For a gas grill, preheat grill. Reduce heat to medium. Place fish on greased grill rack over heat. Cover and grill as above.)
5. Serve fish with relish. If desired, sprinkle with the basil leaves. Makes 4 servings.

EACH SERVING *559 cal, 26 g fat, 100 mg chol, 104 mg sodium, 32 g carb, 2 g fiber, 36 g pro.*

PORT-GLAZED GRILLED SALMON WITH BASIL-PEACH RELISH

PEPPER JELLY AND SOY-GLAZED SALMON

Grilled Shrimp in Coconut Milk Sauce

PREP 25 minutes
MARINATE 30 minutes
COOK 15 minutes   GRILL 7 minutes

 1 pound fresh or frozen extra-large shrimp (about 30 total)
 2 teaspoons lime juice
 1 malagueta, tabasco, or bird chile, finely chopped (see tip, page 35)
 2 cloves garlic, minced
    Salt and black pepper
 1 tablespoon olive oil
 ½ cup chopped red sweet pepper
 ¼ cup finely chopped onion
 1 cup chopped, seeded, peeled tomatoes (2 medium)
 ½ cup unsweetened coconut milk
 1 tablespoon tomato paste
    Snipped fresh parsley or cilantro

1. Thaw shrimp, if frozen. Peel and devein shrimp. Rinse shrimp; pat dry with paper towels. In a medium bowl combine shrimp, lime juice, half of the finely chopped chile pepper, and half of the garlic; add salt and black pepper to taste. Toss to coat. Cover and marinate in the refrigerator for 30 minutes to 1 hour, stirring occasionally.
2. For coconut milk sauce, in a medium skillet heat oil over medium heat. Add sweet pepper, onion, the remaining chile pepper, and the remaining garlic; cook about 10 minutes or until tender, stirring occasionally. Add tomatoes, coconut milk, and tomato paste. Bring to boiling; reduce heat. Simmer, uncovered, about 5 minutes or until sauce reaches desired consistency. Season with salt. Keep warm.
3. Thread shrimp onto four long wooden skewers (see tip, page 167); transfer to a baking sheet. Grease an unheated grill rack. For a charcoal grill, grill kabobs on the greased rack of an uncovered grill directly over medium coals for 7 to 9 minutes or until shrimp are opaque, turning once halfway through grilling. (For a gas grill, preheat grill. Reduce heat to medium. Place skewers on greased grill rack over heat. Cover and grill as above.)
4. Divide sauce among 4 shallow bowls; place shrimp kabobs on top. Sprinkle with parsley. Makes 4 servings.
EACH SERVING *195 cal, 10 g fat, 129 mg chol, 327 mg sodium, 6 g carb, 1 g fiber, 19 g pro.*

Pepper Jelly and Soy-Glazed Salmon

PREP 25 minutes   MARINATE 1 hour
GRILL 15 minutes   COOK 10 minutes

 1 2-pound fresh or frozen skinless salmon fillet, about 1 inch thick
 ⅔ cup green jalapeño pepper jelly
 ⅓ cup rice vinegar
 ⅓ cup soy sauce
 3 green onions, sliced
 1 tablespoons grated fresh ginger
 2 teaspoons toasted sesame oil
 3 cloves garlic, minced
 ¼ teaspoons crushed red pepper
 ¼ cup snipped fresh cilantro
 ¼ cup sliced fresh jalapeños (see tip, page 35) and sliced green onions

1. Thaw fish, if frozen. Rinse fish; pat dry with paper towels. For marinade, in saucepan melt jelly over low heat; remove from heat. Stir in vinegar, soy sauce, green onions, ginger, sesame oil, garlic, and crushed red pepper. Place fish in shallow dish; pour marinade on fish. Cover; refrigerate 1 to 2 hours, turning fish occasionally.
2. Remove fish from marinade; reserve marinade. For a charcoal grill, arrange medium-hot coals around edge of grill. Test for medium heat in center of grill. Place fish on greased heavy-duty foil in the center of grill. Cover. Grill 15 to 18 minutes or until fish flakes when tested with a fork. (For gas grill, adjust for indirect cooking. Grill over medium heat as above.)
3. Bring reserved marinade to boiling; reduce heat. Simmer, uncovered, 10 minutes or until reduced to ½ cup. Drizzle over fish; sprinkle with cilantro, jalapeños, and onions. Makes 8 servings.
EACH SERVING *237 cal, 9 g fat, 6 mg chol, 482 mg sodium, 34 g carb, 3 g fiber, 6 g pro.*

**GRILLED SHRIMP IN
COCONUT MILK SAUCE**

DOUBLE-CHEDDAR
BISCUITS, RECIPE
PAGE 255

side dishes

ROUND OUT DINNER It's time for plain old peas and everyday taters to move over and make room on the plate. These fresh salads, colorful vegetable dishes, and savory breads are ready to move in.

CREAMY BRUSSELS SPROUTS WITH PEPPERED BACON

Creamy Brussels Sprouts with Peppered Bacon

START TO FINISH **35 minutes**

- 4 slices peppered bacon
- 2 pounds Brussels sprouts, trimmed and halved through stem ends
- ¾ cup reduced-sodium chicken broth
- ½ teaspoon kosher salt
- ¼ teaspoon black pepper
- ¾ cup whipping cream
  Cracked black pepper

1. In a large skillet cook bacon over medium heat until browned and crisp. Drain on paper towels, reserving 2 tablespoons drippings in skillet.
2. Add Brussels sprouts to drippings in skillet. Cook over medium heat for 4 minutes, stirring occasionally. Add broth, salt, and pepper. Heat to boiling. Reduce heat. Simmer, covered, for 5 minutes. Uncover; cook for 2 minutes or until liquid is almost evaporated. Add cream. Cook for 4 minutes or until thickened.

3. Transfer sprouts to serving dish. Sprinkle with crumbled bacon and cracked pepper. Makes 8 servings.
EACH SERVING *174 cal, 14 g fat, 38 mg chol, 305 mg sodium, 10 g carb, 4 g fiber, 6 g pro.*

Double-Gingered Orange Carrots

START TO FINISH **30 minutes**

- 1½ pounds baby carrots with tops, trimmed, or 1 pound small to medium carrots
- 2 teaspoons olive oil
- ¼ cup orange juice
- 1 1-inch piece fresh ginger, peeled and shaved or cut into very thin slices
- 2 tablespoons chopped, toasted hazelnuts
- 1 tablespoon chopped crystallized ginger
- ¼ teaspoon salt

1. Halve baby carrots lengthwise. Quarter small carrots lengthwise; cut crosswise into 3-inch pieces.
2. In a nonstick skillet cook carrots in hot olive oil over medium heat for 10 minutes, stirring once. Add orange juice, fresh ginger, and salt; toss to coat. Cook, covered, 6 minutes or until carrots are tender. Uncover; cook 2 minutes or until liquid is reduced by half.
3. To serve, sprinkle with nuts and crystallized ginger. Makes 4 servings.
EACH SERVING *109 cal, 5 g fat, 0 mg chol, 224 mg sodium, 16 g carb, 4 g fiber, 2 g pro.*

Thyme-Roasted Beets

PREP **20 minutes** ROAST **40 minutes** at 400°F COOL **15 minutes**

- 4 pounds baby beets (assorted colors) or small beets
- 6 cloves garlic, peeled
- 3 sprigs fresh thyme
- 5 tablespoons olive oil
- ½ teaspoon kosher salt
- ¼ teaspoon freshly ground black pepper
- 2 tablespoons lemon juice
- 1 tablespoon snipped fresh thyme
  Snipped fresh thyme (optional)

1. Preheat oven to 400°F. Cut tops off the beets and trim the root ends. Wash beets thoroughly. If using small beets, cut into 1- to 1½-inch wedges. Place beets in a 3-quart baking dish. Add garlic and the thyme sprigs. In a small bowl stir together 3 tablespoons of the oil, the salt, and pepper. Drizzle over vegetables in baking dish; toss to coat.
2. Cover with foil. Roast for 40 minutes or until tender. (A knife should easily slide into the beets when they are tender.) Uncover. Let beets cool in pan on a wire rack about 15 minutes. If using small beets, remove skins by wrapping the wedges, 1 at a time, in a paper towel and gently rubbing off the skins. (Baby beets do not need to be peeled.)
3. Remove garlic from dish and finely chop. Discard thyme sprigs. In a small bowl combine finely chopped garlic, the remaining 2 tablespoons oil, the lemon juice, and the 1 tablespoon snipped thyme. Drizzle mixture over beets; toss lightly to combine.
4. Serve warm or at room temperature. If desired, garnish with additional snipped thyme. Makes 8 servings.
EACH SERVING *165 cal, 9 g fat, 0 mg chol, 268 mg sodium, 20 g carb, 6 g fiber, 3 g pro.*

**DOUBLE-GINGERED
ORANGE CARROTS**

FIVE-HERB ROASTED
CARROTS AND
POTATOES

Five-Herb Roasted Carrots and Potatoes

PREP 25 minutes
BAKE 45 minutes at 400°F

- 3 pounds tiny new potatoes, peels on and quartered
- 3 medium carrots, cut into bite-size pieces
- 3 tablespoons snipped fresh chives
- 1 tablespoon butter or margarine, melted
- 2 tablespoons olive oil
- 3 tablespoons snipped fresh oregano
- 1 tablespoon snipped fresh parsley
- 1 tablespoon snipped fresh rosemary
- 4 cloves garlic, minced (optional)
- 1½ teaspoons snipped fresh sage
- ¾ teaspoon salt
- ¼ teaspoon freshly ground black pepper

1. Preheat oven to 400°F. Grease a 15×10×2-inch baking sheet. Place potatoes and carrots in prepared pan.
2. In a small bowl combine chives, melted butter, oil, oregano, parsley, rosemary, garlic (if desired), sage, salt, and pepper. Drizzle over vegetables; toss gently to coat. Cover pan with foil. Bake for 30 minutes. Stir vegetables. Bake, uncovered, for 15 minutes more or until potatoes are tender. Makes 9 servings.

EACH SERVING *202 cal, 9 g fat, 11 mg chol, 254 mg sodium, 28 g carb, 3 g fiber, 4 g pro.*

Caramelized Brussels Sprouts with Lemon

PREP 15 minutes COOK 6 minutes

- ¼ cup extra virgin olive oil
- 2 cups Brussels sprouts, trimmed and halved lengthwise
- 2 tablespoons water
  Juice of lemon half, about 1 tablespoon

1. In an extra-large nonstick skillet heat 3 tablespoons of the olive oil over medium heat. Arrange sprouts in a single layer, cut sides down. Drizzle with remaining olive oil and sprinkle with *salt* and *black pepper*. Cover and cook 3 minutes. Remove lid and

sprinkle sprouts with water. Cover and cook 2 minutes more. Sprouts should just be tender when pierced with a fork and beginning to caramelize.
2. Remove cover and increase heat slightly. When cut sides are well caramelized, toss sprouts in pan, drizzle with lemon juice, and sprinkle with more salt and pepper to taste. Makes 6 servings.

EACH SERVING *106 cal, 9 g fat, 0 mg chol, 209 mg sodium, 6 g carb, 2 g fiber, 2 g pro.*

Braised Cabbage with Spicy Croutons

START TO FINISH 30 minutes

- 2 tablespoons olive oil
- 1 tablespoon butter
- ⅓ 12-ounce baguette, torn into coarse croutons (2 cups)
- ¼ teaspoon garlic powder
- ¼ teaspoon crushed red pepper
- 1 small head green cabbage, cut into 6 wedges
- ½ cup water
  Snipped fresh parsley
  Lemon wedges

1. In an extra-large skillet heat 1 tablespoon olive oil and butter over medium-high heat. Add bread, garlic powder, and crushed red pepper. Cook and stir 3 to 5 minutes until golden brown. Remove croutons from skillet with slotted spoon and cool in a single layer on paper towels.
2. Add cabbage to skillet, overlapping wedges if needed. Season with *salt* and *black pepper*. Add water; bring to boiling. Reduce heat and simmer, covered, 15 minutes or until tender.
3. Place cabbage on platter; drizzle with remaining olive oil. Top with croutons, parsley, and lemon wedges. Makes 6 servings.

EACH SERVING *141 cal, 7 g fat, 5 mg chol, 254 mg sodium, 19 g carb, 4 g fiber, 4 g pro.*

BRAISED CABBAGE WITH SPICY CROUTONS

BROCCOLI RABE
WITH GARLIC

ROASTED MUSHROOM
MEDLEY

Broccoli Rabe with Garlic

START TO FINISH 20 minutes

- 1 pound broccoli rabe or 2½ cups broccoli florets
- 2 teaspoons olive oil
- 2 cloves garlic, minced
- 1½ cups reduced-sodium chicken broth
- ⅛ teaspoon salt
- ⅛ teaspoon black pepper

1. If using broccoli rabe, remove large leaves and, if necessary, cut stems to 6 to 8 inches long. In a 3- to 4-quart Dutch oven cook broccoli rabe or broccoli, half at a time if necessary, in a large amount of boiling water for 3 minutes for broccoli rabe or 6 minutes for broccoli florets. Drain well; gently squeeze broccoli rabe to get it really dry.
2. In the same Dutch oven heat oil over medium heat. Add garlic; cook and stir for 30 seconds. Carefully add drained broccoli rabe or broccoli florets (oil will spatter if the vegetables are not well drained); cook and stir for 1 minute. Add broth and cook, uncovered, until all the broth has evaporated, stirring frequently. Stir in salt and pepper. Serve immediately. Makes 4 servings.
EACH SERVING *48 cal, 3 g fat, 0 mg chol, 98 mg sodium, 4 g carb, 3 g fiber, 4 g pro.*

Roasted Mushroom Medley

PREP 25 minutes
ROAST 20 minutes at 400°F

- 1 pound assorted fresh mushrooms (such as cremini, stemmed shiitake, button, and/or porcini), quartered
- 6 cloves garlic, peeled and thinly sliced
- 2 tablespoons olive oil
- 2 teaspoons Worcestershire sauce
- 2 teaspoons balsamic vinegar
- ¼ teaspoon dried oregano, crushed
- ¼ teaspoon salt
- ¼ teaspoon black pepper
- 1 tablespoon snipped fresh parsley

1. Preheat oven to 400°F. Place mushrooms in a 15×10×2-inch baking pan. Stir garlic slices into mushrooms.
2. Drizzle mushroom mixture with oil, Worcestershire sauce, and balsamic vinegar. Sprinkle with oregano, salt, and pepper. Toss gently to coat.
3. Roast, uncovered, for 20 minutes or until mushrooms are tender, stirring twice. Stir in parsley just before serving. Makes 6 servings.
EACH SERVING *65 cal, 5 g fat, 0 mg chol, 124 mg sodium, 4 g carb, 1 g fiber, 3 g pro.*

Harvest Vegetable Hash

PREP 30 minutes
ROAST 30 minutes at 425°F

- ¼ teaspoon ancho chili powder or chili powder
- ¼ teaspoon coarse sea salt or kosher salt
- ¼ teaspoon cracked black pepper
- ⅛ teaspoon ground turmeric
- 2½ cups coarsely chopped vegetables, such as peeled sweet potatoes, carrots, parsnips, and/or unpeeled tiny new potatoes
- 2 cloves garlic, peeled and cut in half
- 1 tablespoon olive oil or cooking oil
- ½ cup packed spinach leaves

1. Preheat oven to 425°F. In a small bowl combine ancho chili powder, salt, pepper, and turmeric.
2. In a 2-quart baking dish toss vegetables and garlic with the olive oil. Sprinkle with the chili powder mixture; toss again to distribute seasonings.
3. Roast vegetables, uncovered, for 30 minutes or until lightly browned and tender, stirring once or twice. Remove from oven. Add spinach and toss just until wilted. Serve immediately. Makes 6 servings.
EACH SERVING *193 cal, 7 g fat, 0 mg chol, 231 mg sodium, 31 g carb, 5 g fiber, 3 g pro.*

**SMOKED ALMOND
AND ONION BAKE**

Smoked Almond and Onion Bake

PREP 35 minutes
BAKE 30 minutes at 350°F
COOL 15 minutes

- ½ cup smoke-flavor whole almonds
- ½ cup all-purpose flour
- ¼ cup butter
- ½ teaspoon water
- 3 slices bacon, chopped
- 2½ cups halved and sliced onions
- ¼ cup sliced green onions
- 2 eggs beaten
- 1 cup milk
- 1 cup shredded Swiss cheese
- ¼ teaspoon salt
- ⅛ teaspoon black pepper
- ⅛ teaspoon ground nutmeg
- 1 cup shredded romaine
- 1 tablespoon bottled balsamic vinaigrette

1. Preheat oven to 350°F. For crust, place almonds in a food processor. Cover and process until finely ground. Add flour; process until combined. Add butter. Cover and process with several on/off turns until mixture resembles coarse crumbs. Add the water; cover and process with on/off turns until mixture holds together.
2. Evenly press almond mixture into a 2-quart baking pan. Bake, uncovered, for 12 minutes. Transfer to a wire rack.
3. Meanwhile, in a large skillet cook bacon until crisp. Using a slotted spoon, transfer cooked bacon to paper towels, reserving 1 tablespoon drippings in skillet. Add sliced onions to skillet. Cook, covered, over medium-low heat for 20 minutes, stirring occasionally. Uncover. Cook for 5 minutes. Remove from heat; stir in green onions.
4. Spoon onion mixture evenly over crust. Sprinkle with cooked bacon. In a large bowl combine eggs, milk, cheese, salt, pepper, and nutmeg; pour evenly over onion-bacon layers.
5. Bake, uncovered, about 30 minutes or just until top is light brown and egg mixture is set. Cool on a wire rack for 15 minutes. Cut into pieces to serve. In a medium bowl toss romaine with vinaigrette; spoon some on each serving. Makes 4 servings.

EACH SERVING *486 cal, 34 g fat, 172 mg chol, 599 mg sodium, 27 g carb, 3 g fiber, 20 g pro.*

CUMIN-RUBBED SWEET POTATOES WITH SAGE

Cumin-Rubbed Sweet Potatoes with Sage

PREP 25 minutes
ROAST 1 hour at 375°F
COOL 5 minutes

- 4 medium sweet potatoes
- 2 tablespoons coarse salt
- 1 tablespoon cumin seeds, crushed
- ½ cup butter, softened (1 stick)
- 1 tablespoon maple syrup or honey
- 1 teaspoon crushed red pepper flakes
  Canola or peanut oil for frying
  Fresh sage leaves (about 12)

1. Preheat oven to 375°F. Wash and scrub potatoes. Mix together salt and cumin seeds. While skins are still damp, rub all over with salt mixture (reserve any remaining salt mixture for another use). Bake directly on oven rack for 1 hour, turning once to crisp evenly on all sides.
2. Meanwhile, for spiced butter, in a bowl stir together softened butter, maple syrup, and crushed red pepper. Roll into a log using waxed paper; chill.
3. Heat 3 inches of oil in a medium saucepan over medium heat. Fry sage leaves for 2 minutes or until crisp. Drain on paper towels.
4. Cool potatoes for 5 minutes. If desired, brush off some of the salt from the skins. With a sharp knife, slice open lengthwise. Push the ends toward the center to open each potato. Top each with about 1 tablespoon of spiced butter and sage leaves. Makes 4 servings.

EACH SERVING *278 cal, 19 g fat, 31 mg chol, 527 mg sodium, 26 g carb, 4 g fiber, 3 g pro.*

Canola oil, for frying
9   shallots, sliced crosswise into
     ¼-inch rings
½   cup cornstarch, sifted

1. Preheat oven to 350°F. Lightly grease a 2-quart baking dish.
2. Bring a large saucepan of salted water to boiling. Prepare and set aside a large bowl of ice water. Cook green beans in boiling water about 2 minutes, until bright green; drain and place in ice water to cool. Drain.
3. Meanwhile, in a very large skillet melt 2 tablespoons of the butter over medium heat. Cook and stir onion in hot butter about 3 minutes, until soft and translucent. Add 1 tablespoon butter; turn heat to medium-high. Sauté mushrooms about 4 minutes, until golden. Transfer onions, mushrooms, and beans to large bowl.
4. For sauce, in the same skillet melt remaining butter over medium heat; add flour. Stir constantly, about 2 minutes, until flour turns light brown. Slowly pour in milk; cook and stir about 4 minutes, until thickened. Stir in salt, pepper, and nutmeg. Remove from heat; cool completely. Pour cooled sauce over bean mixture; stir to coat evenly. Spoon into prepared baking dish. Bake about 40 minutes, until sauce bubbles around edges.
5. Meanwhile, for topping, pour 3 to 4 inches of oil into a deep saucepan. Heat over medium-high heat until sizzling. Working in batches, separate shallots into rings; toss with cornstarch to coat, shaking off excess. Carefully add to hot oil. Fry for 2 minutes, until golden and crisp. Remove with slotted spoon; drain on paper towels.
6. Remove casserole from oven; sprinkle with shallots. Bake 5 minutes more, until top is crisp and golden. Serve warm. Makes 8 servings.

EACH SERVING *126 cal, 8 g fat, 13 mg chol, 200 mg sodium, 12 g carb, 2 g fiber, 3 g pro.*

Roasted Vegetables and Chickpeas

PREP **30 minutes**
ROAST **45 minutes at 425°F**

1   pound carrots, peeled and cut into 2-inch pieces
1   pounds sweet potatoes, peeled and cut into chunks
1   large red onion, peeled, halved, and cut into 1-inch wedges
1   pound red or russet potatoes, cut into cubes
6   cloves garlic, minced
1   16-ounce can chickpeas (garbanzo beans), rinsed and drained
2   to 3 tablespoons vegetable oil
1   teaspoon dried rosemary, crushed
1   teaspoon packed brown sugar or granulated sugar
½   teaspoon kosher salt
½   teaspoon freshly ground black pepper

1. Position oven rack in center of oven. Preheat oven to 425°F. Place all vegetables, garlic, and chickpeas in a large shallow roasting pan. In a small bowl combine oil, rosemary, brown sugar, salt, and pepper. Drizzle over vegetables; toss well to coat.
2. Roast, uncovered, about 45 minutes or until vegetables are lightly browned and tender, stirring twice. Makes 8 servings.

EACH SERVING *223 cal, 4 g fat, 0 g chol, 301 mg sodium, 42 g carb, 7 g fiber, 6 g pro.*

Creamy Green Beans with Crispy Shallots

PREP **30 minutes**   COOK **15 minutes**
BAKE **45 minutes at 350°F**

2   pounds green beans, trimmed, cut into 3-inch pieces
6   tablespoons unsalted butter (¾ stick)
1   onion, diced
1   pounds button mushrooms, cleaned and sliced
¼   cup all-purpose flour
2½   cups milk
2   teaspoons sea salt
½   teaspoon freshly ground black pepper
2   gratings of fresh nutmeg

**CREAMY GREEN
BEANS WITH CRISPY
SHALLOTS**

Roasted Sweets and Greens

PREP 10 minutes
ROAST 35 minutes at 400°F

1½ to 2 pounds sweet potatoes,
   scrubbed
1 tablespoon olive oil
½ teaspoon salt
¼ teaspoon ground black pepper
2 cloves garlic, sliced or minced
¼ cup chopped hazelnuts
2 cups arugula
¼ cup cider vinegar

1. Preheat oven to 400°F. Cut sweet
potatoes in half lengthwise, then cut
into wedges. Place on a large rimmed
baking sheet. Toss with oil and season
with salt and pepper.
2. Roast for 15 minutes, toss, then
roast 15 minutes more or until tender.
Sprinkle with chopped garlic and
hazelnuts. Return to oven for 5 minutes
or until nuts are toasted and garlic
is softened. Remove from oven and
sprinkle with arugula and vinegar.
Makes 4 servings.
EACH SERVING *236 cal, 9 g fat, 0 mg chol,
387 mg sodium, 37 g carb, 6 g fiber, 4 g pro.*

Corn and Broccoli Bake

PREP 20 minutes
BAKE 35 minutes at 350°F

1 10-ounce package frozen cut
   broccoli
1 egg, lightly beaten
1 14.75-ounce can cream-style corn
⅔ cup crushed rich round crackers
⅛ teaspoon seasoned pepper
3 slices American cheese
   (0.75 ounce each), halved
1 cup crushed potato chips
2 tablespoons butter, melted

1. Preheat oven to 350°F. Place broccoli
in a colander and run cold water over
broccoli to separate. Drain well. In
a medium bowl combine egg, corn,
crushed crackers, and pepper. Stir in
broccoli.
2. Divide broccoli mixture among
six ungreased 6-ounce baking dishes.
Top with cheese. In a small bowl
combine crushed potato chips and
melted butter; sprinkle over broccoli
mixture.

3. Place baking dishes in a shallow
baking pan. Bake, uncovered, about
35 minutes or until heated through.
Makes 6 servings.
EACH SERVING *244 cal, 14 g fat, 55 mg chol,
528 mg sodium, 25 g carb, 2 g fiber, 7 g pro.*

Spicy Green Stir-Fry with Peanuts

START TO FINISH 25 minutes

¼ cup cold water
1 tablespoon reduced-sodium
   teriyaki sauce
½ teaspoon cornstarch
2 teaspoons peanut or sesame oil
1 teaspoon grated fresh ginger
⅓ cup lightly salted peanuts
⅛ teaspoon cayenne pepper or
   crushed red pepper
4 ounces fresh green beans,
   trimmed
½ large green or red sweet pepper,
   seeded and cut into thin bite-
   size strips
⅓ cup shelled frozen sweet
   soybeans (edamame), thawed
1 clove garlic, minced
2 baby bok choy, separated into
   leaves, or 3 cups coarsely
   shredded napa cabbage

1. In a small bowl stir together water,
teriyaki sauce, and cornstarch; set aside.
2. In a wok or large nonstick skillet heat
1 teaspoon oil over medium-high heat.
Add ginger; cook and stir 15 seconds.
Add peanuts; cook and stir 30 seconds.
Transfer peanuts to a small bowl.
Immediately sprinkle cayenne pepper
over peanuts; toss to coat. Set aside.
3. Heat remaining 1 teaspoon oil in the
wok or large nonstick skillet. Add green
beans; stir-fry for 3 minutes. Add green
pepper, edamame, and garlic. Stir-fry
for 3 minutes or until vegetables are
crisp-tender. Stir water mixture; add to
vegetables in wok. Cook and stir until
thickened and bubbly. Cook and stir
for 2 minutes more. Stir in bok choy or
cabbage.
4. Top with gingered peanuts before
serving. Makes 4 servings.
EACH SERVING *130 cal, 9 g fat, 0 mg chol,
142 mg sodium, 8 g carb, 3 g fiber, 6 g pro.*

SPICY GREEN STIR-FRY
WITH PEANUTS

SUMMER VEGETABLE POTATO SALAD

Summer Vegetable Potato Salad

START TO FINISH 35 minutes

- 1 pound small yellow or red new potatoes, sliced
- 2 fresh ears of sweet corn, cooked, or 1 cup frozen whole kernel corn, thawed
- 4 roma tomatoes, sliced or cut into thin wedges
- ¼ cup fresh basil leaves, torn
- ¼ cup olive oil
- 3 tablespoons balsamic vinegar
- 1 tablespoon finely chopped shallot or red onion
- ½ teaspoon Dijon mustard
- ¼ teaspoon sugar
  Salt and black pepper
- ½ cup crumbled feta cheese (2 ounces)
  Fresh basil leaves

1. In a medium saucepan cook potatoes, covered, in enough boiling salted water to cover for 5 minutes or just until tender. Drain and cool. Cut corn from cobs. On a large serving platter arrange potatoes and tomatoes. Sprinkle with corn and the ¼ cup basil.

2. For dressing, in a screw-top jar combine oil, vinegar, shallot, mustard, sugar, salt, and pepper to taste. Cover and shake well. Pour dressing over salad. Sprinkle with feta cheese and basil leaves. Makes 8 to 10 servings.

EACH SERVING *530 cal, 25 g fat, 44 mg chol, 1,017 mg sodium, 60 g carb, 9 g fiber, 17 g pro.*

Shoestring Sweet Potatoes and Beets

PREP 30 minutes   COOK 2 minutes per batch

- 2 small sweet potatoes
- 1 medium beet
- 1 teaspoon coarse salt
  Vegetable oil for deep-frying
  Thyme sprigs with tender stems (optional)
  Coarse salt (optional)

1. Peel sweet potatoes and beet. Cut lengthwise into long narrow strips. Place each vegetable in separate bowls; toss each with ½ teaspoon coarse salt.
2. In a 4-quart Dutch oven or deep-fryer heat 2 to 3 inches of oil to 365°F. To prevent splattering, spread beet strips on a paper towel and pat dry.

Carefully add beet strips and potatoes, about one-fourth at a time, to the hot oil. Fry about 2 minutes per batch or until crisp and golden brown, stirring gently once or twice. Using a slotted spoon, carefully remove fries from hot oil to paper towels to drain. If desired, add thyme sprigs to hot oil with the vegetables (CAUTION: Thyme sprigs will spatter briefly when added to the oil.) Transfer to platter; sprinkle with additional coarse salt if desired. Makes 8 servings.

EACH SERVING *203 cal, 20 g fat, 0 mg chol, 261 mg sodium, 5 g carb, 1 g fiber, 0 g pro.*

Roasted Potato Salad With Chutney Dressing

PREP 25 minutes
ROAST 25 minutes at 425°F

- 3 medium potatoes
- 3 tablespoons olive oil
- ½ teaspoon kosher salt or salt
- ¼ teaspoon cayenne pepper (optional)
- ½ cup mango chutney
- 1 to 2 tablespoons lemon juice
- 1 teaspoon curry powder
- 2 cups lightly packed fresh baby spinach
  Pine nuts, toasted (optional)

1. Preheat oven to 425°F. Scrub potatoes and cut into ¾- to 1-inch pieces. In a 3-quart baking pan combine potatoes, 2 tablespoons of the oil, the salt, and cayenne pepper (if using). Toss to coat. Roast, uncovered, for 25 minutes or until potatoes are tender, stirring occasionally.
2. Meanwhile, for chutney dressing, snip any large pieces of chutney. In a small bowl combine chutney, remaining olive oil, the lemon juice, and curry powder. Add half the chutney dressing to hot potatoes. Toss to coat. Add spinach to hot potato mixture; toss gently. If desired, sprinkle with pine nuts. Serve with remaining chutney dressing. Makes 8 to 10 servings.

EACH SERVING *125 cal, 5 g fat, 0 mg chol, 264 mg sodium, 18 g carb, 1 g fiber, 1 g pro.*

SHOESTRING
SWEET POTATOES
AND BEETS

MASHED SWEET POTATOES WITH WHITE CHEDDAR

Mashed Sweet Potatoes with White Cheddar

PREP 40 minutes BAKE 40 minutes
at 425°F/30 minutes 325°F
COOK 5 minutes

  3 pounds sweet potatoes
  ¼ cup butter
  1 teaspoon kosher salt or salt
  3 ounces aged white cheddar
      cheese, shredded
  ¼ cup bourbon or orange juice
  ¼ cup whipping cream
  ¼ cup packed dark brown sugar
  1 large red onion, cut into thin
      wedges
  2 medium red apples, cored and
      cut into narrow wedges
  2 teaspoons snipped fresh thyme
  ¼ teaspoon black pepper

1. Preheat oven to 425°F. Scrub
potatoes and prick with a fork; place
on foil-lined baking sheet. Bake for
40 minutes or until tender. Remove
from oven. Reduce oven temperature
to 325°F.
2. Butter a 1½-quart baking dish;
set aside. When potatoes are cool
enough to handle, scrape flesh from
skin. Transfer to bowl. Mash with
2 tablespoons of the butter and
¾ teaspoon of the salt. Stir in cheese,
bourbon, cream, and 2 tablespoons of
the brown sugar. Spoon into prepared
dish. Cover; bake for 30 minutes or
until heated through.
3. Meanwhile, in microwave-safe
2-quart casserole combine remaining
butter, brown sugar, and salt; add
onion. Cook, uncovered, on high for
3 minutes or until onion is crisp-tender;
add apples. Cover and cook 2 minutes
more or until apple is tender. Stir in
thyme and pepper. Serve over sweet
potatoes. Makes 8 servings.
EACH SERVING *293 cal, 12 g fat, 37 mg
chol, 421 mg sodium, 38 g carb, 5 g fiber,
5 g pro.*

TUSCAN CHEESE-POTATO BAKE

Tuscan Cheese-Potato Bake

PREP 30 minutes
BAKE 20 minutes at 400°F

  2 pounds red potatoes
  ¼ cup butter
  3 cloves garlic, minced
  1½ teaspoons snipped fresh thyme
      or ½ teaspoon dried thyme
  1 cup buttermilk
  ½ teaspoon salt
  ¼ teaspoon black pepper
  1 cup shredded fontina cheese
  1 cup finely shredded Parmesan
      cheese
  ⅓ cup crumbled blue cheese
  ½ cup panko (Japanese-style bread
      crumbs)
  ¼ teaspoon dried Italian
      seasoning, crushed
  1 tablespoon olive oil
      Snipped fresh parsley (optional)

1. Preheat oven to 400°F. Lightly grease
a 2-quart baking dish; set aside. Scrub
potatoes; cut into 1-inch pieces. In a
large saucepan cook potatoes in enough
boiling, lightly salted water to cover for
12 minutes or until tender; drain.
2. In an extra-large skillet melt butter
over medium heat. Add garlic and
thyme; cook and stir for 1 minute.
Add potatoes; coarsely mash with a
potato masher. Stir in buttermilk, salt,
and pepper. Fold in fontina cheese,
½ cup of the Parmesan cheese, and the
blue cheese. Transfer mixture to the
prepared baking dish, spreading evenly.
3. In a small bowl combine the
remaining ½ cup Parmesan cheese,
panko, and Italian seasoning. Drizzle
with oil; toss gently to combine.
Sprinkle evenly over potato mixture.
4. Bake, uncovered, about 20 minutes
or until mixture is bubbly and top is
golden brown. If desired, sprinkle with
parsley. Makes 8 servings.
EACH SERVING *304 cal, 18 g fat, 47 mg
chol, 653 mg sodium, 23 g carb, 2 g fiber,
14 g pro.*

CHEESE AND VEGETABLE RICE CASSEROLE

Buttermilk Mashed Creamers

PREP 15 minutes COOK 30 minutes
STAND 5 minutes

- 2 pounds Yukon gold or russet potatoes
- 6 tablespoons unsalted butter
- ½ cup well-shaken buttermilk
  Sea salt and freshly ground black pepper

1. Peel potatoes. Cut any large potatoes in half so potatoes are uniform size. Place potatoes in a large saucepan and cover with 2 inches of cold water. Bring to low boiling over medium-high heat. Cover, reduce heat, and simmer about 30 minutes, until potatoes are tender when pierced with the tip of a small knife.
2. Drain potatoes, then return to saucepan. Add unsalted butter; cover and let stand until butter is melted. Add buttermilk; mash with a potato masher or whip with electric beaters until creamy and butter and buttermilk are incorporated. Season to taste with salt and pepper. Makes 8 servings.
EACH SERVING *175 cal, 9 g fat, 24 mg chol, 68 mg sodium, 22 g carb, 2 g fiber, 3 g pro.*

Cheese and Vegetable Rice Casserole

PREP 20 minutes BAKE 35 minutes
at 350°F STAND 10 minutes

- 1 16-ounce package frozen broccoli, cauliflower, and carrots, thawed
- 4 cups cooked rice
- 1 15-ounce can black beans, rinsed and drained
- 1 12-ounce jar roasted sweet red peppers, drained and coarsely chopped
- 1 cup frozen whole kernel corn, thawed
- 2 4-ounce cans diced green chiles, drained
- 2 cups shredded cheddar cheese
- 1¼ cups chicken broth
- ½ cup seasoned fine dry bread crumbs
- 2 tablespoons butter, melted

1. Preheat oven to 350°F. Lightly grease a 3-quart baking dish; set aside.
2. In a large bowl stir together mixed vegetables, cooked rice, beans, roasted peppers, corn, and chiles. Stir in 1 cup of the cheese and the broth. Spoon into prepared baking dish. Sprinkle with the remaining 1 cup cheese.
3. In a small bowl combine bread crumbs and melted butter. Sprinkle over casserole.
4. Bake, uncovered, for 35 to 40 minutes or until casserole is heated through and crumbs are golden brown. Let stand for 10 minutes before serving. Makes 6 servings.
EACH SERVING *471 cal, 18 g fat, 50 mg chol, 1,423 mg sodium, 60 g carb, 8 g fiber, 21 g pro.*

Skillet Corn

START TO FINISH 35 minutes

- 4 slices bacon
- 2 cups fresh or frozen corn kernels
- 1 cup frozen shelled sweet soybeans (edamame)
- 1 cup grape or cherry tomatoes, halved
- ½ small red onion, thinly sliced
- 2 tablespoons snipped fresh cilantro
- 1 small fresh jalapeño, seeded and finely chopped (see tip, page 35)
- 1 tablespoon olive oil
- ½ teaspoon finely shredded lime peel
- 1 tablespoon lime juice
- 2 cloves garlic, minced
- ¼ teaspoon ground cumin
- ⅛ teaspoon salt
- ⅛ teaspoon chili powder

1. In a large skillet cook bacon over medium heat until crisp. Remove bacon and drain on paper towels, reserving 2 tablespoons of the drippings in skillet. Discard the remaining drippings. Crumble bacon; set aside. Add corn and soybeans to the reserved drippings. Cook and stir for 3 minutes or just until corn and beans are crisp-tender.
2. In a large bowl stir together crumbled bacon, corn and soybeans, tomatoes, red onion, cilantro, and jalapeño.
3. For dressing, in a screw-top jar combine oil, lime peel, lime juice, garlic, cumin, salt, and chili powder. Cover and shake well. Pour dressing over corn mixture; toss gently to coat. Makes 6 servings.
EACH SERVING *182 cal, 11 g fat, 9 mg chol, 160 mg sodium, 17 g carb, 3 g fiber, 7 g pro.*

CORN-ON-THE-COB
PUDDING

Corn-on-the-Cob Pudding

PREP 30 minutes   CHILL 2 hours
BAKE 45 minutes at 350°F
STAND 10 minutes

½ cup finely chopped onion
1 tablespoon olive oil
1 cup frozen whole kernel corn, thawed
6 cups 1-inch cubes crusty country Italian bread
2 fresh jalapeños, seeded and finely chopped (see tip, page 35)
2 cups fat-free milk
1 cup refrigerated or frozen egg product, thawed, or 4 eggs, lightly beaten

1. Lightly grease a 2-quart baking dish; set aside. In a large skillet cook onion in hot oil over medium heat for 3 minutes or until tender, stirring occasionally. Stir in corn. Cook and stir for 2 minutes more. Cool slightly.

2. In a large bowl combine corn mixture, bread cubes, and jalapeños. In a medium bowl combine milk and egg. Pour milk mixture over bread mixture; stir gently to combine. Transfer pudding to prepared baking dish. Cover and chill for 2 to 24 hours.

3. Preheat oven to 350°F. Bake, uncovered, about 45 minutes or until center is set and top is lightly browned. Let stand for 10 minutes before serving. Makes 12 servings.

EACH SERVING *136 cal, 2 g fat, 1 mg chol, 225 mg sodium, 22 g carb, 2 g fiber, 7 g pro.*

Boston Baked Beans with Pancetta

PREP 30 minutes   STAND 1 hour
COOK 1 hour   BAKE 1½ hours at 300°F

8 ounces Great Northern beans or dried navy beans
3 ounces pancetta or bacon, chopped
½ cup chopped onion
2 tablespoons packed brown sugar
2 tablespoons pure maple syrup
2 tablespoons Worcestershire sauce
¾ teaspoon dry mustard
¼ teaspoon salt
⅛ teaspoon black pepper
2 ounces pancetta or bacon, chopped, crisp-cooked, and drained (optional)

BOSTON BAKED BEANS WITH PANCETTA

1. Rinse beans. In a 4- to 5-quart Dutch oven combine beans and 4 cups water. Bring to boiling; reduce heat. Simmer, uncovered, for 2 minutes. Remove from heat. Cover and let stand for 1 hour. (Or combine beans and 4 cups water in Dutch oven. Cover and let soak in a cool place overnight.) Drain and rinse beans.
2. Return beans to Dutch oven. Stir in 8 cups fresh water. Bring to boiling; reduce heat. Cover and simmer for 1 to 1¼ hours or until beans are tender, stirring occasionally. Drain beans, reserving liquid.
3. Preheat oven to 300°F. In the same Dutch oven cook the 3 ounces pancetta and the onion over medium heat until pancetta is slightly crisp and onion is tender, stirring occasionally. Add brown sugar; cook and stir until sugar is dissolved. Stir in maple syrup, Worcestershire sauce, dry mustard, salt, and pepper. Stir in drained beans and ¾ cup of the reserved bean liquid.
4. Bake, covered, for 1 hour. Uncover and bake for 30 to 45 minutes more or until desired consistency, stirring occasionally. Beans will thicken slightly as they cool. If necessary, stir in additional reserved bean liquid. If making 6 individual servings, use six 8-ounce ramekins. If desired, sprinkle with cooked pancetta. Makes 6 servings.

EACH SERVING *275 cal, 6 g fat, 12 mg chol, 507 mg sodium, 44 g carb, 7 g fiber, 12 g pro.*

BBQ White Beans with Peppers

PREP **25 minutes** CHILL **overnight**

1 medium green sweet pepper
4 ounces cooked ham, cut into strips

BBQ WHITE BEANS WITH PEPPERS

1 tablespoon vegetable oil
1 large onion, chopped (1 cup)
3 cloves garlic, minced
2 15-ounce cans cannellini beans (white kidney beans) and/or navy beans, rinsed and drained
2 tablespoons yellow mustard
2 tablespoons cider vinegar
2 tablespoons pure maple syrup
1 tablespoon Worcestershire sauce
   Crushed red pepper (optional)
   Fresh oregano leaves (optional)

1. Slice 2 rings from sweet pepper; wrap and refrigerate. Chop remaining pepper; set aside. In a skillet cook ham in hot oil over medium-high heat until browned; remove from skillet. Add onion and garlic to skillet. Cook and stir 3 minutes or until tender.
2. In a 1½-quart casserole combine beans, ham, onion and garlic mixture, chopped sweet pepper, mustard, vinegar, maple syrup, Worcestershire sauce, and crushed red pepper to taste. Cover and refrigerate overnight.
3. Stir 2 tablespoons water into beans. Reheat over medium heat for about 5 minutes or until heated through, adding the pepper rings for the last 2 minutes of reheating. If desired, sprinkle with crushed red pepper and fresh oregano. Makes 6 to 8 servings.

EACH SERVING *169 cal, 5 g fat, 11 mg chol, 565 mg sodium, 29 g carb, 8 g fiber, 12 g pro.*

ROSY BEET
RISOTTO

Rosy Beet Risotto

PREP 15 minutes
ROAST 1 hour 15 minutes at 350°F
COOL 30 minutes COOK 25 minutes

    12 ounces beets
     3 tablespoons olive oil
    ½   cup chopped red onion
    1½ cups Arborio or short grain rice
     2 tablespoons snipped fresh
        basil or 1 teaspoon dried basil,
        crushed
     2 14.5-ounce cans reduced-sodium
        chicken broth
    ½   cup crumbled blue cheese
        Salt and freshly ground black
        pepper
        Fresh basil leaves

1. Preheat oven to 350°F. Place beets in center of an 18-inch square of heavy foil. Drizzle with 1 tablespoon olive oil. Fold together opposite edges of foil in double folds, allowing room for steam to build. Roast 1 hour and 15 minutes or until tender. Cool 30 minutes. Carefully open packet. Remove beets; gently transfer liquid to measuring cup; add water to equal ½ cup; pour into a medium saucepan. Cut beets into wedges; set aside.
2. In a 3-quart saucepan cook onion in remaining oil over medium heat until tender; add rice. Cook and stir 5 minutes. Stir in dried basil if using.
3. Carefully stir 1 cup of hot broth into rice mixture. Cook, stirring constantly, over medium heat until liquid is absorbed. Then add ½ cup broth at a time, stirring constantly until broth is absorbed before adding more broth (about 22 minutes).
4. Stir in any remaining broth. Cook and stir just until rice is tender and creamy.
5. Add beets; heat through. Remove risotto from heat; stir in half the cheese, snipped basil (if using), and salt and pepper to taste. Sprinkle with remaining cheese and basil leaves. Makes 6 servings.
EACH SERVING 185 cal, 7 g fat, 5 mg chol, 441 mg sodium, 26 g carb, 1 g fiber, 5 g pro.

RICE-VERMICELLI PILAF

Rice-Vermicelli Pilaf

START TO FINISH 30 minutes

     1 cup long grain white rice
    ½   cup finely broken (½- to ¾-inch
        pieces) dried angel hair pasta
    ⅓   cup finely chopped onion
     3 tablespoons butter
     1 14.5-ounce can chicken or beef
        broth
    ¼   cup water
    ¼   teaspoon salt
    ¼   teaspoon black pepper
        Snipped fresh basil, dill, and/or
        crisp-cooked crumbled bacon

1. In a medium saucepan cook rice, angel hair pasta, and onion in hot butter over medium heat for 4 minutes or until pasta is lightly browned and onion is nearly tender. Carefully add broth, water, salt, and pepper; bring to boiling. Reduce heat. Simmer, covered, for 15 minutes or until the rice is tender and broth is absorbed.
2. Fluff pilaf with a fork. Sprinkle with basil before serving. Makes 4 servings.
EACH SERVING 336 cal, 9 g fat, 24 mg chol, 607 mg sodium, 55 g carb, 1 g fiber, 7 g pro.

Easy Coconut Rice

PREP 10 minutes
BAKE 30 minutes at 350°F
STAND 5 minutes

     1 cup long grain rice (such as
        basmati or jasmine)
    ½   cup frozen peas, thawed
    1¼ cups water
    ¾   cup unsweetened coconut milk
    ½   teaspoon salt
    ¼   teaspoon ground cinnamon

1. Preheat oven to 350°F. Place rice and peas in a lightly buttered 2-quart casserole or baking dish.
2. In a small saucepan combine the water, coconut milk, salt, and cinnamon; bring to boiling. Pour boiling liquid over rice. Bake, covered, about 30 minutes or until rice is tender. Let stand for 5 minutes. Stir before serving. Makes 4 servings.
EACH SERVING 258 cal, 9 g fat, 0 mg chol, 318 mg sodium, 40 g carb, 1 g fiber, 5 g pro.

SPANISH RICE

SUCCOTASH

Spanish Rice

PREP 25 minutes   COOK 20 minutes
STAND 5 minutes

    4   slices bacon, chopped
    1   cup coarsely chopped onion
    ¾   cups coarsely chopped green
        sweet pepper
    1   clove garlic, minced
    1   14.5-ounce can diced tomatoes
    ½   teaspoon black pepper
    ¼   teaspoon cayenne pepper
    1   cup uncooked jasmine, basmati,
        or long grain rice
    2   teaspoons olive oil
    ½   teaspoon salt
    2   cups water
    ¼   cup chopped green olives
        (optional)
    1   cup shredded cheddar cheese

1. In a large skillet cook bacon until crisp. Remove bacon from skillet; drain on paper towels. Remove all but 1 tablespoon bacon drippings from the skillet. Add onion, sweet pepper, and garlic to skillet. Cook and stir over medium heat for 7 minutes or until tender. Add undrained tomatoes, black pepper, and cayenne pepper. Bring to boiling; reduce heat. Simmer, covered, for 20 minutes.
2. Meanwhile, in a large saucepan stir together rice, olive oil, and salt. Add water. Bring to boiling, stirring occasionally. Reduce heat to low and simmer, covered, about 15 minutes or until rice is tender.

3. Stir the cooked rice, cooked bacon, and, if desired, chopped olives into tomato mixture. Sprinkle with shredded cheddar cheese. Cover and let stand about 5 minutes or until cheese is melted. Makes 6 servings.
EACH SERVING *273 cal, 12 g fat, 28 mg chol, 577 mg sodium, 32 g carb, 2 g fiber, 9 g pro.*

Succotash

START TO FINISH 25 minutes

    4   cups frozen lima beans
    ¼   cup butter
    4   cups fresh corn kernels or frozen
        whole kernel corn
    ½   teaspoon salt
    ¼   teaspoon black pepper
    ½   cup whipping cream
    ½   cup diced cooked ham or
        crisp-cooked, crumbled bacon

1. Cook lima beans according to package directions; drain and set aside.
2. Heat butter in a large skillet over medium heat. Add corn, salt, and pepper. Cook and stir for 2 minutes. Add drained beans. Cook and stir for 1 minute.
3. Add cream and ham. Bring to boiling; reduce heat. Simmer, uncovered, about 2 minutes or until cream thickens slightly. Makes 6 servings.
EACH SERVING *182 cal, 9 g fat, 27 mg chol, 207 mg sodium, 22 g carb, 4 g fiber, 6 g pro.*

Walnut-Lemon Rice Pilaf

START TO FINISH 25 minutes

    ½   cup coarsely chopped walnuts
    1   small yellow sweet pepper, cut
        in bite-size strips
    ½   small red onion, cut into slivers
    2   cloves garlic, minced
    2   teaspoons olive oil
    1   8.8-ounce pouch cooked brown
        rice
    ¼   cup coarsely chopped fresh
        parsley
    ½   teaspoon finely shredded lemon
        peel
    2   tablespoons lemon juice
    ¼   teaspoon salt

1. In a large dry skillet heat walnuts over medium heat for 3 minutes or until lightly toasted, stirring frequently. Remove from skillet; set aside. In the same skillet cook sweet pepper, onion, and garlic in hot oil over medium heat 5 minutes or just until tender, stirring occasionally.
2. Add rice to skillet. Cook and stir to heat through. Stir in nuts, parsley, lemon peel and juice, and salt. Makes 4 servings.
EACH SERVING *238 cal, 14 g fat, 0 mg chol, 152 mg sodium, 26 g carb, 2 g fiber, 5 g pro.*

**WALNUT-LEMON
RICE PILAF**

WALDORF SALAD

CREAMY CUCUMBERS

MAPLE BAKED
STUFFED PEARS

Waldorf Salad

START TO FINISH 20 minutes

- 4 cups chopped apples and/or pears
- 4 teaspoons lemon juice
- ½ cup chopped celery
- ½ cup chopped walnuts or pecans, toasted (see tip, page 31)
- ½ cup raisins, snipped pitted whole dates, or dried tart cherries
- ½ cup seedless green grapes, halved
- ⅔ cup mayonnaise or salad dressing

1. In a large bowl toss apples with lemon juice. Stir in celery, nuts, raisins, and grapes. Stir in mayonnaise until combined. Serve immediately or cover and chill up to 8 hours. Makes 8 servings.

EACH SERVING *245 cal, 20 g fat, 7 mg chol, 107 mg sodium, 18 g carb, 2 g fiber, 2 g pro.*

Creamy Cucumbers

PREP 15 minutes CHILL 4 hours

- ½ cup sour cream or plain yogurt
- 1 tablespoon vinegar
- ½ teaspoon salt
- ¼ teaspoon dried dill
  Dash black pepper
- 3 cups cucumber, peeled, halved lengthwise, and thinly sliced
- ⅓ cup thinly sliced red onion

1. In a medium bowl combine sour cream, vinegar, salt, dill, and pepper. Add cucumber and onion; toss to coat. Cover and chill for 4 hours or up to

3 days, stirring occasionally. Stir before serving. Makes 6 servings.

EACH SERVING *45 cal, 3 g fat, 8 mg chol, 209 mg sodium, 4 g carb, 0 g fiber, 1 g pro.*

Italian Pasta Salad

START TO FINISH 25 minutes

- 4 ounces dried whole wheat rotini pasta, dried whole grain penne pasta, or dried bow tie pasta
- 1 cup fresh sugar snap peas, trimmed
- ½ cup chopped red sweet pepper
- ¼ cup shredded fresh basil
- 2 tablespoons pitted niçoise olives or pitted ripe olives, quartered
- 2 tablespoons red wine vinegar
- 2 tablespoons olive oil
- 1 clove garlic, minced
- ⅛ teaspoon salt
  Dash black pepper

1. Cook pasta according to package directions, adding the sugar snap peas for the last 1 minute of cooking. Drain well. Rinse well with cold water; drain again. In a large bowl combine pasta mixture, sweet pepper, basil, and olives. Set aside.
2. For dressing, in a screw-top jar combine red wine vinegar, olive oil, garlic, salt, and pepper. Cover and shake well. Pour dressing over pasta and vegetables; toss gently to combine. Makes 6 servings.

EACH SERVING *118 cal, 5 g fat, 0 mg chol, 75 mg sodium, 16 g carb, 2 g fiber, 3 g pro.*

Maple Baked Stuffed Pears

PREP 20 minutes
BAKE 40 minutes at 350°F

- 4 medium firm pears with stems
- ¼ cup dried cranberries or dried tart red cherries
- 3 tablespoons chopped walnuts, toasted (see tip, page 31)
- 1 tablespoon lemon juice
- 2½ teaspoons sugar
- ¼ cup water
- ¼ cup pure maple syrup

1. Preheat oven to 350°F. Cut a thin slice from the bottom of each pear so the pears stand up. Use a melon baller through the bottom of each pear to remove the core.
2. In a small bowl combine cranberries, walnuts, lemon juice, and sugar. Spoon cranberry mixture into the hollow bottoms of pears. Stand pears in an ungreased 2-quart baking dish. Add the water to baking dish. Pour maple syrup over and around pears. Sprinkle any remaining cranberry mixture into dish.
3. Bake, covered, for 20 minutes. Uncover; bake for 20 minutes more or until pears are tender, basting occasionally with cooking liquid.
4. To serve, spoon any cooking liquid over pears. If desired, cut pears in half, topping with filling from dish. Serve warm. Makes 4 servings.

EACH SERVING *219 cal, 4 g fat, 0 mg chol, 4 mg sodium, 49 g carb, 6 g fiber, 1 g pro.*

¼ cup honey
1 teaspoon finely shredded lime peel
½ cup coconut, toasted (see tip, page 31)
⅓ cup coarsely chopped macadamia nuts, toasted (see tip, page 31)

1. Place pineapple, papaya, kiwifruits, and mangoes in an extra-large resealable plastic bag. Add honey and lime peel. Seal bag and turn gently to coat.
2. Chill fruit for at least 1 hour or up to 48 hours before serving.
3. Transfer fruit to a large serving bowl. Before serving, sprinkle fruit with toasted coconut and macadamia nuts. Makes 12 servings.

EACH SERVING *142 cal, 5 g fat, 0 mg chol, 17 mg sodium, 26 g carb, 3 g fiber, 2 g pro.*

Corn and Blueberry Salad

PREP 25 minutes CHILL overnight

6 ears fresh sweet corn, husked
1 cup fresh blueberries
1 small cucumber, sliced
¼ cup finely chopped red onion
¼ cup chopped fresh cilantro
1 fresh jalapeño, seeded and finely chopped (see tip, page 35)
2 tablespoons lime juice
2 tablespoons olive oil
1 tablespoon honey
½ teaspoon ground cumin
½ teaspoon salt

1. In a Dutch oven bring salted water to boiling. Add corn. Cook, covered, for 5 minutes or until tender. When cool enough to handle, cut corn from cobs.
2. In a serving bowl combine corn, blueberries, cucumber, red onion, cilantro, and jalapeño. For dressing, in screw-top jar combine lime juice, oil, honey, cumin, and salt. Cover; shake well to combine. Add to salad; toss. Cover and refrigerate up to 24 hours. Makes 6 servings.

EACH SERVING *152 cal, 6 g fat, 0 mg chol, 211 mg sodium, 26 g carb, 3 g fiber, 4 g pro.*

Chunky Oven Applesauce

PREP 30 minutes
BAKE 45 minutes at 400°F

6 medium tart apples (such as McIntosh or Granny Smith), peeled, cored, and cut into ½- to 1-inch pieces
¼ cup packed brown sugar
2 tablespoons butter, cut up
2 tablespoons water
¼ teaspoon salt
5 star anise
½ cup fresh or frozen raspberries and/or blackberries, thawed

1. Preheat oven to 400°F. Place apples in an ungreased 2-quart casserole or baking dish. Stir in brown sugar, butter, the water, salt, and star anise. Cover tightly with foil. Bake for 45 minutes or until apples are tender, gently stirring once or twice (recover with foil after stirring).
2. Top with berries. Discard star anise. If desired, mash gently with a fork or carefully transfer applesauce to a food processor; pulse with several on/off turns until smooth. Serve warm, at room temperature, or chilled. Makes 10 servings.

EACH SERVING *102 cal, 2 g fat, 6 mg chol, 77 mg sodium, 21 g carb, 3 g fiber, 0 g pro.*

Tropical Fruit Bowl

PREP 30 minutes CHILL 1 hour

1 medium pineapple, peeled and cut into bite-size pieces
1 large papaya, halved, seeded, peeled, and cut into 1-inch cubes
4 kiwifruits, peeled and cut into bite-size pieces
2 mangoes, seeded, peeled, and cut into 1-inch cubes

**CORN AND
BLUEBERRY SALAD**

SESAME NOODLE SLAW

FENNEL SLAW

Sesame Noodle Slaw

PREP 20 minutes BAKE 10 minutes at 300°F CHILL 30 minutes

- 1 cup sliced almonds
- ¼ cup sesame seeds
- ⅔ cup vegetable oil
- ⅓ cup rice vinegar or cider vinegar
- ¼ cup reduced-sodium soy sauce
- 2 3-ounce packages chicken-flavor ramen noodles
- 2 teaspoons sugar
- ½ teaspoon black pepper
- 12 cups shredded cabbage or packaged coleslaw mix
- ⅔ cup thinly sliced green onions
- ⅔ cup golden raisins or raisins (optional)

1. Preheat oven to 300°F. Spread almonds and sesame seeds in a shallow baking pan. Bake about 10 minutes or until toasted, stirring once; cool.
2. Meanwhile, for dressing, in a screw-top jar combine oil, vinegar, soy sauce, seasoning packet from noodles, sugar, and pepper. Cover and shake well.
3. In a large bowl layer cabbage, green onions, raisins (if desired), and toasted almonds and sesame seeds. Break noodles into small pieces. Sprinkle onto salad.
4. Add dressing; toss gently to combine. Cover and refrigerate for 30 minutes or up to 4 hours. Makes 8 servings.
EACH SERVING 205 cal, 16 g fat, 0 mg chol, 349 mg sodium, 14 g carb, 3 g fiber, 4 g pro.

Fennel Slaw

PREP 25 minutes CHILL 1 hour

- 2 medium fennel bulbs
- 1 cup large green olives, pitted and sliced
- ⅓ cup chopped fresh parsley
- ⅓ cup olive oil
- 3 tablespoons red wine vinegar
- 4 cloves garlic, minced
- ¼ teaspoon salt
- ¼ teaspoon crushed red pepper

1. Trim any brown spots from fennel; cut a thin slice off base of bulbs. Discard green stems. Cut fennel in half lengthwise, then cut crosswise into thin slices.
2. In a large bowl combine fennel, olives, and parsley. In a small bowl whisk together oil, vinegar, garlic, salt, and crushed red pepper. Add to slaw; toss to coat. Cover and refrigerate 1 to 24 hours. Makes 8 servings.
EACH SERVING 128 cal, 12 g fat, 0 mg chol, 391 mg sodium, 6 g carb, 3 g fiber, 1 g pro.

Peach and Blackberry Slaw

START TO FINISH 30 minutes

- ¼ cup white wine vinegar
- ¼ cup olive oil
- 1 teaspoon sugar
- 1 tablespoon snipped fresh chives, basil, and/or tarragon
  Salt and black pepper
- 1 small head cabbage
- 2 white peaches
- 1 yellow peach
- ½ pint blackberries
- 2 ounces coarsely crumbled blue cheese (optional)
  Snipped fresh chives, basil, and/or tarragon

1. For the dressing, in a small bowl whisk together vinegar, olive oil, sugar, and the 1 tablespoon chives. Season to taste with salt and pepper; set aside.
2. Shred cabbage and place in a large bowl. Halve, pit, and thinly slice peaches and add to bowl with cabbage. Gently toss to combine. Drizzle with about half the dressing; toss to coat. Top with blackberries and, if desired, cheese. Sprinkle with herbs; pass remaining dressing. Makes 4 servings.
EACH SERVING 151 cal, 9 g fat, 0 mg chol, 116 mg sodium, 16 g carb, 5 g fiber, 2 g pro.

**PEACH AND
BLACKBERRY SLAW**

HERB SALAD WITH CREAMY LEMON DRESSING

SICILIAN ESCAROLE SALAD

TOMATO BREAD SALAD

Herb Salad with Creamy Lemon Dressing

START TO FINISH 20 minutes

- 2 medium lemons, peel finely shredded and juiced
- 3 cloves garlic, minced
- 2 teaspoons Dijon mustard
- ¼ teaspoon salt
- ¼ teaspoon black pepper
- ½ cup olive oil
- ½ cup sour cream
- 2 to 3 medium heads butterhead lettuce, torn, or 6 to 8 cups mixed baby salad greens
- 1½ cups assorted fresh herbs, such as chives, basil, parsley, or mint, torn
- 12 to 16 radishes, thinly sliced

1. For dressing, in a small bowl combine lemon peel and juice, garlic, mustard, salt, and pepper. Slowly whisk in oil until thickened. Whisk in sour cream.
2. Toss together lettuce and herbs; transfer to serving platter. Top with sliced radishes; pass dressing. Makes 6 servings.

EACH SERVING *215 cal, 22 g fat, 7 mg chol, 161 mg sodium, 5 g carb, 1 g fiber, 2 g pro.*

Sicilian Escarole Salad

START TO FINISH 20 minutes

- 3 tablespoons olive oil
- 1 tablespoon white wine vinegar
- ½ 2-ounce can anchovy filets, drained and chopped
- 1 cloves garlic, minced
- ¼ teaspoon dried basil
- ¼ teaspoon dried oregano, crushed
- ⅛ teaspoon salt
- ⅛ teaspoon crushed red pepper Dash black pepper
- 3 cups torn escarole
- 3 cups torn leaf lettuce
- 1 small English cucumber, quartered lengthwise and sliced into ½-inch chunks
- ½ cup pitted ripe olives or oil-cured black olives, chopped
- ½ cup thinly sliced red onion
- 1½ cups assorted stir-ins such as chopped roasted red sweet peppers, drained and rinsed cannellini beans, drained and flaked tuna (packed in oil), tomato slices, chopped salami, and cubed Asiago cheese

1. For dressing, in a screw-top jar combine oil, vinegar, anchovies, garlic, basil, oregano, salt, red pepper, and black pepper. Cover; shake well.
2. In an extra-large salad bowl combine escarole, lettuce, cucumber, olives, and onion. Add desired stir-ins. Just before serving, pour dressing over salad and toss well. Makes 6 servings.

EACH SERVING *93 cal, 8 g fat, 0 g chol, 319 mg sodium, 4 g carb, 2 g fiber, 2 g pro.*

Tomato Bread Salad

PREP 35 minutes   CHILL overnight
BAKE 10 minutes at 400°F

- 4 medium roma tomatoes, cut into 1-inch chunks
- ½ medium red onion, cut in thin wedges (½ cup)
- 1 medium yellow sweet pepper, cut into 1-inch pieces
- ¼ cup olive oil
- ¼ cup red wine vinegar
- 1 tablespoon Dijon mustard
- ½ teaspoon Italian seasoning, crushed
- 8 ounces ciabatta or focaccia bread, cut into 1-inch pieces
- 1 tablespoon olive oil
- 1 cup small fresh basil leaves White cheddar cheese shavings (optional)

1. In a large serving bowl combine tomatoes, onion, and sweet pepper. In a screw-top jar combine ¼ cup olive oil, the red wine vinegar, mustard, Italian seasoning, ½ teaspoon *salt*, and ¼ teaspoon *black pepper*. Cover; shake well to combine. Add to vegetables; stir to coat. Cover and refrigerate overnight (up to 24 hours).
2. Preheat oven to 400°F. In a shallow baking pan toss bread cubes with 1 tablespoon olive oil to coat. Bake about 10 minutes or until toasted, stirring once. Remove and cool on pan. Add bread cubes and basil to salad; toss to combine. If desired, top with shaved cheese. Makes 6 servings.

EACH SERVING *225 cal, 13 g fat, 0 mg chol, 453 mg sodium, 23 g carb, 3 g fiber, 5 g pro.*

BEET, CARROT, AND APPLE SALAD

Sweet Potato Spoon Bread

PREP 25 minutes
BAKE 45 minutes at 400°F/35 minutes at 350°F STAND 10 minutes

- 4 tablespoons unsalted butter (½ stick), melted
- 2 medium sweet potatoes (about 1 pound)
- 2½ cups milk
- 1 tablespoon fresh thyme
- 1 tablespoon light brown sugar
- 2 teaspoons coarse sea salt
- ½ teaspoon freshly ground black pepper
- 1 cup finely ground white or yellow cornmeal
- 4 large eggs, separated
- 2 teaspoons baking powder

1. Preheat oven to 400°F. Generously grease a 2-quart soufflé or casserole with 1 tablespoon of the butter.
2. Wrap potatoes in foil. Bake for about 45 minutes or until soft to touch. Remove from oven. Discard foil; cool. When cool enough to handle, remove and discard peels. In a large bowl mash potatoes.
3. Reduce oven to 350°F. In a large saucepan bring milk, thyme, sugar, salt, and pepper to a low boil over medium heat. In a slow steady stream whisk cornmeal into milk mixture. Cook, whisking constantly, about 4 minutes or until mixture is thick and pulls away from bottom of pan. Remove from heat; cool slightly. Add potatoes, egg yolks, remaining 3 tablespoons butter, and baking powder to milk mixture; stir to thoroughly mix.
4. In a large mixing bowl beat egg whites with electric mixer until soft peaks form. Gently fold whites into the potato mixture.
5. Spoon batter into prepared dish. Bake about 35 minutes or until internal temperature reaches 165°F. Edges will be firm and the center a little soft. Remove from oven. Let stand 10 minutes. Serve warm. Makes 8 servings.
EACH SERVING *234 cal, 10 g fat, 127 mg chol, 576 mg sodium, 28 g carb, 1 g fiber, 8 g pro.*

Beet, Carrot, and Apple Salad

START TO FINISH 45 minutes

- 1 orange, zested and juiced
- 1 lime, zested and juiced
- 2 tablespoons sherry vinegar
- ¾ cup extra virgin olive oil
  Sea salt and freshly ground black pepper
- 1 pounds beets, peeled and cut into matchsticks*
- 2 large carrots, peeled and cut into matchsticks*
- 1 Granny Smith apple, cored, peeled, and cut into matchsticks*
- 1 turnip, peeled and cut into matchsticks*
- 1 bunch parsley, stems removed (optional)

1. In a large bowl combine orange zest and juice, lime zest and juice, and vinegar. Slowly whisk in the olive oil and season with salt and pepper to taste.
2. Layer beets, carrots, apple, and turnip in bowl. Season with additional salt and pepper to taste. Toss salad just before serving. If desired, sprinkle with parsley. Makes 8 servings.
*To cut matchsticks, use a mandoline or food processor fitted with a julienne blade or large shredding blade.
EACH SERVING *118 cal, 10 g fat, 0 mg chol, 87 mg sodium, 7 g carb, 2 g fiber, 1 g pro.*

SWEET POTATO
SPOON BREAD

**BRUSCHETTA
BISCUITS WITH FETA**

Bruschetta Biscuits with Feta

PREP 30 minutes
BAKE 15 minutes at 425°F

- ¾ cup milk
- ⅓ cup olive oil
- 1 cup fresh baby spinach leaves, chopped
- ¼ cup fresh basil leaves, chopped
- ¼ cup dried tomatoes (not oil-packed), chopped
- ¼ cup pitted Kalamata olives, chopped
- 2 cups all-purpose flour
- 2 teaspoons baking powder
- ½ teaspoon salt
- 3 tablespoons crumbled feta cheese
- 1 tablespoon pine nuts

1. Preheat oven to 425°F. Line a baking sheet with parchment paper. In a bowl combine milk, oil, spinach, basil, tomatoes, and olives. In a large bowl combine flour, baking powder, and salt. Make a well in center of flour mixture. Add milk mixture all at once; stir with a fork until moistened.
2. On a lightly floured surface gently knead dough until it holds together. Pat into an 8×8-inch square. Cut into nine squares.
3. Place biscuits 1 inch apart on prepared baking sheet. Brush lightly with milk. Sprinkle with feta cheese and pine nuts. Bake 15 minutes or until golden. Cool slightly before serving. Makes 9 biscuits.

EACH BISCUIT *210 cal, 11 g fat, 5 mg chol, 332 mg sodium, 24 g carb, 1 g fiber, 5 g pro.*

Double-Cheddar Biscuits

PREP 20 minutes
BAKE 15 minutes at 425°F

- 2½ cups unbleached all-purpose flour, sifted before measuring
- 2 teaspoons baking powder
- 1¼ teaspoons kosher salt
- ½ teaspoon sugar
  Dash cayenne pepper
- ½ cup shredded extra-sharp white cheddar cheese, at room temperature (about 2 ounces)
- ½ cup shredded sharp orange cheddar cheese, at room temperature (about 2 ounces)
- 3 tablespoons cold unsalted butter, cut into ½-inch pieces
- 1 cup heavy cream
- 2 tablespoons buttermilk

1. Preheat oven to 425°F. Line a baking sheet with foil. In a large mixing bowl whisk together flour, baking powder, salt, sugar, and cayenne. With fingers, work in grated cheeses. Add the cold butter. Quickly rub butter into flour texture with fingers until mixture resembles oatmeal with some large marble-size pieces.
2. Stir in cream; add buttermilk and stir just until absorbed. Dough will look chunky and dry at this point. Turn out onto a lightly floured board. Use your hands to press and knead to a cohesive dough.
3. Roll to ½-inch thickness. Cut out 2½-inch rounds and place ½ inch apart on prepared baking sheet. Gather scraps, reroll, cut out, and place on baking sheet. Dip fork in flour, then prick three sets of evenly spaced holes on each biscuit.
4. Bake on center rack for 15 minutes or until well browned, rotating pans if needed to ensure even browning. Cool slightly before serving. Makes 12 to 14 biscuits.

EACH BISCUIT *197 cal, 12 g fat, 39 mg chol, 259 mg sodium, 18 g carb, 1 g fiber, 5 g pro.*

DOUBLE-CHEDDAR BISCUITS

Crisp Cornmeal Scones

PREP 15 minutes
BAKE 12 minutes at 425°F

- 2 cups all-purpose flour
- 1 cup yellow cornmeal
- 2 tablespoons granulated sugar
- 1½ teaspoons baking powder
- ½ teaspoon salt
- ½ cup cold butter, coarsely shredded or cubed
- 1 cup buttermilk
  Buttermilk
  Coarse sugar

1. Preheat oven to 425°F. In a large bowl whisk together flour, cornmeal, granulated sugar, baking powder, and salt.
2. Add shredded butter to flour mixture; toss to distribute. (Or cut cubed butter into flour mixture with pastry blender to resemble coarse crumbs.) Make a well in center of flour-butter mixture. Add 1 cup buttermilk; stir with spoon until moistened. Do not overmix. (If dough appears dry, add 1 to 2 tablespoons additional buttermilk.)

3. Turn dough out onto floured surface. Gently knead by lifting and folding dough, 4 or 5 times, turning one-quarter after each knead. Roll into 8-inch square, ¾-inch thickness. Cut into 1½- to 2-inch squares. Place squares 1 inch apart on ungreased baking sheet. Brush with buttermilk; sprinkle with coarse sugar. Bake 12 minutes or until lightly browned; cool scones on rack. Serve warm. Makes 16 scones.
EACH SCONE *155 cal, 6 g fat, 16 mg chol, 165 mg sodium, 24 g carb, 1 g fiber, 3 g pro.*

SKILLET SQUASH CORN BREAD

Skillet Squash Corn Bread

PREP 20 minutes
BAKE 25 minutes at 400°F

- 1 cup yellow cornmeal
- ¾ cup whole wheat flour
- 1 tablespoon sugar
- 2 teaspoons baking powder
- 1 teaspoon salt
- ½ teaspoon baking soda
  Nonstick cooking spray
- 1¼ cups buttermilk
- 2 eggs, slightly beaten
- 1½ cups finely shredded yellow summer squash or zucchini
  Honey butter (optional)

1. Preheat oven to 400°F. In a large bowl stir together cornmeal, flour, sugar, baking powder, salt, and baking soda; set aside.
2. Coat a 9-inch cast-iron skillet or 9×1½-inch round metal baking pan with cooking spray. Place in the preheated oven for 2 minutes.
3. Meanwhile, in a medium bowl combine buttermilk and eggs. Add egg mixture all at once to flour mixture. Stir just until moistened. Gently stir in squash. Pour batter into hot skillet or pan. Bake for 25 minutes or until a wooden toothpick inserted near center comes out clean. Serve warm. If desired, serve with honey butter. Makes 8 servings.

EACH SERVING *150 cal, 3 g fat, 50 mg chol, 544 mg sodium, 27 g carb, 2 g fiber, 6 g pro.*

CORN BREAD WITH TOMATO-BACON RIBBON

Corn Bread with Tomato-Bacon Ribbon

PREP 25 minutes
BAKE 35 minutes at 350°F
COOL 15 minutes

  Nonstick cooking spray
- ½ 8-ounce package cream cheese, softened
- 1 tablespoon butter, softened
- 1 tablespoon cornstarch
- ¼ teaspoon black pepper
- 2 eggs
- 2 tablespoons milk
- 2 slices bacon, crisp-cooked, drained, and crumbled
- 2 tablespoons oil-packed dried tomatoes, drained and chopped
- 1 8.5-ounce package corn muffin mix

1. Preheat oven to 350°F. Lightly coat a 2-quart square baking pan with cooking spray; set aside. In a medium mixing bowl beat cream cheese, butter, cornstarch, and pepper with an electric mixer on medium until smooth. Beat in eggs and milk until combined. Stir in bacon and tomatoes; set aside.
2. In a large bowl prepare corn muffin mix according to package directions. Spread about two-thirds of the batter into prepared baking pan. Pour cream cheese mixture evenly over batter. Drop remaining batter in small mounds over cream cheese mixture.
3. Bake, uncovered, about 35 minutes or until top springs back when lightly touched. Cool in pan on a wire rack for 15 minutes before serving. Serve warm. Makes 6 servings.

EACH SERVING *290 cal, 16 g fat , 65 mg chol, 597 mg sodium, 31 g carb, 3 g fiber, 7 g pro.*

**CLASSIC
BUTTERMILK
BISCUITS**

5. Place a baking sheet on rack in upper third of oven. Bake 8 to 12 minutes or until golden brown. Remove. Brush with melted butter. Serve hot. Makes 12 to 16 biscuits.

EACH BISCUIT *231 cal, 12 g fat, 8 mg chol, 200 mg sodium, 26 g carb, 2 g fiber, 6 g pro.*

Cranberry-Buttermilk Muffins

PREP 20 minutes
BAKE 15 minutes at 400°F

    1   cup fresh cranberries
    2   tablespoons sugar
    2   cups all-purpose flour
    ⅓   to ½ cup sugar
    4   teaspoons baking powder
    1   teaspoon finely shredded orange
        peel
    ½   teaspoon salt
    1   egg, lightly beaten
    ¾   cup buttermilk
    ¼   cup butter, melted
        Coarse sugar

1. Preheat oven to 400°F. Grease twelve 2½-inch muffin cups or line with paper bake cups; set aside.
2. In a medium bowl toss cranberries with 2 tablespoons sugar; set aside.
3. In a large bowl combine flour, ⅓ to ½ cup sugar, baking powder, orange peel, and salt; stir well. In a small bowl combine egg, buttermilk, and butter. Make a well in center of flour mixture; add egg mixture and cranberries. Stir just until moistened. Spoon into prepared muffin cups. Sprinkle tops with coarse sugar.
4. Bake muffins about 15 minutes or until golden and a toothpick inserted in centers of muffins comes out clean. Cool on a wire rack. Serve warm. Makes 12 muffins.

EACH MUFFIN *163 cal, 5 g fat, 29 mg chol, 306 mg sodium, 27 g carb, 1 g fiber, 3 g pro.*

Classic Buttermilk Biscuits

PREP 10 minutes
BAKE 8 minutes at 500°F

    5   cups sifted unbleached
        all-purpose flour (measured
        after sifting)
    1   tablespoon plus 1½ teaspoon
        baking powder
    1   tablespoon kosher salt
    ½   cup plus 2 tablespoons packed
        lard or butter, chilled
    2   cups chilled buttermilk
    3   tablespoons unsalted butter,
        melted

1. Preheat oven to 500°F. In a large bowl whisk together flour, baking powder, and kosher salt. Add lard, coating in flour. Working quickly, rub lard between fingertips until roughly half the lard is coarsely blended and half remains in large (about ¾-inch) pieces.
2. Make a well in center of flour mixture. Add buttermilk all at once. With a large spoon, stir dough quickly, just until blended and it begins to mass and form a sticky dough. (If dough appears dry, add 1 to 2 tablespoons buttermilk.)
3. Immediately turn dough onto a generously floured surface. Using floured hands, knead briskly 8 to 10 times until a cohesive ball of dough forms. Gently flatten dough with hands to an even thickness. Using a floured rolling pin, lightly roll dough to ¾-inch thickness.
4. Dip a dinner fork in flour, then pierce dough completely through at ½-inch intervals. Flour a 2½- or 3-inch biscuit cutter. Stamp out rounds and arrange on a heavy baking sheet lined with parchment paper. Add dough pieces to baking sheet (do not reroll dough).

CRANBERRY-
BUTTERMILK
MUFFINS

Italian Spinach Soup

START TO FINISH 35 minutes

- ½ cup chopped onion (1 medium)
- 4 cloves garlic, minced
- 2 teaspoons dried Italian seasoning, crushed
- 2 tablespoons butter
- 2 tablespoons dry sherry (optional)
- 2 14.5-ounce cans chicken broth
- 1 large potato, peeled and chopped
- 2 9-ounce packages fresh spinach or 1¼ pounds fresh spinach, washed and trimmed
- 2 cups watercress, tough stems removed
- 2 ounces Parmesan cheese, shaved
- 2 small tomatoes, quartered, seeded, and thinly sliced

1. In 4-quart Dutch oven cook onion, garlic, and Italian seasoning in hot butter over medium heat for 5 minutes or until onion is tender, stirring occasionally.
2. If using sherry, remove Dutch oven from heat; slowly pour in sherry. Return to heat; cook and stir 1 minute. Add broth and potato. Bring to boiling. Simmer, covered, 10 minutes or until potato is tender. Remove from heat.
3. Set aside 2 cups spinach. Stir remaining spinach, half at a time, into soup just until wilted. Cool about 5 minutes.
4. Transfer soup, half at a time, to food processor or blender; cover and process or blend until smooth. Return to Dutch oven; heat through. Season with salt.
5. To serve, top with reserved spinach, watercress, Parmesan, and tomatoes. Makes 6 servings.

EACH SERVING *151 cal, 7 g fat, 18 mg chol, 881 mg sodium, 16 g carb, 4 g fiber, 8 g pro.*

Rosemary Potato Soup with Crispy Carrots

START TO FINISH 45 minutes

- 1 tablespoon butter
- 1 medium white or yellow onion, chopped
- ½ teaspoon salt
- ¼ teaspoon pepper
- 4 medium russet or white potatoes, peeled and cut into 2-inch chunks (1 to 1½ pounds)
- 4 cups water
- 1 teaspoon dried rosemary, crushed

ROSEMARY POTATO SOUP WITH CRISPY CARROTS

⅓ cup vegetable oil
2 medium carrots, peeled, then
   cut into ribbons with a vegetable
   peeler
   Kosher salt or salt
   Coarse-ground black pepper

1. In a 4- or 5-quart Dutch oven melt butter over medium heat. Add onion, salt, and pepper. Cook, stirring occasionally, until onions are translucent but not brown. Add potatoes, 2 cups of the water, and rosemary. Bring to boiling; reduce heat. Simmer, covered, for 20 minutes or until potatoes are tender and can be pierced with a fork. Remove from heat.
2. With a potato masher, mash potatoes until no lumps remain. Or, for smoother soup, transfer soup, a portion at a time, to a blender or food processor. Cover and blend or process until nearly smooth. Return all to Dutch oven. Add remaining 2 cups of water. Bring to boiling; reduce heat. Simmer, uncovered, about 10 minutes or until thickened and desired consistency, stirring frequently to prevent soup from sticking to pan.
3. While soup is simmering, in a large skillet heat oil over medium-high heat. Add carrot ribbons, a few at a time, to hot oil. Cook for 1 minute or until crisp. Transfer to a cooling rack or paper towels; immediately sprinkle with kosher salt.
4. Spoon soup into serving bowls; top with crispy carrots and sprinkle with coarse pepper. Makes 6 servings.

EACH SERVING *236 cal, 5 g fat, 5 mg chol, 313 mg sodium, 26 g carb, 3 g fiber, 2 g pro.*

PUMPKIN SOUP WITH SPICED CROUTONS

Pumpkin Soup with Spiced Croutons
START TO FINISH 30 minutes

2 medium carrots, sliced
2 tablespoons butter
1 medium onion, finely chopped
1 stalk celery, finely chopped
1 clove garlic, minced
2 15-ounce cans pumpkin
1 32-ounce box reduced-sodium chicken broth
½ cup half-and-half or light cream
½ cup water
3 tablespoons maple syrup
1 teaspoon pumpkin pie spice
1 recipe Spiced Croutons
   Celery leaves (optional)

1. In a large saucepan cook carrots in hot butter over medium heat for 2 minutes; add onion, celery, and garlic. Cook 8 minutes or until vegetables are tender.
2. Stir in pumpkin, broth, half-and-half, water, maple syrup, and pumpkin pie spice. Heat through. Season with *salt* and *pepper*.
3. To serve, top soup with Spiced Croutons and celery leaves. Makes 8 servings.
Spiced Croutons In a bowl toss 3 cups of 1-inch bread cubes with 2 teaspoons pumpkin pie spice. In a large skillet toast bread cubes in 2 tablespoons hot butter for 8 minutes, turning occasionally.

EACH SERVING *200 cal, 9 g fat, 21 mg chol, 590 mg sodium, 28 g carb, 4 g fiber, 5 g pro.*

CHOCOLATE-MALTED MOUSSE,
RECIPE PAGE 282

SPICY GINGERSNAPPERS,
RECIPE PAGE 310

desserts

SWEET TALK Everyone loves a little something sweet—
especially at the end of a homemade meal. And the cakes,
pies, cobblers, cookies, and bars know just what to say.

Honey-Glazed Buttermilk Oatmeal Coffee Cake

PREP 30 minutes
BAKE 25 minutes at 375°F
COOL 10 minutes

- ½ cup honey
- ⅓ cup butter, melted
- 2 tablespoons light-color corn syrup
- 2 teaspoons finely shredded lemon peel
- 4 teaspoons lemon juice
- ½ cup chopped pecans
- 1½ cups rolled oats
- 1 cup all-purpose flour
- ¾ cup packed brown sugar
- ½ cup chopped pecans
- 1 teaspoon baking powder
- ½ teaspoon baking soda
- ½ teaspoon salt
- ⅔ cup buttermilk
- 2 eggs, lightly beaten
- ¼ cup butter, melted
- 1½ teaspoons vanilla

1. Preheat oven to 375°F. Grease a 9×9×2-inch baking pan. In a small bowl combine ½ cup honey, ⅓ cup melted butter, corn syrup, lemon peel, and lemon juice. Stir in ½ cup chopped pecans. Pour into prepared pan; set aside.
2. For cake, in a blender or food processor, blend or process oats until finely ground. Transfer to a large bowl. Stir in flour, brown sugar, ½ cup pecans, baking powder, baking soda, and salt. Make a well in the center of the flour mixture. In a medium bowl combine buttermilk, eggs, ¼ cup melted butter, and vanilla. Add the milk mixture all at once to the flour mixture. Stir just until moistened (batter should be lumpy).
3. Spoon batter evenly over honey mixture in pan. Bake for 25 minutes or until a wooden toothpick inserted in center comes out clean. Remove from oven and immediately invert cake onto a serving plate. Cool about 10 minutes. Serve warm. If desired, drizzled with additional honey. Makes 9 servings.
EACH SERVING *450 cal, 23 g fat, 79 mg chol, 357 mg sodium, 58 g carb, 3 g fiber, 6 g pro.*

CARAMEL APPLE UPSIDE-DOWN CORNMEAL CAKE

DUTCH APPLE CAKE WITH CARAMEL GLAZE

Caramel Apple Upside-Down Cornmeal Cake

PREP 35 minutes   COOK 8 minutes
BAKE 30 minutes at 350°F
COOL 10 minutes

6	tablespoons butter
4	medium apples, peeled, cored, and sliced
½	cup packed brown sugar
2	tablespoons milk
½	cup chopped pecans
⅓	cup dried cranberries
¾	cup all-purpose flour
2	tablespoons granulated sugar
1½	teaspoons baking powder
¼	teaspoon salt
¾	cup cornmeal
1	cup hot water
¼	cup butter, melted
2	eggs, lightly beaten
1½	teaspoons vanilla

1. Preheat oven to 350°F. In a large oven-going skillet melt 2 tablespoons of the butter over medium heat. Add apples; cook and stir 5 minutes or until tender. Remove from skillet. In same skillet combine remaining butter and brown sugar. Cook and stir over medium heat until butter is melted. Bring to boiling. Remove from heat. Stir in milk. Sprinkle with pecans and cranberries. Arrange apple slices on top.
2. In a bowl combine flour, sugar, baking powder, and salt. In a medium bowl combine cornmeal, water, and ¼ cup butter. Stir in eggs and vanilla. Stir in flour mixture. Pour over apples.
3. Bake for 30 minutes or until a toothpick inserted near center comes

out clean. Cool in pan 10 minutes. Invert; serve warm. Makes 8 servings.
EACH SERVING *396 cal, 21 g fat, 91 mg chol, 249 mg sodium, 49 g carb, 4 g fiber, 5 g pro.*

Dutch Apple Cake with Caramel Glaze

PREP 40 minutes
BAKE 1 hour at 325°F
COOL 30 minutes

7	cooking apples, such as Granny Smith, Rome, or Golden Delicious (about 2½ pounds)
3	cups all-purpose flour
1	teaspoon baking soda
1½	teaspoon ground cinnamon
1	teaspoon kosher salt
½	teaspoon freshly grated nutmeg
3	eggs
1½	cups vegetable oil
1	cup packed brown sugar
1	cup granulated sugar
2½	teaspoons vanilla
1¼	cups chopped pecans
1	recipe Caramel Glaze

1. Preheat oven to 325°F. Peel apples; quarter, core, and cut each quarter into 1½-inch chunks. Butter and flour a 3-quart baking pan.

2. In a medium bowl whisk together flour, baking soda, cinnamon, salt, and nutmeg. In an extra-large mixing bowl whisk eggs until combined. Whisk in oil, sugars, and vanilla until well blended. Gradually whisk flour mixture into the egg-sugar mixture just until well blended.
3. Fold apples and pecans into batter (batter will be thick). Spread batter in prepared pan to edges. Bake for 1 to 1¼ hours, until a toothpick inserted in center of cake comes out clean. Cool on a wire rack for 30 minutes while preparing glaze.
Caramel Glaze In a medium skillet melt 6 tablespoons unsalted butter. Add ⅓ cup packed dark brown sugar, ⅓ cup packed light brown sugar, ½ cup whipping cream, and a pinch of salt. Cook and stir over medium-low heat for 2 minutes, until blended. Increase heat and boil for 2 minutes or until dime-size bubbles cover the surface of glaze. Remove from heat. Cool about 5 minutes or until glaze begins to thicken. Spoon glaze over cake. Makes 16 servings.
EACH SERVING *568 cal, 35 g fat, 61 mg chol, 256 mg sodium, 62 g carb, 2 g fiber, 5 g pro.*

**MILK CHOCOLATE
MARBLE LOAF CAKE**

Milk Chocolate Marble Loaf Cake

PREP 30 minutes   STAND 30 minutes
BAKE 65 minutes at 350°F
COOL 50 minutes

4	large eggs
1½	cups sugar
6	tablespoons unsalted butter, melted
½	cup whole milk
2	teaspoons vanilla
1¾	cups all-purpose flour
1	teaspoon baking powder
¼	teaspoon salt
3	ounces milk chocolate, chopped
¼	cup sugar
¼	cup orange juice
4	oranges, segmented
1	small pink grapefruit, segmented
10	kumquats, halved (optional)

1. For the cake, let eggs stand at room temperature 30 minutes. Butter and flour a 9×5×3-inch loaf pan; set aside.
2. Preheat oven to 350°F. In medium bowl whisk together the eggs, sugar, butter, milk, and vanilla. In a separate bowl combine the flour, baking powder, and salt.
3. In a small saucepan bring 1 inch of water to simmering over low heat. Place a small bowl over water. Add chocolate. Stir with a rubber spatula until chocolate is melted. Remove from heat.
4. Stir flour mixture into egg mixture just until combined. Transfer about one-third of the batter (a generous cup) to a separate bowl. Stir melted chocolate into small amount of batter, mixing well. Drop ¼ cup of plain batter into the prepared pan; top with 2 tablespoons chocolate batter. Repeat with remaining batter. Do not stir.
5. Bake in center of the oven for 65 minutes, until a toothpick inserted into center of loaf comes out clean.
6. Meanwhile, prepare citrus compote. In a saucepan combine sugar and orange juice. Cook and stir over medium heat until hot and sugar has dissolved. Transfer to a bowl. Stir in orange and grapefruit segments and, if desired, kumquats. Set aside to cool. (Can be made up to 2 days ahead.)

7. Cool cake in pan on wire rack 10 minutes. Remove from pan, return to the wire rack, and cool at least 40 minutes before slicing. Serve slices topped with citrus compote. Makes 12 servings.
EACH SERVING *330 cal, 10 g fat, 88 mg chol, 123 mg sodium, 55 g carb, 2 g fiber, 5 g pro.*

Busy-Day Cake

PREP 25 minutes   BAKE 30 minutes at 350°F   COOL 30 minutes

1⅓	cups all-purpose flour
⅔	cup sugar
2	teaspoons baking powder
⅔	cup milk
¼	cup butter, softened
1	egg
1	teaspoon vanilla
1	cup whipping cream
2	tablespoons sugar
½	teaspoon vanilla
3	cups assorted fresh berries

1. Preheat oven to 350°F. Grease an 8×1½-inch round cake pan; set aside.
2. In a medium mixing bowl combine flour, sugar, and baking powder. Add milk, butter, egg, and vanilla. Beat with an electric mixer on low until combined. Beat on medium for 1 minute. Spread batter in prepared pan.
3. Bake about 30 minutes or until a wooden toothpick inserted near center comes out clean. Cool cake in pan on a wire rack about 30 minutes.
4. Meanwhile, prepare sweetened whipped cream. In a chilled mixing bowl add whipping cream, the 2 tablespoons sugar, and the ½ teaspoon vanilla. Beat with an electric mixer on medium until soft peaks form.
5. Serve cake warm with berries and sweetened whipped cream. Makes 8 servings.
EACH SERVING *346 cal, 18 g fat, 84 mg chol, 130 mg sodium, 42 g carb, 2 g fiber, 5 g pro.*

APPLE CAKE WITH BUTTERY CARAMEL SAUCE

Mocha Sheetcake with Pecan Frosting

PREP 25 minutes BAKE 20 minutes at 350°F COOL 1 hour

  5 teaspoons instant espresso
     coffee powder
  1 cup boiling water
1⅓ cups butter
  ⅔ cup unsweetened cocoa powder
  2 cups sugar
  2 cups all-purpose flour
  2 eggs, lightly beaten
  1 cup buttermilk
  1 teaspoon baking soda
  2 teaspoons vanilla
  1 teaspoon ground cinnamon
  ½ teaspoon salt

1. Preheat oven to 350°F. Generously grease a 15×10×1-inch baking pan; set aside.
2. Dissolve espresso powder in the boiling water. In a medium saucepan combine espresso, butter, and unsweetened cocoa. Bring to boiling over medium-high heat, stirring constantly. Remove from heat; let cool for 10 minutes.
3. In a large bowl whisk together the sugar and flour. Add the warm cocoa mixture; stir to blend well. Add eggs, buttermilk, baking soda, vanilla, cinnamon, and salt; mix well. Spread batter evenly into prepared pan.
4. Bake for 20 to 25 minutes or until a wooden toothpick inserted near the center comes out clean.
5. Meanwhile, for pecan frosting, in a medium saucepan heat ⅓ cup butter, ½ cup buttermilk, ⅓ cup unsweetened cocoa powder, and 1 teaspoon of the instant espresso coffee powder over medium-low heat, stirring constantly until butter is melted. Remove from heat. With an electric mixer on medium beat in 4½ cups powdered sugar and 1 teaspoon of the vanilla.
6. Immediately frost hot cake. Sprinkle with 1 cup *chopped toasted pecans* (see tip, page 31). Cool to room temperature before serving. Makes 24 servings.
EACH SERVING *330 cal, 14 g fat, 45 mg chol, 192 mg sodium, 50 g carb, 2 g fiber, 3 g pro.*

Apple Cake with Buttery Caramel Sauce

PREP 35 minutes BAKE 45 minutes at 350°F COOL 45 minutes

  2 cups all-purpose flour
  1 teaspoon baking powder
  ½ teaspoon salt
  ½ teaspoon ground nutmeg
  ½ teaspoon ground cinnamon
  ¼ teaspoon baking soda
  ½ cup butter, softened
  2 cups sugar
  2 eggs
  6 cups coarsely chopped, unpeeled
     cooking apples
  1 cup chopped walnuts
  ⅓ cup butter
  ⅓ cup sugar
  ⅓ cup packed brown sugar
  ⅓ cup whipping cream
  ½ teaspoon vanilla

1. Preheat oven to 350°F. Grease a 3-quart rectangular baking dish; set aside. In a medium bowl stir together the flour, baking powder, salt, nutmeg, cinnamon, and baking soda; set aside.
2. In an extra-large mixing bowl beat butter with an electric mixer on medium to high for 30 seconds. Gradually add sugar, about ¼ cup at a time, beating on medium until well combined. Scrape sides of bowl; beat for 2 minutes more. Add eggs, one at a time, beating well after each addition. Add flour mixture to butter mixture, beating on low just until combined. Fold in apples and walnuts. (Batter will be thick.) Spread batter into prepared baking pan.
3. Bake for 45 minutes or until a toothpick inserted near the center comes out clean. Cool in pan on a wire rack for 45 minutes.
4. Meanwhile, for buttery caramel sauce, in a small saucepan melt the ⅓ cup butter over medium heat. Stir in the ⅓ cup sugar, brown sugar, and whipping cream. Bring to boiling, stirring constantly. Remove from heat; stir in vanilla. Serve warm with buttery caramel sauce. Makes 16 servings.
EACH SERVING *369 cal, 17 g fat, 59 mg chol, 188 mg sodium, 23 g carb, 2 g fiber, 4 g pro.*

MOCHA SHEETCAKE WITH PECAN FROSTING

CINNAMON APPLE SPICE CAKE

Cinnamon Apple Spice Cake

PREP 25 minutes
BAKE 40 minutes at 350°F
COOL 10 minutes

1½ cups buttermilk
¾ cup canola oil
½ cup water
2 cups packed brown sugar
2 eggs
2 teaspoons baking powder
1½ teaspoons ground cinnamon
½ teaspoon baking soda
½ teaspoon salt
2 teaspoons vanilla
2½ cups all-purpose flour
2 Gala apples, cored and cut into
½-inch chunks
1 recipe Fruit Topping

1. Preheat oven to 350°F. Line an 8×8×2-inch baking pan with parchment paper. Grease and flour the pans; set aside.
2. In a mixing bowl whisk buttermilk, oil, water, brown sugar, eggs, baking powder, cinnamon, baking soda, salt, and vanilla until combined. Whisk in flour; stir in apples. Divide evenly between prepared pans.
3. Bake for 40 minutes or a until toothpick inserted near centers comes out clean. Cool in pans on wire rack for 10 minutes. Invert cake layers from pans onto racks; remove parchment paper. Cool completely on racks.
4. Prepare Fruit Topping. Place one cake layer, flat side up, on serving platter. Spoon on about two-thirds of fruit topping. Top with second cake layer and remaining topping. Serve immediately. Makes 10 servings.
Fruit Topping In a skillet melt 2 tablespoons unsalted butter over medium heat. Add 4 small apples or firm pears, cored and cut into slices and/or wedges; add ¼ cup granulated sugar. Cook, stirring occasionally, about 8 minutes or just until fruit begins to soften. Remove from heat.
EACH SERVING *532 cal, 20 g fat, 50 mg chol, 319 mg sodium, 84 g carb, 3 g fiber, 6 g pro.*

Rhubarb and Spice Snacking Cake

PREP 25 minutes
BAKE 30 minutes at 350°F
COOL 30 minutes

⅓ cup granulated sugar
⅓ cup chopped pecans
1 tablespoon butter, melted
1 teaspoon ground cinnamon
1 cup all-purpose flour
½ teaspoon baking soda
¼ teaspoon salt
⅛ teaspoon ground nutmeg
¼ cup butter, softened
¾ cups packed brown sugar
1 egg
⅓ cup sour cream
1 cup chopped fresh rhubarb or frozen unsweetened rhubarb, thawed, drained, and chopped
¼ cup golden raisins
1 teaspoon finely shredded lemon peel

1. Preheat oven to 350°F. Grease and flour an 8×8×2-inch square baking pan; set aside. For crumb topping, in a small bowl combine granulated sugar, pecans, the 1 tablespoon melted butter, and ½ teaspoon of the cinnamon until crumbly; set aside. In another small bowl stir together flour, baking soda, the remaining ½ teaspoon cinnamon, the salt, and nutmeg; set aside.
2. In a medium mixing bowl beat the ¼ cup butter with an electric mixer on medium to high for 30 seconds. Beat in brown sugar until well combined. Beat in egg. Alternately add flour mixture and sour cream to butter mixture, beating until combined after each addition (batter will be thick). Stir in rhubarb, raisins, and lemon peel.
3. Evenly spread batter in the baking pan. Sprinkle with crumb topping. Bake for 30 minutes or until a wooden toothpick inserted near the center of cake comes out clean. Cool in pan on a wire rack for 30 minutes. Serve warm or cool completely and serve at room temperature. Makes 9 servings.
EACH SERVING *276 cal, 12 g fat, 45 mg chol, 223 mg sodium, 41 g carb, 2 g fiber, 3 g pro.*

RHUBARB AND SPICE SNACKING CAKE

**CREAM SODA-TOFFEE
CUPCAKES**

Cream Soda-Toffee Cupcakes

PREP 25 minutes BAKE 18 minutes
at 350°F COOL 5 minutes

      2 cups all-purpose flour
  1½ teaspoons baking powder
    ½ teaspoon baking soda
    ¼ teaspoon salt
    ½ cup butter, softened
    ¾ cup granulated sugar
    ¼ cup packed brown sugar
      3 eggs
      1 tablespoon molasses
  1½ teaspoons vanilla
    ½ cup buttermilk
    ½ cup cream soda (not diet)
    ¾ cup toffee pieces
      1 recipe Brown Butter Frosting

1. Preheat oven to 350°F. Line eighteen
2½-inch muffin cups with paper bake
cups; set aside. Combine flour, baking
powder, baking soda, and salt; set aside.
2. In large bowl beat butter with
electric mixer on medium to high
30 seconds. Add sugars; beat until
well combined. Beat in eggs, one at a
time, on low until combined. Beat in
molasses and vanilla.
3. Alternately add flour mixture,
buttermilk, and cream soda to butter
mixture, beating on low after each
addition until combined. Stir in ½ cup
of the toffee. Fill cups three-fourths
full. Bake about 18 minutes or until
tops spring back when lightly touched.
Cool in pans on racks 5 minutes.
Remove from pans; cool. Frost;
top with remaining toffee. Makes
18 cupcakes.
Brown Butter Frosting In a saucepan
heat ¼ cup butter over medium-low
heat about 8 minutes or until lightly
browned; cool. In a bowl beat ¼ cup
softened butter with mixer on medium
for 30 seconds. Add cooled brown
butter; beat until combined. Add 2 cups
powdered sugar, ½ teaspoon vanilla,
⅛ teaspoon ground nutmeg, and a
dash of salt. Beat in 1 to 2 tablespoons
buttermilk until spreadable. Use
immediately. If frosting begins to set
up, stir in a small amount of boiling
water.

EACH CUPCAKE *307 cal, 14 g fat, 69 mg chol,
241 mg sodium, 42 g carb, 0 g fiber, 3 g pro.*

Double-Berry Streusel-Topped Cake

PREP 25 minutes
BAKE 25 minutes at 400°F
COOL 30 minutes

      2 cups all-purpose flour
    ¼ cup sugar
      1 tablespoon baking powder
    ½ teaspoon salt
      6 tablespoons butter
    ¾ cup milk
      1 egg, lightly beaten
      1 teaspoon vanilla
      1 cup frozen blueberries, thawed
         and drained
      3 cups frozen sweetened sliced
         strawberries, thawed
    ⅓ cup all-purpose flour
      3 tablespoons sugar
      3 tablespoons butter
         Sweetened whipped cream
         (optional)

1. Preheat oven to 400°F. Grease the
bottom of a 3-quart rectangular baking
pan or coat with nonstick cooking spray.
2. In a medium mixing bowl stir
together flour, sugar, baking powder,
and salt. Cut in butter until mixture
resembles coarse meal; set aside. In a
small bowl stir together milk, egg, and
vanilla; add to flour mixture, stirring
until moistened. Fold in blueberries.
Spread evenly in prepared pan (batter
will be thin). Spoon undrained
strawberries over batter in pan.
3. For topping, in another small
bowl stir together the ⅓ cup flour
and the 3 tablespoons sugar. Cut in
3 tablespoons butter until mixture
resembles fine crumbs. Sprinkle over
berries. Bake 25 minutes or until set
and top is evenly browned. Cool about
30 minutes before serving. If desired,
serve with whipped cream. Makes
12 servings.

EACH SERVING *256 cal, 10 g fat, 42 mg chol,
231 mg sodium, 38 g carb, 2 g fiber, 4 g pro.*

DOUBLE-BERRY STREUSEL-TOPPED CAKE

CHOCOLATE-FILLED
SWEET POTATO
CUPCAKES

Chocolate-Filled Sweet Potato Cupcakes

PREP 25 minutes
BAKE 19 minutes at 350°F
COOL 10 minutes

- 2 cups all-purpose flour
- 2 teaspoons pumpkin pie spice
- 1½ teaspoons baking powder
- ½ teaspoon baking soda
- ¼ teaspoon salt
- 1 cup unsalted butter, softened
- 1¼ cups granulated sugar
- 3 large eggs
- 1 pounds sweet potatoes, roasted,* peeled, and mashed
- ¼ cup milk
- 1 teaspoon vanilla

- 24 milk chocolate or dark chocolate kisses, unwrapped
- 8 ounces milk chocolate, chopped
- 4 ounces semisweet chocolate, chopped
- 6 tablespoons unsalted butter, softened
- ½ cup powdered sugar

1. Preheat oven to 350°F. Line twenty-four 2½-inch muffin cups with 5×4-inch rectangles of parchment paper or paper bake cups.
2. In a medium bowl combine flour, pumpkin pie spice, baking powder, baking soda, and salt; set aside. In a large mixing bowl beat butter with an electric mixer on medium for 30 seconds. Add granulated sugar; beat about 2 minutes or until light and fluffy. With mixer on low, beat in eggs, one at a time, stopping to scrape down sides of bowl between additions. Add sweet potatoes, milk, and vanilla. Beat on low until combined. Add flour mixture; beat on low just until combined.
3. Fill prepared muffin cups about two-thirds full with batter. Bake 5 minutes. Remove from oven. Gently press a kiss, tip up, about halfway into each cup. Bake 14 minutes more or until tops spring back when touched and chocolate sinks into cakes. Cool in pan 10 minutes; remove and cool completely on wire rack.
4. For the frosting, in a medium saucepan over low heat bring 1 inch of water to simmering. Place chopped milk chocolate and semisweet chocolate in a medium mixing bowl;

set bowl over saucepan. With a rubber spatula, stir until chocolate is melted. Remove from heat; cool 15 minutes. With an electric mixer on low beat chocolate 30 seconds. Beat in butter 1 to 2 tablespoons at a time. Beat in powdered sugar until smooth. Spread on tops of cupcakes. Makes 24 cupcakes.

*Tip To roast sweet potatoes, preheat oven to 425°F. Prick unpeeled potatoes all over with a fork. Place in roasting pan. Roast 50 minutes or until tender. When cool, peel off and discard skin.

EACH CUPCAKE *341 cal, 21 g fat, 68 mg chol, 110 mg sodium, 36 g carb, 1 g fiber, 4 g pro.*

Chocolate Cupcakes with a Kick

PREP 35 minutes
BAKE 18 minutes at 350°F
COOL 10 minutes

- 1 package two-layer chocolate or devil's food cake mix
- 1¼ cups sour cream
- 3 eggs
- ⅓ cup cooking oil
- 2 tablespoons instant coffee crystals
- ½ to 1 teaspoon ground chipotle chile pepper
- 1 11.5-ounce package semisweet chocolate chunks
- 2 teaspoons all-purpose flour
- 1 recipe White Frosting
- 2 ounces semisweet chocolate, chopped
- ¼ cup whipping cream

1. Preheat oven to 350°F. Line twenty-four 2½-inch muffin cups with paper bake cups; set aside. In a large mixing bowl combine cake mix, sour cream, eggs, oil, coffee crystals, and chipotle pepper. Beat with electric mixer on low to combine. Beat on medium for 2 minutes.

CHOCOLATE CUPCAKES WITH A KICK

2. In a bowl toss chocolate chunks with flour. Fold into batter. Spoon into prepared cups. Bake 18 minutes or until tops spring back when lightly touched. Cool in pans on wire rack 5 minutes. Remove from pans; cool completely. Frost with White Frosting.

3. For chocolate drizzle, place chopped chocolate in a bowl. In a saucepan bring cream to boiling. Pour over chocolate; do not stir. Let stand 5 minutes; whisk until smooth. Place chocolate in a resealable plastic bag; seal bag and snip off a small corner. Drizzle over frosted cupcakes. Makes 24 cupcakes.

White Frosting In a large mixing bowl beat one 8-ounce package softened cream cheese and ½ cup softened butter on medium to high for 30 seconds. Beat in ½ teaspoon vanilla. Gradually beat in 2 to 2½ cups powdered sugar until spreadable.

EACH CUPCAKE *335 cal, 21 g fat, 55 mg chol, 251 mg sodium, 37 g carb, 2 g fiber, 4 g pro.*

CARAMEL-APPLE PUDDING CAKE

Caramel-Apple Pudding Cake

PREP 25 minutes
BAKE 25 minutes at 350°F

  2 medium tart cooking apples, such as Granny Smith or Jonathan, peeled, cored, and thinly sliced (2 cups)
  3 tablespoons lemon juice
  ½ teaspoon ground cinnamon
  ⅛ teaspoon ground nutmeg
  ¼ cup raisins
  1 cup all-purpose flour
  ¾ cup packed brown sugar
  1 teaspoon baking powder
  ¼ teaspoon baking soda
  ½ cup milk
  3 tablespoons butter (no substitutes), melted
  1 teaspoon vanilla
  ½ cup chopped pecans or walnuts
  ¾ cups caramel ice cream topping
  ½ cup water

1. Preheat oven to 350°F. Grease a 2-quart baking pan. Arrange apples in bottom of dish; sprinkle with lemon juice, cinnamon, and nutmeg. Top evenly with raisins. Set aside.

2. In a large bowl stir together flour, brown sugar, baking powder, and baking soda. Add milk, 2 tablespoons of the melted butter, and vanilla; mix well. Stir in chopped nuts. Evenly spread batter over apple mixture.
3. In a small saucepan combine caramel topping, water, and remaining melted butter; bring to boiling. Pour caramel mixture over the batter in the baking dish.
4. Bake for 25 minutes or until center is set when dish is gently shaken. While warm, cut into squares, inverting each piece onto a dessert plate. Spoon caramel-apple mixture from dish over each piece. Makes 12 servings.
EACH SERVING *215 cal, 6 g fat, 8 mg chol, 114 mg sodium, 38 g carb, 2 g fiber, 2 g pro.*

Brownie-Raspberry Desserts

PREP 40 minutes
BAKE 30 minutes at 350°F

  ½ cup butter, softened
  ¾ cup sugar
  ½ teaspoon salt
  3 eggs
  1 teaspoon vanilla
  1 cup chocolate-flavor syrup

  1 cup all-purpose flour
  1 cup whipping cream
  2 ounces white baking chocolate, chopped
  5 large marshmallows
  1½ cups fresh or frozen unsweetened red raspberries, thawed
  2 tablespoons powdered sugar
  1 teaspoon vanilla
     Chocolate-flavor syrup

1. Preheat oven to 350°F. Lightly grease a 3-quart rectangular baking pan; set aside. In a large mixing bowl beat butter with electric mixer on medium for 30 seconds. Add sugar and salt; beat on medium until well combined. Add eggs and 1 teaspoon vanilla; beat until combined. Add 1 cup chocolate syrup; beat until combined. Beat in flour until combined. Pour into prepared pan. Bake 30 minutes. Cool completely in pan on a wire rack.
2. Meanwhile, in a small saucepan heat and stir ¼ cup of the whipping cream, the white chocolate, and marshmallows over low heat until melted and smooth; set aside to cool slightly.
3. Place 1½ cups raspberries in a food processor or blender; cover and process or blend until smooth. Press pureed berries through a fine-mesh sieve; discard seeds. Stir raspberry puree into marshmallow mixture.
4. In a large chilled mixing bowl beat remaining ¾ cup whipping cream, powdered sugar, and 1 teaspoon vanilla with electric mixer on medium until soft peaks form. Gradually fold raspberry puree into whipped cream until well combined.
5. Cut brownies into twelve 3-inch squares. For each serving, place a brownie on a dessert plate. Spoon raspberry cream on brownie. Top with fresh whole berries and drizzle with chocolate syrup. Makes 12 servings.
EACH SERVING *382 cal, 18 g fat, 101 mg chol, 207 mg sodium, 50 g carb, 2 g fiber, 4 g pro.*

S'MORES
BREAD PUDDING

S'mores Bread Pudding

PREP 25 minutes   STAND 5 minutes
BAKE 40 minutes at 325°F
COOL 20 minutes

- 4   Hawaiian sweet bread or frankfurter buns, cut into 1-inch pieces
- 4   eggs
- 1   14-ounce can sweetened condensed milk
- ¾   cup milk
- 1   teaspoon vanilla
- ¼   teaspoon ground nutmeg
- 1   cup tiny marshmallows
- ¾   cup semisweet chocolate pieces
- ½   cup coarsely crushed graham cracker squares
- 2   tablespoons milk

1. Preheat oven to 325°F. Grease a 2-quart square baking dish; set aside. Place bread pieces on shallow baking sheet. Bake for 7 minutes or until dry and crisp; cool.
2. In a medium bowl lightly beat eggs. Stir in sweetened condensed milk, ¾ cup milk, vanilla, and nutmeg; set aside.
3. Place bread pieces in prepared baking dish. Sprinkle with ½ cup each of the marshmallows and chocolate pieces. Evenly pour milk mixture over all. Let stand 5 minutes. Sprinkle with crushed graham crackers. Bake, uncovered, for 35 minutes. Sprinkle with ¼ cup of the remaining marshmallows. Bake about 5 minutes more or until a knife inserted near center comes out clean.
4. For drizzle, in a small saucepan heat and whisk remaining marshmallows, remaining chocolate pieces, and 2 tablespoons milk over low heat until melted and smooth. Drizzle over bread pudding. Cool 20 minutes before serving. Serve warm. Makes 9 servings.
EACH SERVING *348 cal, 12 g fat, 111 mg chol, 221 mg sodium, 52 g carb, 1 g fiber, 10 g pro.*

TIRAMISU BREAD PUDDINGS

Tiramisu Bread Puddings

PREP 25 minutes   BAKE 30 minutes at 375°F   COOL 20 minutes

- 1⅓   cups milk
- 1¼   cups whipping cream
- 2   tablespoons instant coffee crystals
- 6   eggs, lightly beaten
- ⅔   cup granulated sugar
- ⅓   cup packed brown sugar
- 2   teaspoons vanilla
- 8   cups torn white bread slices (about 12 slices)
- ⅓   cup powdered sugar
- 1   recipe Cream Cheese Topping

1. Preheat oven to 375°F. In large bowl stir together milk, whipping cream, and coffee crystals until coffee is dissolved. Reserve 1 tablespoon milk mixture; set aside.

2. Stir eggs, the sugars, and vanilla into milk mixture in large bowl. Stir in bread pieces until moistened. Evenly divide among eight ungreased 6-ounce ramekins or custard cups, filling each almost full. Place on a 15×10×1-inch baking pan.
3. Bake for 30 minutes or until puffed, set, and a knife inserted near centers comes out clean. Transfer to a wire rack (puddings will fall slightly as they cool).
4. In a small bowl combine powdered sugar and reserved 1 tablespoon milk mixture; stir until smooth. Drizzle over bread pudding. Top with Cream Cheese Topping. Makes 8 servings.
Cream Cheese Topping In a medium mixing bowl beat ¾ cup whipping cream; 1 ounce cream cheese, softened; and 1 tablespoons powdered sugar on medium until soft peaks form. Makes about 1½ cups.
EACH SERVING *522 cal, 29 g fat, 248 mg chol, 362 mg sodium, 55 g carb, 1 g fiber, 11 g pro.*

PEAR-CINNAMON STREUSEL SQUARES

Pear-Cinnamon Streusel Squares

PREP 30 minutes
BAKE 45 minutes at 350°F

- 2 cups all-purpose flour
- 1¼ cups quick-cooking rolled oats
- ¾ cup packed brown sugar
- 2 teaspoons ground cinnamon
- 1 cup butter
- 2 eggs
- 1 cup granulated sugar
- 2 tablespoons all-purpose flour
- ¼ teaspoon baking powder
- ¼ teaspoon salt
- 2 cups peeled and chopped pears or apples
- ¾ cup cinnamon-flavor pieces
- 1 recipe Powdered Sugar Icing

1. Preheat oven to 350°F. Lightly grease a 3-quart baking dish; set aside. In a large bowl stir together the 2 cups flour, oats, brown sugar, and cinnamon. Using a pastry blender, cut in butter until mixture resembles coarse crumbs. Remove 1½ cups of the oats mixture for topping; set aside. Evenly press the remaining oats mixture into the bottom of the prepared baking pan. Bake for 15 minutes.
2. Meanwhile, for filling, in a medium bowl combine eggs and granulated sugar. Stir in the 2 tablespoons flour, baking powder, and salt. Stir in pears and cinnamon pieces. Spread filling evenly over hot crust. Sprinkle with the reserved oats mixture.
3. Bake for 30 minutes more or until top is golden. Cool in pan on a wire rack. Cut into bars. Drizzle with Powdered Sugar Icing. Makes 32 bars.
Powdered Sugar Icing In a small bowl stir together 1 cup powdered sugar and 1 tablespoon milk. Stir in additional milk, 1 teaspoon at a time, until icing is drizzling consistency.
EACH BAR *193 cal, 8 g fat, 29 mg chol, 81 mg sodium, 29 g carb, 1 g fiber, 2 g pro.*

Berry-Glazed Cheesecake Dessert

PREP 25 minutes   BAKE 30 minutes
at 350°F   CHILL 4 hours

- 1 cup all-purpose flour
- ¼ cup sugar
- 2 teaspoons finely shredded lemon peel
- 1 teaspoon baking powder
- ½ cup butter
- 1 egg, beaten
- ¼ cup milk
- ½ teaspoon vanilla
- 2 8-ounce packages cream cheese, softened
- 1 3-ounce package cream cheese, softened
- 1¼ cups sugar
- 1 egg
- 1 tablespoon lemon juice
- 2 teaspoons vanilla
- 4 cups fresh strawberries, sliced
- ½ cup currant jelly
- ¼ cup sliced almonds, toasted (see tip, page 31)

1. Preheat oven to 350°F. Lightly grease a 3-quart baking pan; set aside. For bottom layer, in a medium bowl stir together flour, the ¼ cup sugar, the lemon peel, and baking powder. Using a pastry blender, cut in butter until mixture resembles coarse crumbs. Make a well in the center.
2. In a small bowl combine beaten egg, the milk, and the ½ teaspoon vanilla; add all at once to flour mixture. Stir just until dough clings together. Spread dough into prepared pan; set aside.
3. For cheesecake layer, in a medium mixing bowl combine cream cheese, the 1¼ cups sugar, 1 egg, the lemon juice, and the 2 teaspoons vanilla. Beat with an electric mixer on high until smooth and creamy. Spread over dough in pan.
4. Bake, uncovered, for 30 minutes or until top is golden brown. Cool in pan on a wire rack. Cover and chill for at least 4 hours or up to 24 hours.
5. Not more than 3 hours before serving, arrange sliced strawberries over cake. Stir jelly to soften; drizzle over berries. If desired, sprinkle with almonds. Cover and chill until serving. Makes 12 servings.
EACH SERVING *441 cal, 25 g fat, 105 mg chol, 226 mg sodium, 49 g carb, 2 g fiber, 6 g pro.*

BERRY-GLAZED CHEESECAKE DESSERT

CARROT
CHEESECAKE

Carrot Cheesecake

PREP 40 minutes BAKE 1½ hours
plus 8 minutes at 325°F
COOL 45 minutes CHILL 4 hours

- 1 package 2-layer-size carrot cake mix
- 1 cup water
- ½ cup cooking oil
- 6 eggs
- ½ cup raisins
- 3 8-ounce packages cream cheese, softened
- 1½ cups granulated sugar
- 2 teaspoons vanilla
    Nonstick cooking spray
- 2 tablespoons powdered sugar
- 1 tablespoon water
- 1 teaspoon ground cinnamon
- ½ cup coarsely chopped walnuts
- 1 cup powdered sugar
- 3 to 4 teaspoons milk

1. Preheat oven to 325°F. Grease and flour a 10-inch springform pan; set aside. In a large mixing bowl combine carrot cake mix, the 1 cup water, oil, and 3 of the eggs. Beat with electric mixer on low for 30 seconds, scraping sides of bowl constantly. Beat on medium for 3 minutes. Fold in raisins. Pour into pan.
2. In another large mixing bowl beat cream cheese with an electric mixer on medium until smooth. Beat in granulated sugar and vanilla until smooth. Beat in remaining 3 eggs just until combined. Slowly pour over carrot cake layer. Place cheesecake pan on a baking sheet.
3. Bake for 1½ to 1¾ hours or until center is set (top will be uneven and center may fall slightly as it cools). Cool in pan on a wire rack for 15 minutes. Using a small sharp knife, loosen cake from sides of pan. Cool 30 minutes. Remove sides of pan; cool completely. Refrigerate at least 4 hours before serving.
4. For sugared nut topping, preheat oven to 325°F. Line a small baking pan with foil; lightly coat foil with cooking spray. In a bowl combine the 2 tablespoons powdered sugar, 1 tablespoon water, and cinnamon. Stir in walnuts. Evenly spread nuts into baking pan. Bake 8 minutes or until nuts are lightly toasted, stirring once.

5. For icing, in a bowl combine 1 cup powdered sugar and enough milk to make icing drizzling consistency. Cut cheesecake into wedges. Drizzle each wedge with some of the icing and top with walnuts. Makes 16 servings.
EACH SERVING *506 cal, 28 g fat, 126 mg chol, 373 mg sodium, 59 g carb, 0 g fiber, 8 g pro.*

Chocolate-Malted Mousse

PREP 30 minutes COOL 30 minutes
CHILL 1 hour

- 2 ounces malted milk balls (about ⅔ cup)
- 4 ounces milk chocolate, coarsely chopped
- 3 ounces bittersweet chocolate, coarsely chopped
- 3 cups whipping cream
- ⅓ cup chocolate malted milk powder
- 2 tablespoons chocolate liqueur, almond liqueur, or milk
- ½ teaspoon vanilla
- 1 tablespoon sugar
- 2 teaspoons unsweetened cocoa powder
    Malted milk balls (optional)

1. Place the 2 ounces malted milk balls in a large resealable plastic bag; finely crush with a rolling pin. Set aside.
2. For mousse, in a small saucepan heat milk chocolate and bittersweet chocolate with ¼ cup of the whipping cream over low heat until smooth, stirring constantly. Stir in malted milk powder, liqueur, and vanilla. Cool to room temperature.
3. In a large chilled mixing bowl with chilled beaters beat 1¾ cups whipping cream to stiff peaks (tips stand straight). Stir about ½ cup of the whipped cream into melted chocolate mixture; fold chocolate mixture into remaining whipped cream. Fold in crushed malted milk balls. Spoon into a 1½- to 2-quart dish or 8 to 10 small bowls or glasses. Cover and refrigerate for 1 to 24 hours.
4. In a medium chilled bowl combine remaining 1 cup whipping cream, sugar, and cocoa powder; beat to soft peaks. Spoon on mousse. If desired, top with malted milk balls. Makes 8 to 10 servings.
EACH SERVING *520 cal, 43 g fat, 127 mg chol, 90 mg sodium, 31 g carb, 2 g fiber, 4 g pro.*

CHOCOLATE-MALTED MOUSSE

**PANNA COTTA
WITH PEACHES IN
LIME SYRUP**

Panna Cotta with Peaches in Lime Syrup

PREP 20 minutes   STAND 5 minutes
CHILL 4 hours

 1   envelope unflavored gelatin
 ¼   cup water
 ½   cup sugar
 2   cups half-and-half or light cream
 2   cups whole-fat or 2% plain Greek
     yogurt
 1   teaspoon vanilla
 1   recipe Lime Syrup
 3   to 4 medium peaches, cut in
     wedges
     Thin lime slices (optional)
     Pistachio nuts (optional)

1. Place eight small glasses in a shallow baking pan; set aside.
2. In a small bowl sprinkle gelatin over the water. Do not stir. Let stand 5 minutes.
3. Meanwhile, in a medium saucepan stir together the sugar and ½ cup of the half-and-half. Heat over medium heat until hot but not boiling. Add gelatin; stir until gelatin is dissolved. Remove from heat. Whisk in yogurt until smooth. Stir in remaining half-and-half and the vanilla. Pour into glasses. Cover and refrigerate for 4 to 24 hours or until set.*
4. Meanwhile, prepare Lime Syrup. Toss peaches in the Lime Syrup. To serve, top panna cottas with peaches and some of the syrup. Top with lime slices and pistachios. Makes 8 servings.

Lime Syrup In a small saucepan combine 3 tablespoons lime juice, 1 cup sugar, and ½ cup water. Bring to boiling, stirring to dissolve sugar. Reduce heat and simmer, uncovered, for 8 minutes or until slightly thickened. Syrup will thicken more as it cools.
***Set Method** Prepare as directed, except cover and freeze 20 minutes before transferring to the refrigerator to chill for 1½ hours or until set.
EACH SERVING *336 cal, 13 g fat, 32 mg chol, 49 mg sodium, 48 g carb, 1 g fiber, 9 g pro.*

Very Raspberry Frappés

START TO FINISH 15 minutes

 1½ cups frozen or fresh raspberries
 3   tablespoons raspberry liqueur or
     milk
 1   tablespoon seedless raspberry
     jam
 2   cups raspberry or other berry
     gelato or ice cream
 ¼   cup milk
 ⅓   cup chopped chocolate bars,
     crushed shortbread cookies, or
     chocolate wafer cookies
     To top drink: Chocolate bars,
     shortbread cookies, or chocolate
     wafer cookies

1. Thaw raspberries, if frozen. Place 1 cup of the berries in a blender or food processor. Cover and blend or process until smooth. Press pureed berries through a fine-mesh sieve into a bowl. Discard seeds. Add liqueur and jam to pureed berries; whisk until smooth.
2. For frappé, in a blender or processor combine berry mixture, gelato, and milk. Cover and blend or process just until combined, stopping blender to scrape down sides as needed. Stir in chopped chocolate or crushed cookies.
3. Divide the remaining berries and frappé between two chilled glasses. Top with chocolate or cookies. Serve with long-handled spoons. Makes 2 servings.
EACH SERVING *574 cal, 10 g fat, 9 mg chol, 46 mg sodium, 109 g carb, 7 g fiber, 5 g pro.*

**VERY RASPBERRY
FRAPPÉS**

STRAWBERRY
SHORTCAKE

Strawberry Shortcake

PREP 30 minutes BAKE 15 minutes
at 375°F COOL 10 minutes

- 1 32-ounce carton plain low-fat yogurt*
- 1 recipe Yogurt Cream
- 1¼ cups all-purpose flour
- ¼ cup whole wheat flour
- 2 tablespoons sugar
- 2 teaspoons baking powder
- 1 teaspoon finely shredded lemon peel
- ¼ teaspoon salt
- ¼ cup butter
- 1 egg, lightly beaten
- 2 tablespoons fat-free milk
- 6 cups sliced strawberries

1. Set aside ½ cup of the yogurt for shortcake. Use remainder for the Yogurt Cream. Prepare Yogurt Cream. **2.** Preheat oven to 375°F. For the shortcake, grease a large baking sheet; set aside. In a large bowl combine flours, sugar, baking powder, lemon peel, and salt. Cut in butter until mixture resembles coarse crumbs. In a small bowl combine the egg, milk, and the reserved ½ cup yogurt. Add to flour mixture. Stir just to moisten. With a spatula, spread dough to an even 8-inch-diameter circle on baking sheet. **3.** Bake 15 minutes or until a wooden pick inserted near center comes out clean. Cool pan on a wire rack for 10 minutes. Remove from pan. Cut into 8 wedges. Top wedges with Yogurt Cream and strawberries. Makes 8 servings.

Yogurt Cream Line a strainer with three layers of 100%-cotton cheesecloth or a clean paper coffee filter. Suspend lined strainer over bowl. Spoon in remaining yogurt from the carton. Cover and refrigerate 12 to 24 hours. Discard liquid. Transfer thickened yogurt to a bowl. Stir in ¼ cup honey and 1 teaspoon finely shredded lemon peel. Makes about 2 cups.
*Tip Use a brand of yogurt that contains no gums, gelatin, or fillers. These ingredients may prevent the whey from separating.
EACH SERVING *264 cal, 8 g fat, 45 mg chol, 213 mg sodium, 41 g carb, 3 g fiber, 9 g pro.*

Apple Crisp

PREP 30 minutes BAKE 50 minutes at 375°F COOL 15 minutes

APPLE CRISP

1½ cups unbleached all-purpose flour
1 cup granulated sugar
⅓ cup packed brown sugar
¾ teaspoon cinnamon
½ teaspoon kosher salt or ¼ teaspoon salt
⅔ cup unsalted butter, cut in pieces
8 cups peeled apples, sliced ½ inch thick
2 tablespoons fresh lemon juice
¼ to ⅓ cup granulated sugar
1 tablespoon unbleached all-purpose flour
½ teaspoon kosher salt or ¼ teaspoon salt
⅛ teaspoon freshly grated nutmeg
Butter for baking dish
Whipping cream
1 recipe Rich Custard Sauce

1. Preheat oven to 375°F. For topping, in a large bowl combine the 1½ cups flour, 1 cup granulated sugar, brown sugar, cinnamon, and ½ teaspoon salt. Work butter into flour mixture with your fingers just until it begins to cling together.

2. For the filling, in a 4-quart bowl toss together apples and lemon juice. In a small bowl combine the ¼ cup sugar (use the lesser amount of sugar for sweeter apples), 1 tablespoon flour, salt, and nutmeg. Sprinkle apples with sugar-nutmeg mixture and gently toss to combine.

3. Spoon apples into a lightly buttered 2-quart baking dish. Cover the top of the apples with the crumb mixture, breaking up large pieces as necessary to cover apples. Cover the crisp first with parchment, then foil. Place on a foil-lined baking sheet and bake or 20 minutes. Carefully remove foil and paper from the opposite side of the pan. Return to oven; bake 30 to 40 minutes more or just until top is golden and apples are tender when pierced with the tip of a paring knife. To ensure the flour in filling is cooked, bake until thickened juices bubble from the fruit. Cool 15 to 30 minutes before serving. Serve with whipping cream and/or Rich Custard Sauce. Makes 10 servings.

Rich Custard Sauce In a medium-size nonreactive saucepan heat 1 cup milk and 1 vanilla bean (twisted to bruise but not split) to just below the boiling point. Remove from the heat. Let stand, covered, for 10 minutes to allow the vanilla bean to infuse the milk. Meanwhile, whisk together 4 egg yolks and ¼ cup plus 2 tablespoons sugar. Remove the vanilla bean and slowly whisk the hot milk into the egg yolk mixture. Transfer back to saucepan. Cook over medium heat, stirring constantly, until the custard coats the back of the spoon. Do not let custard reach a simmer or boil. Remove from heat and stir in 1 cup whipping cream. Pour through a fine-mesh strainer and stir in 2 teaspoons vanilla extract and ¼ teaspoon salt. Cool slightly; cover and chill.

EACH SERVING *368 cal, 13 g fat, 33 mg chol, 237 mg sodium, 64 g carb, 2 g fiber, 2 g pro.*

CHUTNEY-STYLE
APPLE COBBLER

Chutney-Style Apple Cobbler

PREP 35 minutes
BAKE 25 minutes at 400°F
COOL 30 minutes

 1 lemon
 3 pounds cooking apples, cored and thinly sliced
 1¼ cups packed dark brown sugar
 3 tablespoons cornstarch
 ½ cup chopped dried apricots
 ¼ cup dried cranberries
 1 small jalapeño, seeded and finely chopped (see tip, page 35)
 1 teaspoon pumpkin pie spice
 2 cups all-purpose flour
 ¼ cup granulated sugar
 1 tablespoon baking powder
 1 teaspoon salt
 ½ cup butter
 1¼ cups buttermilk
    Vanilla yogurt

1. Preheat oven to 400°F. Shred 1 teaspoon peel from lemon; set aside. In a bowl squeeze 2 tablespoons juice from lemon. Add apples; toss to coat.
2. In a 4- to 6-quart Dutch oven stir together brown sugar and cornstarch. Stir in ⅔ cup water, apricots, cranberries, jalapeño, and pie spice. Cook and stir over medium heat until boiling. Cook and stir 1 minute more. Remove from heat; stir in apples. Evenly spoon into a 3-quart baking dish.
3. In a large bowl combine flour, granulated sugar, baking powder, salt, and lemon peel. Cut in butter until pieces are pea size. Stir in buttermilk just until combined. Drop dough into 12 mounds on top of fruit.
4. Bake for 25 minutes or until top is golden and filling is bubbly. Cool on rack 30 minutes. Serve warm with yogurt. Makes 12 servings.
EACH SERVING *393 cal, 9 g fat, 24 mg chol, 415 mg sodium, 75 g carb, 4 g fiber, 7 g pro.*

WARM BANANA BREAD COBBLER

Warm Banana Bread Cobbler

PREP 20 minutes   BAKE 25 minutes at 375°F   COOL 30 minutes

 1 cup self-rising flour
 1 cup granulated sugar
 ¾ cup milk
 ½ cup butter, melted
 1 teaspoon vanilla
 4 medium bananas, peeled and sliced
 1 cup rolled oats
 ¾ cup packed brown sugar
 ½ cup self-rising flour
 ½ cup butter
 ½ cup chopped walnuts
    Vanilla ice cream

1. Preheat oven to 375°F. Butter a 3-quart baking dish; set aside.
2. In a medium bowl stir together the 1 cup self-rising flour and the granulated sugar; add milk, melted butter, and vanilla. Stir until smooth. Spread evenly in the prepared baking dish. Top with sliced bananas.
3. In a large bowl combine oats, brown sugar, and ½ cup self-rising flour. Use a pastry blender to cut in ½ cup butter until crumbly. Stir in walnuts. Sprinkle topping over bananas.
4. Bake for 25 to 30 minutes or until browned and set. Serve warm with vanilla ice cream. Makes 12 servings.
EACH SERVING *560 cal, 28 g fat, 74 mg chol, 378 mg sodium, 75 g carb, 3 g fiber, 7 g pro.*

EGGNOG TRIFLES

Eggnog Trifles

PREP 15 minutes   COOK 10 minutes
STAND 10 minutes   CHILL 4 hours

1   7.2-gram envelope unflavored gelatin
3   tablespoons water
2½ cups whipping cream
1   cup eggnog
⅔   cup sugar
    Large pinch salt
¼   teaspoon freshly grated nutmeg
¾   cup strawberry or raspberry jam
2   teaspoons lemon juice
    Purchased or homemade star cookies sprinkled with sugar and nutmeg (optional)

1. For eggnog custard, in a small bowl stir together gelatin and water. Let stand for 5 minutes.
2. Meanwhile, in a medium saucepan combine cream, eggnog, sugar, and salt. Heat over medium heat, stirring occasionally, until hot. Remove from heat. Stir in gelatin. Cool slightly for about 10 minutes, stirring occasionally. (Stirring prevents the gelatin from sinking.) Immediately divide the eggnog custard among ten 6-ounce coffee cups or custard dishes. Loosely cover with plastic wrap. Refrigerate about 2 hours, until set.
3. For layer 2, sprinkle the nutmeg on custard. For layer 3, in a small bowl whisk together jam and lemon juice. Spoon into each cup, spreading to cover custard. Refrigerate for 2 hours or overnight. For the final layer, top each trifle with a sugar cookie. Makes 10 servings.
EACH SERVING *363 cal, 24 g fat, 97 mg chol, 68 mg sodium, 35 g carb, 0 g fiber, 3 g pro.*

Blueberry Ice Cream Pie

PREP 30 minutes
BAKE 8 minutes at 350°F
CHILL 2 hours   FREEZE 8 hours

1½ cups slivered almonds
2   tablespoons packed light brown sugar
¾   teaspoon kosher salt
3   tablespoons unsalted butter, melted
5   cups blueberries, rinsed, well drained
⅓   cup granulated sugar
1   teaspoon cornstarch
1   teaspoon grated lemon zest
2   teaspoons freshly squeezed lemon juice
1   tablespoon water
⅛   teaspoon freshly ground nutmeg
1   quart vanilla ice cream
½   cup crème fraîche or sour cream
½   cup heavy cream
1   tablespoon sugar

1. Preheat oven to 350°F. In bowl of food processor combine almonds, brown sugar, and ½ teaspoon of the salt. Pulse until coarsely ground. Transfer to a bowl and stir in melted butter. Turn into 9-inch pie plate. With fingers press onto bottom and up sides.
2. Bake 8 to 12 minutes until lightly golden. Allow to completely cool on a rack. Transfer to freezer until ready to use.
3. For the blueberry sauce, in a large nonreactive skillet combine 3 cups of the blueberries, sugar, cornstarch, and ¼ teaspoon of the salt, stirring well. Add zest, lemon juice, water, and nutmeg; stir to blend. Cook and stir over medium heat until blueberries begin to pop, give off juice, and come to a full simmer. Simmer, stirring gently for 1 additional minute until sauce is lightly thickened. Set aside to cool; refrigerate sauce until completely chilled.
4. Transfer ice cream to a mixing bowl and let stand in the refrigerator 30 minutes or just until softened. Spoon half into prepared crust. Spread in even layer and top with ¾ cup of the chilled blueberry sauce. Spoon remaining ice cream on pie and spread to edges. Cover surface of ice cream with plastic wrap and freeze at least 8 hours or overnight until firmly set.
5. To serve, in chilled mixing bowl whisk crème fraîche, heavy cream, and sugar just until thickened to spreading consistency. Do not overbeat. Spread cream mixture on pie; top with remaining 2 cups blueberries. Reheat remaining blueberry sauce; serve with the pie. Makes 10 servings.
EACH SERVING *363 cal, 22 g fat, 53 mg chol, 200 mg sodium, 39 g carb, 4 g fiber, 6 g pro.*

BLUEBERRY ICE CREAM PIE

CHOCOLATE
MERINGUE PIE

Chocolate Meringue Pie

PREP 45 minutes BAKE 29 minutes
at 350°F COOL 1 hour CHILL 2 hour

- 1 recipe Pastry for Single-Crust Pie
- 3 cups milk
- 3 eggs, separated
- 1 cup granulated sugar
- ⅓ cup all-purpose flour
- 2 tablespoons unsweetened cocoa powder
- ¾ teaspoon kosher salt
- 3 ounces unsweetened chocolate, finely chopped
- 3 tablespoons unsalted butter
- 2½ teaspoons vanilla
- ¼ teaspoon cream of tartar
- 6 tablespoons superfine granulated sugar

1. Preheat oven to 450°F. Prepare pastry. Prick bottom and sides of the pastry with a fork. Line pastry with a double thickness of foil. Bake for 8 minutes. Remove foil. Bake 6 minutes more or until crust is golden. Cool on a wire rack.
2. For the filling, in a medium saucepan heat 2½ cups of the milk over medium almost to simmering.
3. In a medium bowl whisk remaining ½ cup milk into the 3 egg yolks. In a second bowl combine 1 cup sugar, flour, cocoa powder, and ½ teaspoon of the kosher salt; whisk into egg yolk mixture until smooth. Gradually whisk in hot milk; return the mixture to saucepan.
4. Over medium-high heat cook and stir mixture until it comes to a full boil. Boil for 30 seconds and remove from heat. Whisk in chocolate and butter until melted and smooth. Stir in 2 teaspoons of the vanilla. Strain mixture through a sieve, pushing it through with a spatula as needed. Keep filling hot while preparing meringue.
5. For meringue, in a large mixing bowl beat egg whites with an electric mixer on medium-high until foamy. Whisk in the remaining ½ teaspoon vanilla, cream of tartar, and ¼ teaspoon of the kosher salt until blended. Whisk rapidly until whites begin to mound. Beat in superfine sugar, 2 tablespoons at a time, sprinkling the sugar over the whole bowl. Continue to beat until tips form stiff glossy peaks (stand straight), and sugar is dissolved.

6. Pour hot filling into pastry shell. Immediately spread meringue on top of pie filling. With a spatula, spread meringue from center to edges, sealing to crust all the way around. Bake for 15 minutes or until top is golden. Cool on a wire rack for 1 hour. Refrigerate at least 2 hours before serving. Makes 8 servings.

EACH SERVING 539 cal, 11 g fat, 140 mg chol, 444 mg sodium, 68 g carb, 3 g fiber, 11 g pro.

Molasses-Bourbon Pecan Pie

PREP 20 minutes BAKE 55 minutes
at 350°F COOL several hours

- 1 recipe Pastry for Single-Crust Pie
- 1 cup molasses
- 1 cup sugar
- 4 large eggs, beaten
- 3 tablespoons bourbon (optional)
- 2 tablespoons unsalted butter, melted
- 1 tablespoon vanilla
  Pinch salt
- 2 cups pecan halves

1. Preheat oven to 350°F. Prepare pastry. Do not prick pastry.
2. For filling, in a bowl stir together molasses, sugar, eggs, bourbon (if using), butter, vanilla, and salt. Evenly spread pecans in unbaked pie shell. Pour filling over pecans.
3. Place pie on center rack of oven with a foil-lined baking sheet on the rack below to catch any filling that bubbles over. Bake for 55 minutes or until firm around the edges and slightly loose in the center. Cool pie on a wire rack for several hours. Makes 10 servings.
Pastry for Single-Crust Pie In a medium bowl stir together 1¼ cups flour and ¼ teaspoon salt. Using a pastry blender, cut in ¼ cup shortening and ¼ cup butter until pieces are pea size. Sprinkle 1 tablespoon water over part of the flour mixture; toss with a fork. Push moistened pastry to side of bowl. Repeat moistening, using 1 tablespoon water at a time, until flour mixture is moistened (¼ to ⅓ cup water total). Gather pastry into a ball; knead gently until it holds together. On a lightly floured surface slightly flatten pastry with hands. Roll pastry from center to edges into a circle about 12 inches in diameter. Wrap pastry around rolling pin. Unroll into a 9-inch pie plate. Ease pastry into plate without stretching. Trim pastry to ½ inch beyond edge of pie plate. Fold under extra pastry. Crimp edge as desired.
EACH SERVING 514 cal, 27 g fat, 113 mg chol, 153 mg sodium, 63 g carb, 3 g fiber, 7 g pro.

Peach Turnovers

PREP 25 minutes
BAKE 15 minutes at 400°F

2 tablespoons granulated sugar
1 tablespoon all-purpose flour
⅛ teaspoon ground cinnamon
1⅓ cups chopped peaches, nectarines, or chopped, peeled apple
½ 17.3-ounce package frozen puff pastry sheets, thawed
  Milk
  Coarse sugar (optional)
¾ cup powdered sugar
1 tablespoon butter, softened
½ teaspoon vanilla
  Dash salt
2 teaspoons milk

1. Preheat oven to 400°F. Line a large baking sheet with parchment paper; set aside. In a small bowl stir together granulated sugar, flour, and cinnamon. Add peaches; toss to coat.
2. Unfold pastry. Cut pastry into 4 squares. Brush edges of squares with milk. Evenly spoon peach filling onto centers of squares. Fold one corner of each square over filling to opposite corner, forming triangles. Press edges with the tines of a fork to seal. Place turnovers on prepared baking sheet. Prick tops of turnovers several times with a fork. Brush with additional milk and, if desired, sprinkle with coarse sugar.
3. Bake for 15 minutes or until puffed and golden brown. Cool slightly on baking sheet on a wire rack.
4. Meanwhile, in a small bowl stir together the powdered sugar, butter, vanilla, and salt. Add enough milk to make icing drizzling consistency. Drizzle over warm turnovers. Makes 4 servings.

EACH SERVING *507 cal, 27 g fat, 8 mg chol, 213 mg sodium, 63 g carb, 2 g fiber, 5 g pro.*

Roasted Peach Pies with Butterscotch Sauce

PREP 40 minutes   CHILL 30 minutes
BAKE 13 minutes at 450°F/20 minutes at 350°F

1 cup all-purpose flour
½ teaspoon baking powder
¼ teaspoon salt
¼ cup unsalted butter
½ cup sour cream
1 tablespoon milk
6 small or 4 medium peaches
1 recipe Butterscotch Sauce
  Vanilla ice cream (optional)
  Fresh mint leaves (optional)
  Freshly ground nutmeg (optional)

1. In a large bowl combine flour, baking powder, and salt. Using a pastry blender or two knives, cut in butter until mixture resembles coarse cornmeal. Stir in sour cream and milk just until combined. Cover and refrigerate for 30 minutes or up to 2 days.
2. Preheat oven to 450°F. For two 7-inch pies, divide dough in half. On a lightly floured surface roll two 8½-inch circles. Transfer to two 7-inch pie plates. (For a 9-inch pie, do not divide dough; roll to an 11-inch circle; transfer to a 9-inch pie plate.) Trim crusts even with top of pie plates. With a lightly floured fork, press sides of crust into pie plate. Line with a double thickness of foil coated with *nonstick cooking spray.* Bake for 8 minutes. Remove foil; bake 5 minutes more or until crust is golden; cool. Reduce oven to 350°F.
3. Cut peaches into thick slices, slicing around the pits. Add peaches to cooled crusts. Cover edges of pies with foil.
4. Bake for 20 minutes or just until peaches are tender. Transfer to a rack. While pies are warm, drizzle with ¼ cup of the Butterscotch Sauce. Serve immediately (crust becomes soggy as pie sits). If desired, serve with ice cream, sprinkle with mint and/or nutmeg. Pass remaining Butterscotch Sauce. Makes 6 to 8 servings.

Butterscotch Sauce In a small saucepan melt ¼ cup unsalted butter over medium heat. Stir in ⅓ cup packed brown sugar and 1 tablespoon light-color corn syrup. Bring to boiling and boil gently, uncovered, for 5 minutes, stirring frequently. Stir in 2 tablespoons whipping cream. Cool slightly. Serve immediately. Makes ½ cup.

EACH SERVING *357 cal, 21 g fat, 56 mg chol, 142 mg sodium, 41 g carb, 2 g fiber, 4 g pro.*

ROASTED PEACH
PIES WITH
BUTTERSCOTCH
SAUCE

Carrot Spice Bars

PREP 25 minutes
BAKE 25 minutes at 350°F

Nonstick cooking spray
¾ cup whole wheat flour
¾ cup rolled oats
½ cup unbleached all-purpose flour
1 teaspoon baking powder
½ teaspoon ground ginger
½ teaspoon ground cinnamon
¼ teaspoon baking soda
¼ teaspoon salt
3 egg whites lightly beaten
2 cups finely shredded carrots
¾ cup packed brown sugar
½ cup canola oil
¼ cup honey
1 teaspoon vanilla
½ cup pecans, chopped and toasted (see tip, page 31)
1 recipe Cream Cheese Frosting (optional)
Ground cinnamon (optional)

1. Preheat oven to 350°F. Line a 3-quart rectangular baking pan with foil, extending foil over edges of pan. Lightly coat the foil with cooking spray; set aside.
2. In a large bowl stir together whole wheat flour, oats, unbleached flour, baking powder, ginger, cinnamon, baking soda, and salt. In a medium bowl stir together egg whites, carrots, brown sugar, oil, honey, vanilla, and pecans. Add carrot mixture to flour mixture, stirring just until combined. Spread batter in prepared pan.
3. Bake about 25 minutes or until a wooden toothpick inserted near the center comes out clean. Cool in pan on a wire rack. If desired, frost with Cream Cheese Frosting. Use foil to lift uncut bars from pan. If desired, sprinkle with cinnamon and cut into bars. Makes 30 bars.

EACH BAR *113 cal, 6 g fat, 0 mg chol, 54 mg sodium, 15 g carb, 1 g fiber, 2 g pro.*

Cream Cheese Frosting In a large mixing bowl beat 4 ounces cream cheese, softened, ¼ cup butter, softened; and 1 teaspoon vanilla with an electric mixer on medium until light and fluffy. Gradually beat in 2½ to 3 cups powdered sugar to reach desired consistency. Cover and store frosted bars in the refrigerator.

SOUR CREAM AND RAISIN BARS

Sour Cream and Raisin Bars

PREP 30 minutes
BAKE 30 minutes at 350°F
COOL 1 hour CHILL 2 hours

1¾ cups quick-cooking rolled oats
1¾ cups all-purpose flour
1 cup packed brown sugar
1 teaspoon baking soda
1 cup butter, melted
1½ cups granulated sugar
4 egg yolks
3 tablespoons cornstarch
2 cups raisins, dried cherries, dried cranberries, or snipped dried apricots
2 cups sour cream

1. Preheat oven to 350°F. Line a 3-quart baking pan with foil, extending foil over edges of pan; set aside. For crust, in a large bowl combine oats, flour, brown sugar, and baking soda. Add melted butter and stir until well combined. Press 3 cups oat mixture on the bottom of prepared dish. Set remaining mixture aside. Bake about 15 minutes or until set and lightly browned. Cool in pan on a wire rack.
2. Meanwhile, for filling, in a medium saucepan combine granulated sugar, egg yolks, cornstarch, raisins, and sour cream. Cook and stir over medium heat until thickened and bubbly. Pour filling over crust in pan; sprinkle with reserved oat mixture. Bake for 15 minutes more or until filling is set and top is lightly browned. Cool in pan on a wire rack for 1 hour. Cover and chill at least 2 hours. Using the edges

CHEWY CHERRY-ALMOND BARS

of the foil, lift the uncut bars out of the pan. Cut into bars. Makes 24 bars.
EACH BAR 286 cal, 129 g fat, 64 mg chol, 125 mg sodium, 64 g carb, 1 g fiber, 3 g pro.

Chewy Cherry-Almond Bars

PREP 20 minutes
BAKE 35 minutes at 350°F

1 cup butter, softened
2 cups packed brown sugar
2 teaspoons baking powder
1 egg
1 teaspoon almond extract
2 cups all-purpose flour
2 cups regular rolled oats
½ cup sliced almonds
1 12-ounce jar cherry preserves

1. Preheat oven to 350°F. Line a 3-quart baking pan with foil, extending foil over edges of pan. Grease foil.

2. In a large mixing bowl beat butter with an electric mixer on medium to high for 30 seconds. Add brown sugar and baking powder. Beat until combined, scraping sides of bowl occasionally. Beat in egg and almond extract until combined. Beat in as much of the flour as you can with the mixer. Using a wooden spoon, stir in any remaining flour, the oats, and almonds.
3. Remove ½ cup of the dough and set aside. Evenly press the remaining dough into prepared baking pan. Spread with preserves. Crumble the reserved ½ cup dough evenly over preserves layer.
4. Bake, uncovered, about 35 minutes or until lightly browned. Cool in pan on a wire rack. Using edges of foil, lift uncut bars out of pan. Cut into long narrow bars. Makes 36 bars.
EACH BAR 170 cal, 6 g fat, 19 mg chol, 58 mg sodium, 27 g carb, 1 g fiber, 2 g pro.

SALTED PEANUT BARS

3. For caramel layer, in a large heavy saucepan over medium-low heat stir caramels and milk until melted and smooth. Pour caramel evenly over peanut layer. Cool in pan on wire rack. Using the foil, lift uncut bars out of the pan. Cut into bars. Makes 48 bars.

EACH BAR *127 cal, 6 g fat, 17 mg chol, 81 mg sodium, 17 g carb, 1 g fiber, 2 g pro.*

Gooey Mixed-Nut Bars

PREP **25 minutes**
BAKE **45 minutes at 350°F**

> Nonstick cooking spray
> ½ cup butter
> 1 package 2-layer-size yellow cake mix
> 4 eggs, lightly beaten
> 1 cup packed brown sugar
> ½ cup light-color corn syrup
> ⅓ cup butter, melted
> 1 teaspoon vanilla
> ½ teaspoon ground cinnamon
> 2 cups mixed nuts, coarsely chopped

1. Preheat oven to 350°F. Line a 3-quart rectangular baking pan with foil, extending foil over the pan edges. Coat foil with cooking spray; set aside. In a large bowl, use a pastry blender to cut ½ cup butter into cake mix until mixture resembles coarse crumbs. Press mixture evenly onto the bottom of the prepared pan. Bake for 15 to 20 minutes or until lightly browned and set.

2. Meanwhile, in a large bowl combine eggs, brown sugar, corn syrup, the ⅓ cup melted butter, vanilla, and cinnamon; whisk to combine. Stir in mixed nuts. Pour nut mixture over warm crust. Bake about 30 minutes more or until bubbly around the edges and golden brown. Cool in pan on a wire rack. Using the edges of the foil, lift the uncut bars out of the pan. Cut into bars. Makes 32 bars.

EACH BAR *207 cal, 11 g fat, 39 mg chol, 155 mg sodium, 26 g carb, 1 g fiber, 3 g pro.*

Salted Peanut Bars

PREP **25 minutes**
BAKE **12 minutes at 350°F**

> ½ cup butter, softened
> ⅔ cup packed brown sugar
> 2 egg yolks
> 2 teaspoons vanilla
> 1 cup all-purpose flour
> ½ cup crushed pretzels
> ½ teaspoon baking powder
> ¼ teaspoon baking soda
> 1 7-ounce jar marshmallow creme
> ½ cup creamy peanut butter
> ¼ cup powdered sugar
> 1 cup salted cocktail peanuts
> 1 14-ounce package vanilla caramels, unwrapped
> 3 tablespoons milk

1. Preheat oven to 350°F. Line a 3-quart rectangular baking pan with heavy foil, extending foil over the edges of the pan; set pan aside. In a large mixing bowl beat butter with an electric mixer on medium to high for 30 seconds. Add brown sugar, egg yolks, and vanilla. Beat until combined, scraping bowl occasionally. In a small bowl combine flour, pretzels, baking powder, and baking soda. Beat in as much of the flour mixture as you can with the mixer. Using a wooden spoon stir in any remaining flour mixture. Press mixture into the prepared pan.

2. Bake for 12 minutes or until lightly browned. Meanwhile, for peanut layer, in a medium microwave-safe bowl combine marshmallow creme and peanut butter. Heat on high power for 1 minute or until softened and slightly melted, stopping to stir after 30 seconds. Stir in powdered sugar. Spread mixture over crust. Sprinkle with salted peanuts.

GOOEY
MIXED-NUT BARS

LUSH LEMON BLONDIES

Lush Lemon Blondies

PREP 30 minutes
BAKE 30 minutes at 325°F

- 1½ cups all-purpose flour
- 1 teaspoon baking powder
- ¼ teaspoon salt
- ½ cup butter, softened
- ¾ cup packed brown sugar
- ½ cup granulated sugar
- 2 eggs
- 2 teaspoons vanilla
- ½ cup chopped macadamia nuts, toasted (see tip, page 31)
- 1 10-ounce jar lemon curd

1. Preheat oven to 325°F. Line a 9×9×2-inch baking pan with foil, extending the foil over edges of pan. Grease foil; set pan aside.
2. In a medium bowl stir together flour, baking powder, and salt. In a large mixing bowl beat butter with an electric mixer on medium to high for 30 seconds. Add brown sugar and granulated sugar. Beat for 5 minutes, scraping bowl occasionally. Add eggs, one at a time, beating well after each addition. Beat in vanilla. Gradually add flour mixture, beating on low until combined. Stir in ⅓ cup of the macadamia nuts.
3. Spread one-third of the batter in the prepared baking pan. At 1-inch intervals drop large spoonfuls of lemon curd onto batter Top with the remaining batter. Gently swirl a knife through the batter and lemon curd layers to marble. Sprinkle with the remaining macadamia nuts.
4. Bake about 30 minutes or until golden and set. Cool in pan on a wire rack. Remove bars from pan, using the foil to lift. Place on cutting board; cut into bars. Makes 20 bars.
EACH BAR *204 cal, 8 g fat, 44 mg chol, 107 mg sodium, 32 g carb, 2 g fiber, 2 g pro.*

FRESH STRAWBERRY BARS

Fresh Strawberry Bars

PREP 25 minutes
BAKE 25 minutes at 350°F

- ¾ cup butter, softened
- ¾ cup peanut butter
- 1 cup packed brown sugar
- ½ cup granulated sugar
- 2 teaspoons baking powder
- ¼ teaspoon salt
- 2 eggs
- 1 teaspoon vanilla
- 2¼ cups all-purpose flour
- ½ cup strawberry jam
- 4 cups small whole strawberries, halved or quartered

1. Preheat oven to 350°F. Line 3-quart rectangular baking pan with foil, extending foil beyond edges. Set aside.
2. In a large mixing bowl beat butter and peanut butter on medium to high for 30 seconds. Beat in sugars, baking powder, and salt until combined. Add eggs and vanilla; beat until combined. Beat in as much flour as you can with mixer. Stir in remaining flour with a wooden spoon.
3. Spread dough in prepared pan. Bake for 25 minutes or until top is lightly browned and a toothpick inserted near center comes out clean.
4. Cool completely on a rack. Remove from pan by lifting foil. Spread jam, then top with berries. Cut into bars. Serve at once or refrigerate up to 6 hours. Makes 24 bars.
EACH BAR *225 cal, 10 g fat, 33 mg chol, 143 mg sodium, 30 g carb, 1 g fiber, 4 g pro.*

ALMOND BRITTLE BROWNIES

Almond Brittle Brownies

PREP 30 minutes
BAKE 37 minutes at 350°F

⅓ cup slivered almonds
¼ cup sugar
1 tablespoon butter
½ cup butter, softened
½ cup sugar
1 cup all-purpose flour
¾ cup butter
4 ounces unsweetened chocolate, coarsely chopped
2 cups sugar
2 teaspoons vanilla
4 eggs
1½ cups all-purpose flour

1. Preheat oven to 350°F. Line a baking sheet with foil. Butter foil; set baking sheet aside. Grease and flour a 3-quart rectangular baking pan; set aside.
2. For almond brittle, in a medium skillet combine almonds, the ¼ cup sugar, and the 1 tablespoon butter. Cook over medium-high heat until sugar starts to melt, shaking skillet occasionally. Do not stir. When sugar starts to melt, reduce heat to low and cook until sugar is golden brown, stirring as needed with a wooden spoon. Pour onto the prepared baking sheet; cool.
3. Place almond brittle in a heavy plastic bag. Using a rolling pin or meat mallet, coarsely crush brittle; set aside.
4. For crust, in a medium mixing bowl combine the ½ cup softened butter and ½ cup sugar. Beat with an electric mixer on medium to high until smooth. Stir in the 1 cup flour until combined. Press mixture evenly onto the bottom of the prepared baking pan. Bake about 10 minutes or until edges are lightly browned.
5. Meanwhile, in a medium saucepan combine the ¾ cup butter and chocolate. Stir over low heat until melted. Remove from heat. Stir in 2 cups sugar and vanilla. Add eggs, one at a time, beating with a wooden spoon after each addition just until combined. Stir in the 1½ cups flour. Pour batter over hot crust, spreading evenly.
6. Bake for 15 minutes. Sprinkle with crushed almond brittle; press lightly into chocolate layer. Bake for 12 minutes or until top is set. Cool in pan on a wire rack. Cut into bars. Makes 36 bars.
EACH BAR 164 cal, 10 g fat, 41 mg chol, 56 mg sodium, 20 g carb, 1 g fiber, 2 g pro.

Macadamia-Eggnog Bars

PREP 25 minutes
BAKE 25 minutes at 350°F

2 cups granulated sugar
⅔ cup butter
2 eggs
1¼ teaspoons vanilla
2 cups all-purpose flour
1 teaspoon baking powder
½ teaspoon ground nutmeg
1 cup chopped macadamia nuts
1 cup powdered sugar
1 tablespoon eggnog

1. Preheat oven to 350°F. Line a 3-quart rectangular baking pan with foil, grease foil; set aside. In a medium saucepan heat and stir granulated sugar and butter over medium heat until butter is melted. Remove from heat. Cool slightly.
2. Stir eggs and 1 teaspoon vanilla into sugar mixture. Stir in flour, baking powder, and nutmeg. Stir in nuts.
3. Spread mixture evenly into prepared pan. Bake for 25 minutes or just until edges begin to pull way from the sides of the pan. Cool in pan on a wire rack. Use foil to remove bars from pan; place on cutting board. Cut into bars.
4. Meanwhile, for eggnog icing, in a small bowl combine powdered sugar, ¼ teaspoon of the vanilla, and eggnog. Stir in additional eggnog, 1 teaspoon at a time, until icing reaches drizzling consistency. Drizzle icing over bars. Makes 36 bars.
EACH BAR 144 cal, 7 g fat, 21 mg chol, 39 mg sodium, 21 g carb, 1 g fiber, 1 g pro.

MACADAMIA-
EGGNOG BARS

Caramel-Hazelnut Brownies

PREP 30 minutes
BAKE 45 minutes at 350°F

- 3 cups all-purpose flour
- 1½ cups unsweetened cocoa powder
- 2 teaspoons baking powder
- 1 teaspoon salt
- 2⅔ cups sugar
- 1½ cups butter, melted
- 4 eggs
- 2 teaspoons vanilla
- 1 14-ounce package vanilla caramels, unwrapped
- 2 tablespoons milk
- 1 cup hazelnuts (filberts), toasted and chopped*
- 2 tablespoons hazelnut liqueur
- 2 cups dark or bittersweet chocolate pieces

1. Preheat oven to 350°F. Line a 3-quart rectangular baking pan with foil, extending foil over edges of pan. Generously grease foil; set aside. In a large bowl stir together flour, cocoa powder, baking powder, and salt.
2. In an extra-large mixing bowl combine sugar and melted butter. Beat with an electric mixer on low until well mixed. Beat in eggs and vanilla until combined. Add flour mixture, ½ cup at a time, beating well after each addition (batter will be thick). Evenly spread batter in prepared pan.
3. In a large microwave-safe bowl combine caramels and milk. Heat on high for 1¼ to 2 minutes or until caramels are melted, stirring every 30 seconds. Stir in half of the hazelnuts and the liqueur. Drizzle caramel mixture over batter in pan.

4. Bake, uncovered, for 45 minutes. Remove from oven. Immediately sprinkle with chocolate pieces. Let stand about 2 minutes or until chocolate is softened. Spread chocolate evenly over brownies. Sprinkle with the remaining hazelnuts.
5. Cool in pan on a wire rack. (If necessary, chill until chocolate is set.) Using edges of foil, lift brownies out of pan. Cut into bars. Makes 36 bars
*To toast hazelnuts, preheat oven to 350°F. Spread nuts in a single layer in a shallow baking pan. Bake for 8 minutes or until lightly toasted, stirring once to toast evenly. Cool nuts slightly. Place the warm nuts on a clean kitchen towel; rub with the towel to remove the loose skins.

EACH BAR *311 cal, 15 g fat, 45 mg chol, 183 mg sodium, 40 g carb, 1 g fiber, 4 g pro.*

FIVE-LAYER BARS

Five-Layer Bars

PREP 10 minutes
BAKE 37 minutes at 350°F

2 13-ounce packages soft coconut macaroon cookies
¾ cup sweetened condensed milk
¾ cup semisweet chocolate pieces
¾ cup raisins or dried cranberries
1 cup coarsely chopped peanuts

1. Preheat oven to 350°F. Arrange cookies in a greased 3-quart baking dish or pan. Press cookies together to form a crust.
2. Bake for 12 minutes. Evenly drizzle crust with condensed milk. Sprinkle with chocolate pieces, raisins, and peanuts.
3. Bake for 25 minutes or until edges are light brown. Cool in pan on a wire rack. Cut into bars. Makes 30 bars.
EACH BAR *181 cal, 7 g fat, 3 mg chol, 86 mg sodium, 28 g carb, 1 g fiber, 3 g pro.*

Loaded Oatmeal Cookies

PREP 30 minutes
BAKE 9 minutes per batch at 350°F

¼ cup butter, softened
½ cup packed brown sugar
⅓ cup sugar
1 teaspoon ground cinnamon
½ teaspoon baking soda
⅛ teaspoon salt
1 egg
1 teaspoon vanilla
¾ cup all-purpose flour
¾ cup rolled oats
¼ cup flaxseed meal
¼ cup wheat germ

LOADED OATMEAL COOKIES

2 ounces dark chocolate, finely chopped
¼ cup dried cranberries
¼ cup chopped walnuts, toasted (see tip, page 31)

1. Preheat oven to 350°F. In a large mixing bowl beat butter with an electric mixer on medium to high for 30 seconds. Add brown sugar, granulated sugar, cinnamon, baking soda, and salt. Beat until combined, scraping sides of bowl occasionally. Beat in egg and vanilla until combined. Beat in flour. Stir in rolled oats, flaxseed meal, wheat germ, chocolate, cranberries, and walnuts (dough will be crumbly).
2. Drop dough by rounded teaspoons 2 inches apart onto ungreased cookie sheets. Bake for 9 minutes or until tops are lightly browned. Cool on cookie sheet for 1 minute. Transfer cookies to wire rack to cool. Makes about 30 cookies.
EACH COOKIE *79 cal, 4 g fat, 11 mg chol, 45 mg sodium, 12 g carb, 1 g fiber, 2 g pro.*

DOUBLE-DARK
CHOCOLATE
COOKIES

Whole Wheat Carrot-Raisin Cookies

PREP 30 minutes
BAKE 8 minutes per batch at 375°F

- ½ cup butter, softened
- 1 cup packed brown sugar
- 2 teaspoons baking soda
- 1 teaspoon ground cinnamon
- 1 teaspoon ground ginger
- ¼ teaspoon salt
- 1 egg
- ¼ cup applesauce
- 1 teaspoon vanilla
- 2 cups whole wheat flour
- 1 cup finely shredded carrots
- ¾ cup raisins
- ¾ cup finely chopped walnuts

1. Preheat oven to 375°F. In a large mixing bowl beat butter with an electric mixer on medium for 30 seconds. Add brown sugar, baking soda, spices, and salt; beat until combined. Beat in egg, applesauce, and vanilla. Beat in as much of the flour as you can with the mixer. Stir in any remaining flour, carrots, raisins, and walnuts just until combined.
2. Drop by slightly rounded teaspoons 2 inches apart onto ungreased cookie sheets. Bake for about 8 minutes or until edges are firm. Transfer cookies to a wire rack to cool. Makes about 36 cookies.

EACH COOKIE *98 cal, 4 g fat, 13 mg chol, 111 mg sodium, 14 g carb, 1 g fiber, 2 g pro.*

Double-Dark Chocolate Cookies

PREP 30 minutes
BAKE 12 minutes per batch at 350°F

- ¼ cup butter, softened
- ¼ cup canola oil
- ½ cup packed brown sugar
- ¼ cup granulated sugar
- 1 egg
- 1 teaspoon vanilla
- ½ cup whole wheat pastry flour
- ½ cup all-purpose flour
- ¼ cup unsweetened cocoa powder
- ½ teaspoon baking powder
- ⅛ teaspoon salt
- 4 ounces bittersweet chocolate, chopped

1. Preheat oven to 350°F. Line cookie sheets with parchment paper. In a large mixing bowl beat butter with an electric mixer on medium for 30 seconds. Beat in oil, brown sugar, and granulated sugar until well combined. Beat in egg and vanilla until combined. In a medium bowl whisk together flours, cocoa powder, baking powder, and salt; beat into sugar mixture. Stir in chocolate.
2. Drop dough by slightly rounded teaspoons 2 inches apart onto prepared cookie sheets. Bake about 12 minutes or just until edges are set. Cool 1 minute on cookie sheets. Transfer cookies to wire rack to cool. Makes about 36 cookies.

EACH COOKIE *237 cal, 9 g fat, 6 mg chol, 482 mg sodium, 34 g carb, 3 g fiber, 6 g pro.*

Vanilla-Salted Peanut Cookies

PREP 35 minutes
BAKE 7 minutes per batch at 375°F

- ¾ cup shortening
- 2 cups packed brown sugar
- ½ teaspoon baking soda
- ¼ teaspoon salt
- 2 eggs
- 1 tablespoon vanilla
- 1½ cups all-purpose flour
- 2 cups rolled oats
- 1 cup dry-roasted peanuts
- ½ cup raisins
- ½ cup flaked coconut

1. Preheat oven to 375°F. In a large mixing bowl beat shortening with an electric mixer on medium to high for 30 seconds. Add brown sugar, baking soda, and salt. Beat until combined, scraping sides of bowl occasionally. Beat in eggs and vanilla until combined. Beat in flour. Using a wooden spoon, stir in oats, peanuts, raisins, and coconut.
2. Drop dough by rounded teaspoons 2 inches apart onto an ungreased cookie sheet. Bake about 7 minutes or until edges are light brown. Let stand for 2 minutes on cookie sheet. Transfer to a wire rack to cool. Makes about 60 cookies.

EACH COOKIE *107 cal, 5 g fat, 7 mg chol, 28 mg sodium, 15 g carb, 1 g fiber, 2 g pro.*

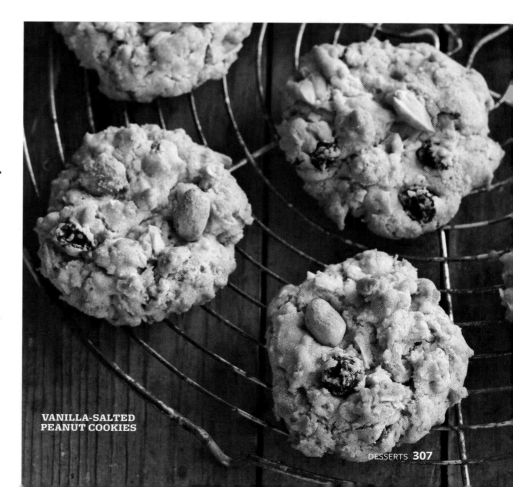

VANILLA-SALTED PEANUT COOKIES

WHOOPIE PIE
TREATS

Whoopie Pie Treats

PREP 1 hour
BAKE 8 minutes per batch at 350°F

½	cup shortening
1	cup granulated sugar
⅔	cup unsweetened cocoa powder
1	teaspoon baking soda
⅛	teaspoon salt
1	egg
1	teaspoon vanilla
2	cups all-purpose flour
1¼	cups buttermilk
¾	cup milk
¼	cup all-purpose flour
¾	cup butter, softened
2	cups powdered sugar
1	teaspoon vanilla
¼	cup unsweetened cocoa powder
3	tablespoons butter
2	cups powdered sugar
2	tablespoons milk
½	teaspoon vanilla
	Milk (optional)

1. Preheat oven to 350°F. In a large mixing bowl beat shortening with an electric mixer on medium to high for 30 seconds. Add granulated sugar, the ⅔ cup cocoa powder, baking soda, and salt. Beat until combined, scraping sides of bowl occasionally. Beat in egg and 1 teaspoon vanilla. Alternately add the 2 cups flour and buttermilk, beating well after each addition.
2. Drop dough by rounded tablespoons 2 inches apart onto an ungreased cookie sheet. Bake for about 8 minutes or until edges are firm. Transfer to a wire rack; cool.
3. For filling, in a small saucepan combine the ¾ cup milk and the ¼ cup flour. Cook and stir over medium heat until thickened and bubbly. Cook and stir for 2 minutes more. Cool.
4. In a medium mixing bowl beat the ¾ cup butter on medium to high for 30 seconds. Add 2 cups powdered sugar; beat until fluffy. Add 1 teaspoon vanilla. Gradually beat in cooled milk mixture. Beat on high about 1 minute or until smooth and fluffy. Spread about 2 tablespoons of the filling on bottoms of half the cookies. Top with the remaining cookies, bottom sides down.
5. For frosting, in a medium bowl beat together the ¼ cup cocoa powder and the 3 tablespoons butter. Gradually beat in 1 cup powdered sugar.

Beat in the 2 tablespoons milk and the ½ teaspoon vanilla. Gradually beat in the remaining 1 cup powdered sugar. Beat in additional milk, if necessary, to make frosting spreading consistency. Frost cookies. Store in an airtight container in the refrigerator. Makes 14 sandwich cookies.
EACH COOKIE *478 cal, 21 g fat, 50 mg chol, 234 mg sodium, 68 g carb, 1 g fiber; 5 g pro.*

Bittersweet Chocolate-Walnut Meringue Kisses

PREP 25 minutes
BAKE 1½ hours at 300°F/200°F
STAND 30 minutes

2	egg whites
¼	teaspoon cream of tartar
½	cup superfine or regular granulated sugar
2	ounces bittersweet chocolate, coarsely chopped (⅓ cup)
⅓	cup chopped walnuts, toasted (see tip, page 31)

1. Let egg whites stand in large mixing bowl at room temperature for 30 minutes. Preheat oven to 300°F. Line a cookie sheet with parchment paper or lightly greased foil.
2. For meringue, beat egg whites and cream of tartar with an electric mixer on medium to high until soft peaks form (tips curl). Gradually add sugar, about 1 tablespoon at a time, beating until glossy and stiff peaks form (tips stand straight). Fold in ¼ cup of the chocolate and ¼ cup of the nuts.
3. Drop meringue in six mounds 2 inches apart on prepared sheet. Using back of spoon, swirl the top of each meringue into a high tip that curls.
4. Place meringues in oven; immediately decrease oven temperature to 200°F. Bake 1½ hours or until crisp and dry on outsides. Cool completely on sheet on wire rack. Gently peel cooled meringues off parchment or foil. To serve, sprinkle with remaining chocolate and nuts.
5. Store meringues in an airtight container at room temperature up to 24 hours. Makes 6 meringue kisses.
EACH KISS *160 cal, 8 g fat, 0 mg chol, 19 mg sodium, 23 g carb, 1 g fiber, 3 g pro.*

BITTERSWEET CHOCOLATE-WALNUT MERINGUE KISSES

SPICY GINGERSNAPPERS

Spicy Gingersnappers

PREP **45 minutes**
BAKE **12 minutes per batch at 350°F**
COOL **2 minutes per batch**

- 1 cup raisins
- 1 cup unsalted butter, softened
- 2 cups packed brown sugar
- 2 eggs
- 1 tablespoon chopped crystallized ginger
- 1 teaspoon finely shredded orange peel
- 1 teaspoon vanilla
- 3⅔ cups all-purpose flour
- ½ cup chopped pecans
- 1½ teaspoons ground cinnamon
- 1 teaspoon baking soda
- ½ teaspoon baking powder
- ½ teaspoon ground nutmeg
- ¼ teaspoon ground ginger
- ¼ teaspoon salt
- 1 recipe Pecan Topping
- 1 recipe Orange Glaze

1. Preheat oven to 350°F. Place raisins and butter in food processor; process until raisins are chopped and combined with butter. Transfer to an extra-large mixing bowl. With an electric mixer beat in brown sugar, eggs, crystallized ginger, orange peel, and vanilla until creamy.

2. In a medium bowl combine flour, pecans, cinnamon, baking soda, baking powder, nutmeg, ginger, and salt. Gradually beat flour mixture into butter mixture. Mix until well combined.

3. With a 2-tablespoon cookie scoop, drop dough 4 inches apart on an ungreased cookie sheet. Flatten tops lightly. Spoon 1 teaspoon Pecan Topping on the center of each unbaked cookie.

4. Bake 12 minutes or just until edges are set. Cool on sheet for 2 minutes; transfer cookies to cooling rack. Cool completely.

5. Drizzle cooled cookies with Orange Glaze. Makes 36 large cookies.

Pecan Topping In a small bowl combine ½ cup chopped raisins, ½ cup chopped pecans, 3 tablespoons sour cream, and 2 tablespoons caramel topping.

Orange Glaze In a small bowl combine 1½ cups powdered sugar and 2 tablespoons orange juice.

EACH COOKIE *210 cal, 8 g fat, 26 mg chol, 70 mg sodium, 34 g carb, 1 g fiber, 2 g pro.*

Bananas Foster Gelato

PREP **30 minutes** CHILL **8 hours**
FREEZE **per manufacturer's directions**

- ⅔ cup packed brown sugar
- 5 egg yolks
- ¼ teaspoon ground cinnamon
- 1¾ cups whole milk
- ¼ cup whipping cream
- ½ teaspoon salt
- 2 ripe bananas
- 1 teaspoon lemon juice
- 2 tablespoons dark rum or ½ teaspoon rum extract
- 1 teaspoon vanilla
  Sliced bananas (optional)
  Caramel-flavored ice cream topping (optional)

1. In a medium mixing bowl beat brown sugar, egg yolks, and cinnamon with an electric mixer about 4 minutes or until light; set aside.

2. In a medium saucepan heat and stir the milk, cream, and salt just until simmering. Slowly stir about 1 cup of the hot milk mixture into the egg yolk mixture. Return all egg yolk mixture to saucepan. Heat and stir constantly (do not boil) until mixture thickens. Remove pan from heat and place in bowl of ice water; stir 2 to 3 minutes to cool.

3. Mash the 2 bananas with the lemon juice. Stir into thickened milk mixture along with rum and vanilla (mixture may appear slightly curdled). Transfer to a large bowl. Cover; refrigerate overnight.

4. Freeze in a 1½- or 2-quart ice cream freezer according to manufacturer's directions. If desired, serve with sliced bananas and caramel topping. Makes 8 servings.

EACH SERVING *198 cal, 7 g fat, 147 mg chol, 180 mg sodium, 28 g carb, 1 g fiber, 4 g pro.*

**BANANAS FOSTER
GELATO**

Recipe Index

D

E

F